MEMBERSHIP CARD
1963 SEASON
Ending 31st December, 1963

1st Performance 6-30
WEDNESDAY
NOVEMBER 20
FRONT STALLS 10/6
XD 35

LEYTON SUPER BATHS, - LEYTON, E.10
MONDAY 8th APRIL, 1963
The Fabulous
Beatles
Bus Routes, 35, 38, 38a, 69, 249, 257, 234, 70, 170, 26 .
NEAREST UNDERGROUND: LEYTON (CENTRAL)

CASINO BALLROOM
LEIGH
NEMS ENTERPRISES PRESENT THEIR FABULOUS

SHOWDANCE

Monday, 25th Feb., 1963
Sensational Opening Attraction
THE GREAT HIT PARADERS
BEATLES
Stars of TV, BBC and Parlophone Records
Also Jiving to Resident Band
7-30—11-0 p.m.   Tickets 5/-
Available in advance or on night from Ballroom

Don't Miss This Great Event!
BIG, BIG Monday Re-Opening
at the
PLAZA Ballroom
DUKE STREET, ST. HELENS
MONDAY, 25th JUNE, 1962
Non-Stop JIVE Session — 7-30 to 11-0 p.m.
HARRY WESTOCK presents his
"BIG BEAT BARGAIN NIGHT"
Starring the Merab's No 1 Rock Combo!
THE BEATLES
Just back from their Sensational German Tour
Now Recording Exclusively for Parlophone
They're Terrific — You must see them!
FIRST EVER APPEARANCE IN ST. HELENS
PLUS
The Big Three
Star Group of the JERRY LEE LEWIS "Rockerscope" Show
The Show will be presented by **BOB WOOLER**
The Well-Known Compere and **DEE JAY**
These Fabulous Attractions Can only be seen at the Plaza !
TELL YOUR FRIENDS.   Come early and see the full Show.
ADMISSION ONLY 2/6 Note the Date
Wilsock Press - St. Helens 1960   Monday, 25 June

SUBSCRIPTION ROOMS
STROUD
SAT. 31st MAR.
8.30 TO 11.45 P.M.
JAYBEE CLUBS present Liverpool's Top Vocal and Instrumental
Group—Stars of Polydor Records—THE
SENSATIONAL
BEATLES
plus
THE REBEL ROUSERS
ADMISSION 5/- • REFRESHMENTS
BY COUNCIL REGULATION   NO TEDDY BOY SUITS
LADIES PLEASE BRING A CHANGE OF SHOES AS STILETTO HEELS ARE NOT ALLOWED
NO ADMISSION AFTER 9 P.M.
Next Week - LEE ATKINS !

No 23 U

MECCA Ltd. - RIALTO, YORK
ARTHUR HOWES presents
THE BEATLES
Wed., 27th Nov., 1963
at 8-45 p.m.
SECOND HOUSE
STALLS 8/6
Tickets cannot be exchanged or money refunded.
No responsibility will be taken for the loss of this ticket.
THIS PORTION TO BE RETAINED

4 TUESDAY [155—210]

Saw Beatles at Town Hall absolutly Great fab. and all the rest LOVE THEM ALL. J.L. especially

5 WEDNESDAY [156—209]
Ember Day

all our loving
a people's history of
the beatles

Richard Houghton

Published in Great Britain 2023
Spenwood Books Ltd, 2 College Street
Higham Ferrers, NN10 8DZ

spenwoodbooks.com

A CIP record for this book is available from the British Library

ISBN 978-1-915858-08-5 (hardback)
ISBN 978-1-915858-19-1 (paperback)

Hardback printed in the Czech Republic via Akcent Media Limited
Paperback printed and bound by Ingram Sparks

Design by Bruce Graham, The Night Owl

Front cover image: Lee Thacker
Rear cover images: Diane Hicks, Norman Scott, Dena Hubbard,
Garth Cawood, Bethena Smith

All other image copyrights: as captioned

all our loving
a people's history of
the beatles

Richard Houghton

Spenwood Books
Manchester, UK

ABOUT THE AUTHOR

Richard Houghton lives in Manchester, UK with his wife Kate and his pomapoo Sid. He is the author of more than 20 music books. His *People's History* titles, published by Spenwood Books, are a series of fan memories that tell the story of legendary rock acts in a brand-new way. Acts covered to date include Led Zeppelin, Jimi Hendrix, Pink Floyd, Black Sabbath, Bruce Springsteen, The Beatles, The Who, Cream, Thin Lizzy, Queen and the Faces. He has also compiled fully authorised 'fan histories' of Jethro Tull, Simple Minds, Orchestral Manoeuvres in the Dark, the Stranglers, Fairport Convention, Shaun Ryder and The Wedding Present.

Did you see The Beatles live? Send your classic gig memory (of the Fab Four, or any other band) to Richard at iwasatthatgig@gmail.com.

For more information go to spenwoodbooks.com.

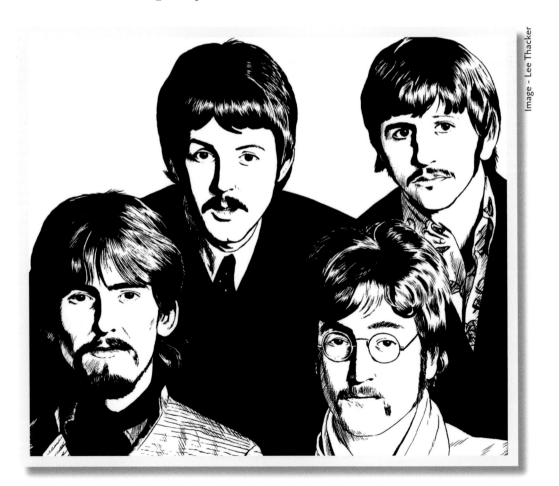

Image – Lee Thacker

ACKNOWLEDGEMENTS

I could not have written this book without the help of a number of people. I am indebted to the many local and regional newspapers in the UK that kindly featured my initial appeal in 2016 for people to come forward with their Beatle memories. Several papers, not just in Britain but also in Australia and New Zealand, were more than happy to run a follow up piece, knowing that their readerships would volunteer further information, reflecting the great affection with which The Beatles are held to this day by the public. In particular, I'd like to thank Terry MacCallum at the Dundee *Courier* and Mike Hill at the *Lancashire Evening Post* for their assistance. I should like also to thank my many Beatle friends on Facebook who contacted me with memories that I have included.

The Beatles have been the subject of almost as much analysis in the digital age as they were before the internet became part of our everyday lives. As an online resource, I found myself referring to beatlesbible.com in order to check key dates, although a number of the shows described in here had to be verified through other research.

I'd like to thank: Des Henly and Richard Whitehouse, for permission to use an extract from their blog about The Beatles visit to Weston-super-Mare; Beth Kaplan for permission to quote from her book, *All My Loving: Coming of Age with Paul McCartney in Paris*; Ray Douglas at Aberdeen Council for the background information about the Beach Ballroom in Aberdeen; David Dills for the Two Red Shoes, Elgin advertisement; the *Lancashire Evening Post* for permission to reproduce quotes from Mike Dryland, Mick Garry and Derry Jackson; Norman Scott and Garth Cawood for permission to reproduce their Beatle photographs; Bruce Pegg, for permission to quote from his book, *Goin' Down De Mont – A People's History of Rock and Pop Concerts at Leicester's De Montfort Hall*; Andy Gillespie, for linking me up via Facebook with various Beatles fans from his hometown of Middleton; Alan Hope, for permission to use his story about The Beatles in Aldershot.

I'd like to thank all my contributors for taking the time to share their Beatle memories and in particular Andi Lothian, Fraser Elder, Ron Watson and John Gordon.

Finally, I should like to thank: Bruce Graham for his design and layout skills; Lee Thacker, for the cover illustration; my wife, Kate Sullivan, for her patience and her willingness to feed me at regular intervals; and my mother, who took me to see The Beatles at the tender age of four. I don't remember anything of it, but others can testify to the fact that – I was there!

SPECIAL THANKS

Des Henly, Edward Fagan, Leslie Reynolds, Christine Parrella, John Bezzini, Seamus Hayes, Edward Fagan, Nancy Richy, Dan Smith, Nancy McFadden Lloyd Kerfoot, Bryan Wyatt, Elaine McAfee Bender, Donna Peterson-Casenove, Benjamin Dobie, JoAnn Grubbs, Norman Humphreys, Margaret E Paterson, Paul Bakewell, Anthony Carpenter, Margaret Vincent, Stuart Hopwood, Roger Hill, Bethena Smith, Margaret Mayberry, Rodger Brownlee.

INTRODUCTION

This is not a complete history of The Beatles. The Beatles are probably the most written about band in history and there are already many excellent and extremely thorough and well-researched books about them. This volume is not seeking to emulate those. What it does, however, is to attempt to capture memories that might otherwise never have been recorded. It contains previously unpublished stories from people who saw The Beatles live and who have never had the chance to tell their tale before. Many of the memories relayed within this book are those of paying customers, audience members who witnessed the group either during their rise to stardom, when Beatlemania was starting to grip Britain and then the world or when they had become a global phenomenon. It is a series of recollections which gives a portrait of their live performances, starting out in Liverpool and going around Britain and the world. But it also contains more mundane brushes with the Fab Four, whether walking home from school with George Harrison or brushing past John Lennon in central London.

There are no memories from when The Beatles performed in Hamburg and no memories from their last live show at Candlestick Park in San Francisco in 1966 or of their appearance on the rooftop of the Apple building on 30 January 1969. But, these gaps apart, there are memories throughout their career from people who saw The Beatles and who can rightly claim 'I was there.'

It's now been almost 57 years since The Beatles' retirement from live performance. The stories relayed in this book in some cases go back more than 60 years, and while teenage diaries have sometimes helped the contributors to this book to put together their stories, many memories are faded by time or embellished through years of retelling. My mother took me to see The Beatles Christmas Show at London's Hammersmith Odeon. For years, I would tell anyone who would listen that I remembered going to see a department store Santa Claus before the show and opening my present – a set of wooden skittles – as we sat in the theatre. In so doing, I dropped one of the wooden balls on the floor and it rolled away to the front of the auditorium never to be seen again. The trouble with that story is that The Beatles performance I witnessed, my mother assures me, was in January 1965. Santa would have long since packed up his grotto and gone home and it seems I have conflated two memories.

I cannot therefore vouch for the accuracy of any of the accounts in this book. Where possible I have tried to verify claims made by my contributors as to when and where they saw individual performances, but I have sought to avoid altering people's stories unnecessarily. Where the 'facts' are mis-remembered I have limited myself to a handful of 'author's notes' to confirm or deny what has been claimed. In the same way that it does not claim to be a complete history of The Beatles, this book does not claim to be an entirely accurate history. I have left out a few stories that were sent to me because it was not possible to verify the performances contributors said they witnessed. In other instances, I have made educated guesses about the shows that people remembered attending because dates, venues and the other acts on the bill on that evening did not triangulate. But the dissonance is all part of the charm of history.

Ultimately, what comes through all these stories is the affection with which The Beatles were – and still are – held. It may have been more than 50 years since people saw them perform, but for many it is a much-cherished memory and one that they recall with great warmth.

Richard Houghton
Manchester, England
September 2023

EARLY DAYS

John Lennon and Paul McCartney first meet at Woolton Village Fete. John is performing with his band the Quarrymen.

ST PETER'S CHURCH
6 JULY 1957, WOOLTON, LIVERPOOL, UK

I WAS THERE: MARK FISCHER

I was three or four when I saw the Quarrymen at the village fete. I was with my mum. I remember meeting Julia Lennon, a playful woman who loved music. She always nurtured the kids. When I was three and a half, I lived with my father and mother on Newcastle Road, right across from Julia Lennon. My mother Phyllis and Julia were best friends and cousins. As my father told it to me, they would hang out quite frequently, baking together and sharing each other's recipes such as a strawberry cherry pie. They would go out together, taking me with them while my father was at work. They brought me to the first Quarrymen show. I remember John holding me after the show when he came to greet his mom, Julia. Julia and her friends would sometimes come over for dinner with John. My father and mother adored John over dinner, with his sarcasm and blunt jokes. Julia would often tell John to hush, thinking my mother and father would get offended but my mother and father only laughed and enjoyed his company all the more.

Mark's claim to have been at Woolton and to have known the Lennons is disputed by others.

ST SILAS SCHOOL
1947, LIVERPOOL, UK

I WAS THERE: ANDREA CREED

I was in the same class as Richard Starkie at St Silas School. He was just one of my class mates. I remember him because, as a result of a playground scrap we had at the age of about seven, I was smacked on the back of my legs by the head teacher in front of the whole school. I was a bit of a teacher's pet with the head teacher and it didn't seem fair. After junior school, we went our separate ways although there was a shop at the end of our street which repaired bikes and radios, and which recharged the large batteries which were used to power the wireless. Richard spent a lot of time in that shop. I don't know whether he was paid or just had an interest in what went on. I next saw Richard when I was working as an air hostess for a small Liverpool based airline. 'Love Me Do' was becoming popular and Richard was flying to London. He looked at me and said in his strong Liverpool accent 'I know you, don't I? You're...'. We spent some time talking about the old days at primary school.

LIVERPOOL INSTITUTE
1958, LIVERPOOL, UK

I WAS THERE: GEOFF GRIPTON

I was at the Liverpool Institute through the late '50s and both Paul and George were pupils a couple of years ahead of me. My brother Cliff was in the same form as George and, for a period, we would walk across town in a group from school towards the Hardman Street area, where George and others would get their buses home. We would then walk on to Skelhorne Street for our bus. I can recall George with his quiff and grey waistcoat and school tie, reversed to be as thin as possible.

LIVERPOOL SCHOOL OF ART
1958, LIVERPOOL, UK

I WAS THERE: RICHARD AUSTIN

I was a late developer and passed the 13+ exam, ending up at the Liverpool School of Art in Gambier Terrace, Liverpool, the junior school to the Liverpool College of Art five minutes away. Cynthia Powell was in the year ahead of me. She was quite good-looking and very quiet, giving the impression of being aloof since she lived in Hoylake. In her book, *John*, Cynthia indicates she first met John Lennon at the College of Art. But I believe she became acquainted with him during her time at Gambier Terrace, ie. before attending the College of Art.

The first time I heard the name Lennon was when my school friend Tony Campbell, who was in love with Cynthia, said he couldn't understand why she liked John Lennon. I was soon to learn by observation that John was a bit of a Ted. On the occasions that he came over to the junior school – to see Cynthia – trouble followed him. He would be accompanied by a group of his hangers on, who were other Teddy Boys from the College of Art. His companions, although having a very similar disposition, appeared to be in awe of him. Fights would start and he would be warned off the school property by the teaching staff.

My cousin David attended Quarry Bank Grammar School at the same time as John Lennon. I asked him about Lennon a couple of times and all David would say was 'oh, him!' I then worked in a commercial art studio in Duke Street, close to Ye Cracke Pub. Rice Street was a few minutes' walk from the College of Art. I spent a lot of time drinking there, probably too much time. On the odd occasion Lennon would be there with Cynthia. I'd met him a couple of times but we were just on nodding terms. I always formed the impression that when he was in the pub something would happen. A fight or a fierce argument would erupt. He seemed to have all the trappings of a catalyst.

ST JOHN'S YOUTH CLUB
1959, ORRELL PARK, LIVERPOOL, UK

I WAS THERE: IRENE EDWARDS, AGE 13

My friend and I knew them when they used to play opposite our youth club band, the Flamingos, who later became the Ravens, at gigs around the dance halls in Liverpool. It was when Pete Best and Stuart Sutcliffe were with Paul and John, before Ringo arrived on the scene. The leader of our youth club group went to the same school as Paul and John. In the early days, when no one had any money, the youth club girls would support the group by helping with the transport of the instruments on the Liverpool buses, taking it to the various dance halls. We would help to put the instruments behind the stage and see The Beatles during change over time halfway through the evening. The Beatles would be on for the second set, so we'd take equipment into the back of the stage and swap it over. I never really had any conversations with them, but when they started playing, we'd be in the front of the stage dancing and you'd get a nod of recognition out of them. The Beatles were quite frightening really, because they used to dress all in black leather.

The Beatles undertake a short Scottish tour in May 1960.

I WASN'T THERE: ARTHUR SCOTT

They went on a tour of Scotland in 1960 backing Johnny Gentle, starting at Alloa on 20th May, the Northern Meeting Rooms in Inverness on 21st May, Fraserburgh on the 23rd, Keith on the 25th, Forres Town Hall on the 26th, the Regal Ballroom in Nairn on the 27th and finishing at Peterhead on the 28th.

In 1960 The Beatles make their first visit to Hamburg in Germany, where they stay for more than three months. They begin 1961 by playing around the Liverpool area. In February 1961 they appear for the first time at the Cavern Club in Liverpool.

CAVERN CLUB
1961, LIVERPOOL, UK

I WAS THERE: JOHN GORDON

The Cavern was a jazz club. I was in the Clyde Valley Stompers, one of the main Scottish bands touring up and down the country, and I also joined one of the bands in Manchester, which was called the Jazz Aces. We used to appear fairly regularly at the Cavern, once every two or three months. Liverpool was like most of the cities in the UK in late 1961, '62. You had two camps of fans. You had the ones who liked rock 'n' roll and the popularity of the *Oh Boy!* show, and this other half which liked traditional jazz. Trad jazz was hugely supported, mainly by the student elements throughout all the universities up and down the country, the art schools and so on. A lot of these little independent clubs up and down the country would feature generally nothing but trad jazz. They very much made an allowance by allowing skiffle groups to appear in jazz clubs, and then it was decided 'they are popular, these skiffle groups, so we'll make it so that they do an interval spot.' So that was the general format that you would come across in some of the regional jazz clubs – there'd be a popular local skiffle group sharing part of the bill with the main bands.

The PA at the Cavern wasn't very good. It consisted of two mics and fairly small speakers attached to the wall of the Cavern. It wasn't sophisticated; it was very, very basic because, generally speaking, the six-piece jazz bands played acoustic. You only had one microphone, at the front, and that was for announcements and vocals. Maybe the clarinet player would bring the clarinet nearer to the microphone, but that was the only sort of amplification people used.

The Cavern was unlicensed, inasmuch as you couldn't get a drink in the place. We didn't really stay in the club long enough to get to know The Beatles because we headed out to go and have a drink at the interval, and that's when they would come on. We shared the same dressing area, which was located just at the side of the small stage of the Cavern. It was only a small room and there'd be nine, ten of us in there. I remember them in the form of a skiffle group heading towards a bluesy type of sound. I can remember times when we played there and they would come on at the interval and the crowd would follow us out to the bars. The audience for The Beatles would shrink to maybe 25 people, sitting around chatting and talking.

They'd be doing their thing on stage and then we would come back in. We usually hung around and gave them the nod that 'after the next number, we'll come on' sort of thing. And then it would be the general melee in the changing room – us trying to grab our instruments, them trying to grab their instruments. One day we did a gig and… we didn't exactly have an altercation but it was a case of they weren't getting out of the way fast enough for us to grab our gear. It was John Lennon and Paul McCartney. We had a bit of a tussle, shoving them out the way while we got our gear because the dressing room was so restricted.

The local Manchester musicians would be all right with them but the Scottish musicians, the type that I was playing with, who were typical Glaswegians, were not very friendly at the best of times. We played at the Cavern roughly twelve to 15 times when The Beatles were on. We never got to a situation where we as a band thought 'well, they're more popular than we are'. The audience had actually come to hear us and not them. It wasn't a particularly big place, it didn't hold a helluva lot of people. And financially it wasn't a particularly good gig. I don't think they go paid much. The appearance that they try to convey in programmes now about that period of time is that, sensationally and overnight, they took the world by storm. To a certain extent it was pretty fast, but it wasn't as fast as that. They put in a lot of playing time before they got any recognition.

CAVERN CLUB,
14 JULY 1961, LIVERPOOL, UK

I WAS THERE: RON WATSON, AGE 16

I saw The Beatles play many times, including twelve times at the Cavern between July and December 1961, eight times in Southport and five more at the Cavern in 1962 and in March at the Southport Odeon and May at the Liverpool Empire in 1963. That's 27 times altogether. The band that emerged after Epstein's influence was a different group but probably had to change in order to get the degree of success they wanted. They were a tough bunch but were style-setters both in terms of clothes, ie. Cuban heel boots, and indeed their material that went right through the R&B and rock 'n' roll era. They put their own stamp on it to great effect.

The nearest you get to getting some idea is probably the BBC recordings because the Hamburg tapes are a bit rough. I was in the Cavern the first time Brian Epstein came down and remember it well, and also when George Harrison got a black eye after Pete

Clockwise from top left: The Woolton stage where John and Paul first met – photo Johnny Parisi; Jazz was still king when The Beatles first appeared on the scene, as Andi Lothian was able to testify; Norman Humphreys was a Cavern regular on Wednesday afternoons in 1961 & '62 but never saw The Beatles (four photos); John Gordon shared a dressing room with The Beatles at the Cavern Club.

Clockwise from top left: Richard Austin was at the Cavern; Ron Watson saw The Beatles several times in the early days, including lunchtimes at the Cavern; Rhona Simon (right) saw the Pete Best line up; Sam Leach with George Harrison and John Lennon drinking Watney's Pale Ale that Sam had bought from the White Hart pub; Roger Brown feels like he almost discovered The Beatles because of seeing them before they were famous; Jennifer Fabb saw The Beatles at Stroud's Subscription Rooms; Paul McCartney dancing on his own at the Aldershot Palais on 9th December 1961 – photo Dick Matthews.

Best was sacked. George would always chat at lunchtime about music and was serious about it, Paul was the ladies' man and John was usually disagreeable whilst Pete was the most popular with the girls. During the same period, '61-'62, Ringo also appeared in Southport at a small club as a member of Rory Storm and the Hurricanes and he was the most experienced member as he was the oldest and the most experienced and also had a stage name.

I'm half-Canadian. My mother was Canadian. I went to the local grammar school and then went to work for a company called Canadian Pacific that was in the Royal Liver Buildings in Liverpool, on the front. So it was easy to go to the Cavern for the lunchtime sessions, and I was told off by the boss every day because I came back late. The Beatles were an interesting phenomenon, because the audiences were relatively small – 50 to 100 people. The Cavern lunchtime sessions were very informal. But that was nice because they would talk to you, even people like me. They didn't have any money so if you bought them a Coke or a hot dog you were a friend for life.

I'd started taking an interest in music when I was eleven years old. My mum bought me a copy of Elvis's 'Hound Dog'. A lot of the stuff that people thought was new I was actually quite familiar with, because it would be B-sides of The Coasters or something like that which I'd originally had on 78s, so I perhaps had a bit more background knowledge than most. But they'd often come up with stuff I'd never heard of. And I'd immediately rush round to NEMS to try and find the original and get a copy of it. Was George Harrison's version of 'Roll Over Beethoven' as good as Chuck Berry's? No. Was John Lennon's version of 'Twist and Shout' better than the Isley Brothers? Yes, it was. They were highly distinctive. If you shut your eyes, you knew who they were.

When I started to go down there, the Cavern had switched from being a jazz club to a rock 'n' roll club. The Beatles would play two or three lunchtime sessions and Gerry and the Pacemakers would play the other two. And they played from half past twelve to ten past one and half past one to ten past two. That was the schedule, the two sets. But they got two different lots of audiences. We were all doing our one-hour lunch breaks, so you'd get those that came to the first ones, and they then had to get back to work. And then there were the people like me that went to the second ones, so the change in the Cavern was pretty profound. It literally was a jazz club and then it completely switched and went on to purely rock 'n' roll. And they brought out quite a lot of innovation.

They'd play one or two original numbers but essentially The Beatles were a covers band. They would find the more obscure American rhythm and blues-type music – Arthur Alexander, Richie Barrett, a whole raft of people – which was often brought in on the ships from people that worked for Cunard. You can get some idea of the music on the BBC recordings, but you don't get the depth or the fact that they were as loud as they were from recordings like that. They were loud in the Cavern, big style, but they weren't the loudest band.

The loudest band was a band called The Big Three, and they were the best band on Merseyside too. The other groups would go and see them. Epstein took them on but they didn't get anywhere because they wouldn't do what The Beatles did, which was to conform. They were lots of bands around but often the repertoire was the same. The Beatles had found them out first. Most bands did 'A Shot of Rhythm and Blues' but The Beatles were the first to do it. The most popular of their numbers didn't actually make it onto the albums.

At lunchtime they weren't under any pressure in terms of appearance. They'd come in in whatever they wanted to come in. John Lennon turned up one day in a corduroy suit. Well, nobody had ever seen a corduroy suit before: 'Where did you get that from?' There was a slight class element in it. The audiences at lunch time were all basically office and shop workers. They weren't what you might describe, for lack of a better phrase, as working class. At the evening shows, there was more of a mixture of people. But they were still wearing the black leather stuff. And then Epstein took the view that that had to change and he put them in suits. Basically, they went along with it because they craved success, or John and Paul did. So they were prepared to compromise. Quite a few of the Merseyside groups wouldn't compromise.

And they had the black leather gear, which Astrid had introduced them to. Nobody had ever done that before. The boots that they wore weren't actually the ones that became known as Beatle boots. They bought them when they were over in Germany and they were a different design. The first time I saw them I thought 'these are good', but Liverpool being Liverpool, at the Cavern somebody shouted out 'what are you doing wearing girls high-heeled shoes?', hich George didn't take too kindly to.

There was no discernible Beatlemania, although they had a lot of people there that liked them. You didn't get the screaming and all that sort of stuff. The lunchtime sessions were informal. And the audience was slightly different because they were people like me who were in what you might call white collar jobs. The lunchtime audience was also different from the audience at night, because word got round. A lot of the girls worked in the local offices, like Cilla Black. Cilla was a typist but she took my coat and hung it up for me in the Cavern.

They would open their shows with one of three numbers – 'Hippy Hippy Shake', 'A Shot of Rhythm and Blues' or 'Some Other Guy'. They used to play two 30-minute sets. McCartney said they'd never been better than when they did those sessions. When they became very popular all that was lost. When they became popular, you might pay 15 shillings (75p) to listen to 25 minutes of girls screaming, when I used to pay a shilling (5p) to watch them play for an hour. It was a different product.

I WAS THERE: RICHARD AUSTIN

During lunch times I would be at the Cavern where The Beatles, resembling mini-Gene Vincents, would put on a tremendous show. However, The Beatles were just one of the many groups playing at numerous venues across Merseyside at the time.

CAVERN CLUB
13 SEPTEMBER 1961, LIVERPOOL, UK

I WAS THERE: RON WATSON

John was a troubled character. He would come across as being aggressive, disagreeable. I remember going up to him one lunchtime session in the break and saying 'I really enjoyed that number. Where did it come from?' He just said 'eff off'. Whereas George Harrison would stop and he would tell you 'oh it's the B-side of so and so' and 'it's on this label', that type of conversation. John rebelled as much as he could, so when they went on stage and started wearing suits, he was the always the one who wouldn't do up his tie.

Two of them were grammar school boys. Two weren't. Paul was the PR guy. George was the serious one. He would talk to you about music. He would practice even in the breaks. He bought himself a new Gretsch guitar when they started getting a bit of money and you could really tell it was his pride and joy. Most of the time I was there, Pete Best was the drummer. I was there when Ringo stood in for Pete Best for the first time because Pete had a sore throat but I don't particularly remember it. On some days seeing them wasn't that big a deal. It was something you could do three times a week. So why would you put it in your diary every single time you went? It was quite a big issue when Pete Best was booted out. That did not go down at all well. Ringo had to work pretty hard to get over that. Pete Best is a really nice guy and he wasn't treated well. He was very popular because he was a good-looking guy and the girls loved him. Whether technically he was a better drummer than Ringo Starr, I don't know. Ringo played on a Sunday afternoon at one of our local places in Southport with Rory Storm and he had his own feature spot. He was the actually the most experienced and the oldest. And he had all the gear. But he had to fight hard to gain acceptance and it took quite a while.

I WAS THERE: IRENE EDWARDS

As our youth club group became more proficient, they joined up with Billy Jones and renamed themselves as The Ravens and would then be on the opposite half of the evening at the Cavern. I went a lot then to the Mardis Gras and to the Cavern. I went with my girlfriend who I went to Queen Mary High School with. I was just going to see whoever performed. I never went at lunchtime. It was always night time. It was rock 'n' roll. There were other groups in Liverpool whose music I liked better at the time. My Cavern days slowed down in autumn 1961 because I was then studying for A levels and the amount of homework I had clipped my wings. I was only going out at weekends then.

CAVERN CLUB
9 NOVEMBER 1961, LIVERPOOL, UK

I WAS THERE: RON WATSON

I remember when Brian Epstein came down to see them because, when you're 16 or 17, the guy who's 24 or 25 and comes down wearing a cravat tends to stand out. I remember him standing at the back, in what were the arches, looking somewhat bewildered. I think he had Alistair Taylor with him at the time. And you could tell from the look on his face that he was mesmerised. He'd never seen anything like it. But to him they were a bit scruffy, ill disciplined. So Epstein made them the offer and the rest, as they say, is history.

CIVIL SERVICE CLUB
14 NOVEMBER 1961, LIVERPOOL, UK

I WAS THERE: RHONA SIMON (NEE CHRISTIAN)

I grew up on the outskirts of Liverpool and was a teenager in late Fifties and early Sixties. I was a civil servant and consequently joined the Civil Service Club in the city. It was a club for young people, and many of the groups that became part of the Mersey Sound performed there on a regular basis. Rory Storm and the Hurricanes, The Big Three, Gerry and the Pacemakers, the Four Jays and many other future household names were regulars. We were located in a little alley called Lower Castle Street, near to Liverpool Town Hall, and were open Tuesday, Thursday and Sunday. I was a committee member and we were responsible for booking the groups. As Tuesday nights were being quite poorly attended, we decided to try and boost the night by booking The Beatles. We paid them £20 per night for three consecutive Tuesdays. They played for the first time on 14th November 1961. Pete Best was still part of the line up then. We knew Ringo as Rory Storm's drummer. Pete was the heartthrob of the night – for me at least! I recently came across my diary from that year and the entry for 14th November reads 'Club, Beatles OK. Had good time.' What an understatement that turned out to be. It has always been one of my regrets that I never did go to see them at the Cavern. It certainly was a great era to be a teenager in our great city!

I WAS THERE: JIM FINN

We used to go to the lunchtime sessions in the Cavern from 12 noon to 2pm. It was two shillings (10p) to get in. The Beatles would be on one day and Gerry and The Pacemakers the next, and it would alternate like that. There was great rivalry between them. One time, when Pete Best was the drummer for The Beatles, they were belting out a song and Gerry Marsden sneaked into the Cavern. He worked his way round to the electrical sockets at the back of the stage and pulled the plugs out. He ran out of the Cavern accompanied by some of the foulest language from John Lennon you have ever heard.

One of the elements of The Beatles' popular appeal was the contrast between the two frontmen – John Lennon, the rough and ready type, and Paul McCartney, the ever-polite smoothie. George Harrison sometimes looked as though he had just got out of bed and come straight to the Cavern whereas Pete Best, who I knew at school, was always immaculately turned out. When we would leave the Cavern, grown ups (shoppers and office workers) walking past would look disapprovingly at us teenagers, probably because of the very loud music coming from within and spilling out into Matthew Street. It's very narrow but back then was able to accommodate a two-way traffic system.

I WAS THERE: GORDON VALENTINE

We played in a *Battle of the Bands*-type talent competition at the Cavern. We pulled up outside and loaded our gear in. The walks were dripping. The place was just smelling of disinfectant that they threw around on the floor. It was an horrendous place. How it got past any fire regulations beats me. But the acoustics were fantastic.

PALAIS DE DANSE
9 DECEMBER 1961, ALDERSHOT, UK

I WAS THERE: ALAN HOPE, AGE 19

The Beatles came to Aldershot in December 1961 and ended up playing to an audience of only 18 people. I'm to blame.

I was an aspiring young pop star, chasing my big break as 'Kerry Rapid' with my group, the Blue Stars. In November 1961 Bob Potter, agent and promoter for the Aldershot Palais, was contacted by Sam Leach, aspiring manager of The Beatles, with a request to book the Aldershot Palais for five consecutive Saturday nights. The Beatles were completely unknown outside of Liverpool. Convinced they were going to be bigger stars than Elvis, Sam paid for five successive Saturdays at the Palais to showcase The Beatles to leading agents, press and promoters in London and the South East. It was his final opportunity to impress The

Beatles and take them away from Liverpool and the potential clutches of Brian Epstein.

As well as the Palais, Bob Potter was also the agent and promoter for Kerry Rapid and the Blue Stars. We regularly played at the Palais on Saturday nights and had built up a very loyal teenage following, ensuring our events were complete sell-outs. When I saw the poster advertising The Beatles' shows, I was very disappointed we had not been asked to be one of the advertised two star supporting groups. Instead, this group I had never heard of were coming onto my patch, meaning we wouldn't be able to play our favourite local venue on the Saturday nights over Christmas and the New Year.

With the help of my drummer, Rocky Ford, and Mike Burton, agent and promoter for the Central Ballroom, I arranged for Kerry Rapid and the Blue Stars to appear at the Central Ballroom on Saturday 9th December and the following Saturday, only a short walk from the Palais. I was well aware we would be in competition with The Beatles for customers, but determined that Kerry Rapid and the Blue Stars would come out on top. I worked hard on promotion with my local fan base and local connections. There was no need for newspaper adverts and posters on the wall. Promotion was all word-of-mouth in those days.

Word soon got around and my event was a complete sell-out, with over 300 people in attendance. And there was a steady build up of local resentment regarding this unknown group from Liverpool trying to take over the Aldershot live music scene, especially during the run up to Christmas and New Year. As the date drew near, the few Beatles posters that had not been torn down were badly damaged and unreadable.

Travelling into Aldershot on the bus that Saturday, I reminded fellow passengers that Kerry Rapid and the Blue Stars were appearing at the Central Ballroom and not the Palais. The band all went in the surrounding pubs to do the same. We were determined to see off The Beatles.

During our interval break, I popped into the White Hart pub for a quick drink. Somebody with a strong Liverpool accent (who I later found out to be Sam Leach) was at the bar, buying bottles of Watney's Pale Ale to take away and unsuccessfully offering the pub's customers free tickets to come and see The Beatles appearing live, less than two minutes' walk away.

I looked in the Palais. There were only about 12 people there. The Beatles - John, Paul, George and Pete Best – were there but there were no other groups and certainly no London agents, press or promoters. The London group advertised on the poster, Ivor Jay and the Jaywalkers, never turned up. The Beatles were messing about, joking and clowning around on stage. Two of them were not even on the stage. It all seemed to be a big laugh to them but it certainly was not to any of the customers. The Beatles poster referred to 'The Battle of the Bands' at the Palais. But the real battle of the bands contest was taking place against Kerry Rapid and the Blue Stars.

I recognised a few people in the Palais and invited them to the Central Ballroom for the second half of my show. Afterwards, two people said that my versions of Chuck Berry's 'Johnny B Goode', 'Memphis, Tennessee' and 'Roll Over Beethoven' were much better than the Beatles' versions played earlier that evening.

We also appeared at the Central Ballroom the following Saturday and during the interval break I again went to see what was going on at the Palais. The Beatles were not appearing 'for five consecutive Saturdays' as advertised. Another Liverpool group, Rory Storm and the Hurricanes, were performing to an audience of around 250 and I remember thinking how much better they were than The Beatles. The Hurricanes' drummer, a showman with a big personality who got everybody up and dancing, really caught my eye. I found out later that this drummer was Ringo Starr.

I still remember my fans being so pleased about our return to Aldershot Palais just before Christmas in 1961 and chanting 'Kerry, Kerry, Kerry' when I came on the stage. It was a great welcome and probably our best ever live performance. If only Sam Leach or Brian Epstein had been there to see it.

The Palais fiasco proved to be a turning point in Sam Leach's relationship with The Beatles. Shortly after returning to Liverpool, they informed Sam they were appointing Brian Epstein as their manager. I met Sam in July 2013 at his house in Liverpool. He opened the door, took one look at me and said, 'C'mon in you bastard, I've always wanted to meet you.' He launched straight into telling me how he still blamed me for The Beatles going off with Brian Epstein. But we shook hands and parted as friends. Alas, I never saw him again, as Sam died in December 2016.

 # KINGSWAY CLUB
22 JANUARY 1962, SOUTHPORT, UK

I WAS THERE: FAITH BARTON, AGE 18

I worked in NEMS at the time that Brian Epstein became interested in The Beatles. I was alone in the staff rest room above the shop one day when the internal phone rang so I answered it. It was Brian. He wanted to know if I had ever heard of The Beatles. Obviously, we had a good chat about them. Lots of people were coming into the pop music department downstairs asking for the record they were on. Shortly after, that he saw them for himself and the rest, as they say, is history. I used to go to the Cavern most lunchtimes and lots of evenings. The Cavern had a unique smell! Before the first time they played at the Kingsway, Brian asked me to organise a coach trip to Southport to support them. This I did with help from a part time employee, who was a student who was waiting to join the RAF. It wasn't easy, and we really had our work cut out convincing the Cavern

Club audience that they wanted to go. If I remember correctly, it cost them five shillings (25p) for transport and entry. Even with the bus load there, I don't think it was overly full.

I WAS THERE: CHRIS RIMMER

I was on the circuit in the '60s with lots of bands. My band was Chris and the Quiet Ones. The name came from being asked to turn it down because we were too loud at a local dance. We started playing spots of 20 minutes between proper dances. We played a lot at the Palace Hotel, Birkdale and at the YMCA, the Clifton, the Queens and various venues on Lord Street. But our favourite venue was the Kingsway, run by Mr Ruane. He was an Irishman and a great fellah who loved us. He ran the Marine Club on the top floor. Our claim to fame was that we played support group to The Beatles the first four times they appeared in Southport. Pete Best was still playing drums. We talked to Brian Epstein. We had a good rapport with the boys, swapping guitars and all that stuff. George Harrison told our rhythm guitar player, Ray, that one day he might be able to afford a guitar like Ray's pink Fender Strat.

KINGSWAY CLUB
29 JANUARY 1962, SOUTHPORT, UK

I WAS THERE: KEVIN FINLAYSON

I was in a band called The Diplomats and we played the Kingsway with The Beatles. They used to have a lot of rock bands up there. We didn't see them much. Pete Best was with them. They had a heck of a job to carry their gear up three floors you know. They had a good sound. They were just together. They were nice lads. They weren't big time or anything.

KINGSWAY CLUB
5 FEBRUARY 1962, SOUTHPORT, UK

I WAS THERE: RON WATSON

I saw them six times at the Kingsway. Those dates at the Kingsway, where they did slightly longer sets than at the Cavern on a lunchtime, was when they were at their peak as a band, and of course very few people actually saw that. Those of us that did were lucky. The set up at the Kingsway was roughly two 45-minute sets. They were good and they knew it, so there was a slight arrogance about the performance because they knew they could blow everybody else off the stage. They had a wide repertoire. They'd often come up with numbers and you'd think 'where did they find that from?' The Kingsway ones were noted in my diary because they were tremendous shows. If you saw them in that local context, you saw a band that the rest of the world never saw. It was the clothes and the general attitude. Remember, in '61, '62, people were watching the Shadows doing things in shiny suits, doing funny little steps. And then all of a sudden – bang! – this band appears on stage in black leather jeans, belting out this very loud music. The contrast was tremendous. It was Jerry Lee Lewis that said during that period of time all of America was full of Bobbies – Bobby Rydell, Bobby Vee, all this sort of sanitised stuff – and the one thing The Beatles weren't in those days was sanitised.

SUBSCRIPTION ROOMS
31 MARCH 1962, STROUD, UK

I WAS THERE: ROGER BROWN, AGE 19

The Beatles came to our local weekly dance at Stroud Sub Rooms before they released their first real hit, 'Love Me Do', so I did not know who they were. They were billed as 'Liverpool's Number One Group', which did not mean as much to us in Gloucestershire as maybe it would in Liverpool. But although we did not know them, we were at a critical age and knew our music, going to Subs each week where different groups played, and buying all the good hits we could afford. This may seem a strange way to be impressed and become a great fan, even before their record was released, but every Saturday night before I went out I always watched *Jukebox Jury* on TV. The records would be brand new, some due to be released the following week, and they were normally played for the first time on the programme. 'Hey Baby' by Bruce Channel was played on the TV that night, and was so good I remembered it. It is a great record and has a wonderful harmonica part in it.

That night, John Lennon said he was going to play this new record. Knowing the quality of the normal Saturday night groups, I waited for them to spoil the song and backing, as it is not easy to play. Wow – was I surprised! John Lennon on the harmonica was really great and their version was better than the original in my opinion. I was a fan from that day. What a great, never to be forgotten night. I was not surprised at their success. It is funny when the rest of the world likes them too. You almost feel cheated as you foolishly think you discovered them.

I WAS THERE: JENNIFER FABB (NEE FARRANT), AGE 18

My mum, Hazel Farrant, provided refreshments at the Stroud Subscription rooms for various clubs including the Freemasons and the chess club during the week. At the weekends, she provided refreshments for visiting singers and bands on Saturday evenings. I was working at Stroud Shambles Nursery School during the week but usually helped Mum at these functions. I looked forward to Saturdays when I would hear new bands and singers. I would be given plastic caps to wear on my stiletto heels to protect the floor at The Subs. Mum particularly remembers when The Beatles came, because Paul asked her for some hot water so he could shave. I am sorry to say I never spoke to any of The Beatles. What a shame!

I WAS THERE: GEORGE LODGE, AGE 22

The Beatles came more as a band to dance to. No chairs were put out. The Subs, as we called them, was a weekly dance. I arrived when the music was in full swing. You just had to pay on the door to get in. I believe it was the Rebel Rousers on stage when I got there. The crowd was already dancing away. Ten minutes after they finished their stint, The Beatles took the stage for the dancing to begin again. I remember the dancing slowly stopped as the crowd were all turning towards the stage to watch and listen to the band. It was soon obvious that these young men were something special. I recall two numbers they performed – Leroy Van Dyke's 'Walk On By' and Bruce Chanel's 'Hey Baby'. The latter they were begged to play three times. After their time was up, they left the stage down the steps. Many of the young people came and crowded round them, shaking their hands. There was no screaming but very warm feelings towards them. I was told later that the boys went for a beer in the Post Office pub opposite.

TOWER BALLROOM
29 JUNE 1962, NEW BRIGHTON, UK

I WAS THERE: RICHARD AUSTIN

I remember being at a dance at the Tower Ballroom, New Brighton and Lennon yelling and screaming at a heckler who seemed to be having a problem with the band. Lennon had to be restrained by George and Paul from jumping off the stage and getting it on within the crowd.

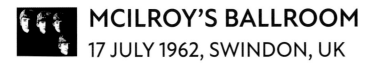

MCILROY'S BALLROOM
17 JULY 1962, SWINDON, UK

I WAS THERE: IAN TITCOMBE

I was one of the 160-odd people there with my then girlfriend. We were regulars at the dances and saw quite a few of the rock 'n' roll groups at that time. To be honest, The Beatles were just another group but they did play a lot of the R&B-type music that I liked, plus they played a Buddy Holly and the Crickets number which, as a big Buddy Holly fan, put them right up in my estimation! I was a frustrated guitar player and remember being taken by John Lennon's Rickenbacker which I had not seen before and Paul McCartney's Hofner bass. I've got to say there was nothing that made me think that they were shortly going to be the biggest group the world has ever seen, but I would love to be a time traveller and be able to go back to that night knowing what I know now!

BELL HALL
20 JULY 1962, WARRINGTON, UK

I WAS THERE: SUE BURKE, AGE 15

I was at the Bell Hall the night The Beatles played. They had live music with a band every Friday – a modern day disco. I was almost 16 and I used to go to keep my brother's girlfriend company as he would leave us there (she is now my sister-in-law). Pete Best was the drummer. It was a brilliant night and my eyes were only for Paul. I thought he was brilliant. They were marvellous and it was a great evening. My only regret was that I never got their autographs. My dad liked music and I told him about the brilliant band I had seen and that they were going to be on a programme called *6 Five Special* on what is now Granada. What they played I can't remember, but Dad said they were rubbish. But it wasn't long before he changed his mind, possibly because I bought all their records and played them all the time.

KINGSWAY CLUB
23 JULY 1962, SOUTHPORT, UK

I WAS THERE: MIKE RUANE

I didn't actually see The Beatles myself. I was too young. However, my father owned the Kingsway Club in the early Sixties and he employed The Beatles several times. I remember him saying he paid them £8 for their last appearance at the Kingsway.

I WAS THERE: RON WATSON

I well recall helping Pete carry his drums up the stairs and I think on the last date Ringo stood in for him as he was ill.

CAVERN CLUB
19 AUGUST 1962, LIVERPOOL, UK

I WAS THERE: FRANK MURPHY

I was outside the Cavern and Brian Epstein was standing in front of me, talking to Paddy, who was on the door. Paddy was telling Epstein that some of Pete Best's fans were heading for the Cavern as they were upset at his sacking and there was going to be trouble. Paddy was telling him to leave but Brian went in. Later, I was watching The Beatles when they came off for their break, led by George. I was talking to the person I came in with, who was the cousin of a friend. As George walked past us, this person punched George in his face.

CAMBRIDGE HALL
26 JULY 1962, SOUTHPORT, UK

I WAS THERE: GARTH CAWOOD

My parents had a ballroom. They were ballroom dancers. I started as a disc jockey, with a record player with a spindle where you put eight records on. But there were horrible pauses in between so I started to introduce the dances just to fill the pauses up. I was doing something at the Cavern Club in Liverpool and Joe Brown and His Bruvvers were playing and I knew two of the Bruvvers so I turned up that night, just as a punter really, because I was in Liverpool. And they said 'we're doing a show for Brian Epstein in Southport. Why don't you come with us?' So I went with them. Joe was top of the bill because 'A Picture of You' was number one and the supporting bands were all Brian Epstein's bands. I was sat with the Bruvvers in the dressing room. We were all sat with our backs to the mirrors and Brian came in. I had met him at the Cavern and spoken to him before.

He came in and he said, 'Joe, I'd like you to meet two protégés of mine. This is Paul Beatle and this is John Beatle.' He always called them John and Paul 'Beatle' at that time. Later on, I spoke to him. I said, 'Look Brian, I've got these clubs and these ballrooms in Yorkshire and I'd like to bring a couple of the bands over. Will they travel?' He said 'yes' so I said, 'Can you give me some clues as to the prices?' He took out a NEMS Enterprises business card and wrote on the back: 'Beatles, £35; Gerry and the Pacemakers, £18; Billy J Kramer and the Coasters, it was then, £15; and The Big Three £11.'

I went back to the friend I was working a couple of these places with and we said 'let's take it steady' so we booked The Big Three for three nights at £11 a night. They came and played in Yorkshire but drove back to Liverpool each night. There were no motorways then of course. And I got to know The Beatles very well.

MARINE HALL
25 AUGUST 1962, FLEETWOOD, UK

I WAS THERE: ALAN WRIGHT

I was a member of a well-known and very popular Fleetwood band called The Trespassers. I stood in the wings watching The Beatles literally die on stage that night. We played the Marine Hall quite a few times before and after and had a loyal following in the area. A number of people have claimed to have played at the Marine Hall on that night, and over the years more than a few have approached me to confirm that they made the story up. Having done our set, we were approached by an associate of The Beatles who offered a 'well done, lads' and told us that if we were interested, he could arrange for us to get work in Hamburg. I wonder how different our lives might have been if we had taken up the offer.

I WAS THERE: RICKY WRIGHT

My friend, Les Hall, and I decided to form a rock 'n' roll group with myself playing guitar and vocals and Les playing the bass. We were joined by Bob Hopwood, a great boogie woogie pianist, and Keith Jackson on drums. We called ourselves the Rainbow Rockets. We started by getting bookings into working men's clubs and then we recruited a lead guitarist from Blackpool called Harry Cole, who was engaged to a girl from Fleetwood. Luckily, our reputation grew and we were offered to appear at the Marine Hall on a Saturday night. We gladly accepted the date and were paid £5 (to be shared between us). At the time, there were a few skiffle groups in Fleetwood using washboards and tambourines but the Rainbow Rockets were purely a rock 'n' roll outfit. Jerry Lee Lewis, Little Richard, Bill Haley – that was our kind of music. When the Marine started to book big-name groups, we were always the main support group. We supported The Beatles when they played the Marine. Unfortunately, the Beatles didn't go down very well with the audience.

I WAS THERE: JANET LEATHERBARROW

My dad was the drummer in The Haloes on that particular night.

CAVERN CLUB
AUGUST 1962, LIVERPOOL, UK

I WAS THERE: JAN BOUNDEN (NEE BIRD)

I'd gone up to Liverpool to meet a school friend who had a cousin there and we went to the Cavern. I didn't see The Beatles in the Cavern but I did experience the atmosphere you get with the Cavern Club and I remember quite distinctly the look of it, the steaminess you used to get. Because you went underground to the old Cavern. And I remember doing something called the Liverpool Stomp.

I WAS THERE: JENNY MASKELL, AGE 15

We just turned up and paid on the door. When I used to go it was just like ordinary blokes. John Lennon was sarcastic, very sarcastic. I didn't really like him very much because I was so young. I couldn't cope with his sarcastic attitude. I'm sure some of the older girls could. But I used to love George. George was lovely. He used to treat everybody the same. And Paul was the same. We all loved George and Paul. But John was very sort of sarcastic all the time. You felt as though you couldn't just have a chat with him. But the others seemed to appreciate the fact that they had the fans there and they used to give you photographs and sign things. George and Paul were my favourite Beatles. I used to like John Lennon's music. I used to like his vocals. In fact, I preferred them to the other two really. But personality-wise it was definitely George and Paul.

The Cavern was very small. It was just like a tunnel really. There was no alcohol and that was great because my parents were happy with that, because I was under age. I went with older people from Huddersfield, who were about 18 or 19, and nobody checked your age. But obviously there wasn't any drinking. The licensing age was 21 in those days and I was only about 14, 15.

They used to just come on and do the odd set in between other people. They didn't play in long sections. I didn't care who else was playing. We just used to hope there were a few sets played while we were there. At the beginning, they were very accessible people, and then they started bringing their LPs out and became untouchable for us really quite quickly. We went over to Liverpool once and went to George Harrison's mother's house for tea. She invited us in, which was quite odd. It would sound strange to a parent now, allowing your 15-year-old to do that, but people seemed a bit safer in those days. And that's why we were able to go around on the train or the bus and go to these places. Our parents thought we were quite safe.

TOWN HALL
31 AUGUST 1962, LYDNEY, UK

I WAS THERE: ALAN LAVERY

I was in a band called the Rebel Rousers. We were a local band based in Cirencester and we supported a lot of the groups – Gene Vincent, the Barron Knights, most of the top people in those days – because we were on the circuit playing Forest of Dean, Lydney,

Birmingham, Bristol. I played lead guitar. We had a contract to do all the American bases. On a Saturday night, if you were playing, it was for squaddies and we played rock. But when you did a Sunday night in the officers' mess, you had to play waltzes and things like that. We did a lot of country and western. We could play most things.

I supported The Beatles when they played in Stroud, and in Lydney the night before. When we got that first booking, for The Beatles they weren't known round here so all the posters said 'The Sensational Beatles' and that, because they were more known up in Liverpool. Both places were packed. They had good PR in Epstein. He sort of got the word about. They were just in ordinary suits. We sat in the dressing room with them and talked, like you do with most other groups. They said to us 'what do you do between the gigs?', because we went on for three quarters of an hour and they went on for three quarters of an hour. In between that we sat and chatted. 'What do you do now?' 'Oh, we go over the pub now' so they said 'well, that's what we'll do then.' At the end of the evening, we just sat down and chatted with them like you normally do with most groups, about who you'd played with and things like this. We didn't get a sense that they were going to be anything big. We played with most bands and some of them were brilliant, but you never got the same sort of vibe with The Beatles. We played with Sounds Incorporated a lot, and musically, they were much better really than The Beatles. They were brilliant.

I had a day job as a mechanic. I can't remember what we got paid as a band, but it wasn't a lot in those days. Those days there were so many different bands, so many different styles, and so we used to practice on a Tuesday and Thursday. We always aimed to get two new numbers out a week to try and keep up with everything. Cozy Powell used to come and listen to our practices. Our drummer taught him to play. Our drummer – he's dead now. I'm the last one standing in the Rebel Rousers.

 # SUBSCRIPTION ROOMS
1 SEPTEMBER 1962, STROUD, UK

I WAS THERE: TONY MARTIN

I was at this dance. I was jiving with a few friends right in front of the stage all night and so was very well aware of what went on. I'm not saying they were bad, but they weren't very good. Their performance was absolutely nothing like their subsequent performances and recordings. These weekly Saturday night dances had been going on for years and we were used to hearing a lot of really tight bands. That was our benchmark and yardstick. By comparison, The Beatles didn't make a great impression. There were probably many mitigating factors for this. I remember Jock, the Subscription Rooms manager, telling us that they'd driven all the way down from Liverpool and had arrived exhausted, penniless and hungry. He took them to the local fish and chip shop and bought them a meal. Not a good start.

They also had Pete Best playing drums and, as was subsequently proved, he was not the best of drummers. Their repertoire was all standards. This may have been at the suggestion or insistence of the promoters. There was certainly no sign of what was to come. If they'd given any hint of 'Love Me Do', 'Please Please Me' or 'I Saw Her Standing There', it would have been unforgettable. They didn't, and it wasn't. We also have to remember that Stroud does not compare in any way to Liverpool or Hamburg. I don't recall the hall being empty – I would say it was comfortably full.

Pete Best left The Beatles on 16 August 1962.

 # BRS BALLROOM, CHARLES RUSSELL HALL
27 SEPTEMBER 1962, BIRMINGHAM, UK

I WAS THERE: TONY NEWSON

It was in Ward End. Sadly, they knocked it down a couple of years ago. The Charles Russell Hall was the actual British Road Services social club the rest of the week. It's where they went to have their sandwiches during the day. It had a stage at the one end and it wasn't too big a size. It was just the job for how The Beatles were then. I think the promoter was Reg Calvert, an agent from Rugby way who ran it. He was the one that brought them down. The dance was called the Teen Beat. It was there for a few years. It went through from pre-Beatles, through the Joe Browns and people like that.

They were in their leathers. We loved them. They were great. They looked a bit rougher than what we were used to, the likes of Joe Brown in his smart suit and tie. And then you got the scruffy-looking Beatles. At that time, we all dressed smart as well, in suits and ties, so they were a bit of a revelation. But it was the music that did it. The music stood out for me. And the picture of The Beatles at that period, with Pete Best slumping over his drums looking very insolent, that was just how they were. They did have that rebellious outlook but it was the music that sold it. Pete Best was still drumming for them the first time I saw them. My ex-wife, who I met down there, has got that photo. I'm sure that, if Ringo was with them, then wouldn't have been giving those pictures out. I remember them announcing on stage that they were about to issue their first single and then playing 'Love Me Do'.

"WHEN BLUES TURN TO GREY"

THE MIGHTY AVENGERS

Clockwise from top left: Joe Ruane paid The Beatles £8 for their last appearance at Southport's Kingsway Club; Tony Newson remembers The Beatles at the BRS Ballroom in Birmingham; Tony Campbell was in The Mighty Avengers, who supported The Beatles the day 'Love Me Do' was released; Arthur McKerron didn't like The Beatles after watching them following rugby practice – but it wasn't for a lack of trying; The Beatles wanted Adeline Reid to take their temperature; Alan Vaughan lent George his Vox amplifier when their bands auditioned together; Val Newson got a signed photo from The Beatles, but was invited into the back of their van for something more.

Clockwise from top left: Despite a disappointing show at the Bridge of Allan in January 1963, Andi Lothian realised The Beatles were going to be huge; Elizabeth Walker remembers a great night in Aberdeen; Gail Laing had the boys' autographs until her mum threw them out, thinking they were rubbish; James Strachan was at the Beach Ballroom; Norman Shearer (sat on amp) recalls an unforgettable night at Aberdeen's Beach Ballroom in January 1963; Liz Wilson and her friends got talking to 'four scruffy-looking guys'; Louise Simpson was at the Beach Ballroom.

I was a service engineer then. I used to get about quite a bit and I remember being on my way back from Stoke-on-Trent and going into a cafe and hearing it being played in there and thinking 'wow, I remember them saying that on stage.' It felt like I was a part of it. Of course, I was mainly there for the girls in those days.

I WAS THERE: VAL NEWSON, AGE 15

My friend Linda and I went every Thursday to see groups. We were groupies in those days. It was before they'd done the first record, so they weren't really famous. They came on and we were really impressed with them. They were still in leathers then. They were rock 'n' roll. They announced that they'd made a record, and we followed them out to their tour van, stalking them. As you do.

As they went to get in the van, we asked if we could have their autographs. They gave us pictures of them with the autographs and we got chatting. And then had a bit of a snog! But I wasn't really pleased, because Linda and I both liked Paul and she got Paul and, unfortunately, I got John. Then they invited us into the tour van, with the beds and everything, and I think we got a bit frightened. I don't think we had a drink. We just had a little chat. They signed the autographs and that was about it.

And then we saw them at the Plaza in Handsworth in '63. By then, they'd had the hit record and were all smartened up, in suits. I've got Paul McCartney's and John Lennon's autographs on a picture of Pete Best, but he wasn't actually with the group then. I was gonna sell the photo but my daughter Anna's such a Beatles fan I had it framed and gave it to her because she wanted it. I was more of a Stones fan myself. I saw the Stones at the Plaza. That's where all the big acts in Handsworth were at the time and we saw a lot of the early groups up there. We were groupies. We used to hang about. Shane Fenton. Screaming Lord Sutch – I had a little snog with him. I was terrible! I never kept all the autographs. I should have done. When I first met my husband, he had the round collar and the Beatle haircut. That's why I first liked him – because he looked like one of The Beatles!

The Beatles first single, 'Love Me Do', is released on 5 October 1962.

CO-OP HALL
5 OCTOBER 1962, NUNEATON, UK

I WAS THERE: TONY CAMPBELL

I was in a band called The Mighty Avengers and worked with The Beatles at Nuneaton Co-op Hall on the Friday that their first single, 'Love Me Do', was released.

TOWER BALLROOM
12 OCTOBER 1962, NEW BRIGHTON, WALLASEY, UK

I WAS THERE: PETE MORRIS, AGE 14

I managed to see The Beatles perform three times. The first time was at the New Brighton Tower Ballroom when, along with a multitude of other groups, they supported Little Richard. I thought that The Beatles that night were phenomenal. 'Love Me Do' had just been released and they had a charismatic energy about them that was just irresistible. They looked so very different for a start. Most group members still had Teddy Boy hairstyles back then, Ringo included. They had better gear than the other groups and a great raw driving sound with wonderful harmonies to match. The fact that they had three front line vocalists also set them apart from most of the other groups on that night, notably The Big Three and Lee Curtis and the All Stars (with Pete Best on drums). The Beatles put them all in the shade, and Little Richard too, in my opinion.

PUBLIC HALL
26 OCTOBER 1962, PRESTON, UK

I WAS THERE: ALAN PARKINSON

I was at both the Preston gigs. At the first one, only about a hundred people were there. We went backstage at the interval because we recognised the drummer, who was at Butlins with Rory Storm and the Hurricanes. Of course, that was Ringo and my cheeky mate said 'remember us from Butlins?' to which he said 'yes'. I'm not sure he did.

I WAS THERE: PETE MORRIS

The second time I saw them, exactly two weeks after the first, was at Preston Public Hall. That night remains one of the greatest memories of my teenage years and is still fresh in my mind now, even after 54 years. The Beatles were second on the bill to Mike Berry and the Outlaws, who had recently been in the hit parade and were supplemented by a local dance band, The Syd Munson Orchestra. All these assorted musicians shared a large communal dressing room to the right of and behind the stage at the Public Hall. There was no need for any security, because nobody was actually famous at this time, and you could wander freely in and out of the backstage area without anybody questioning you. Only being 14, I wasn't interested in drinking in the bars, so I spent the whole evening either watching the groups on stage or hanging out in the dressing room. I managed to observe The Beatles at close quarters. As a young teenager, it seemed to me that they had arrived from another planet. I had never met anybody remotely like them. They looked so different from everybody else, they sounded different in conversation and they had a really wacky, Goon-like humour between them that was unique.

That night, they played three sets of about two hours in total. I remember leaning up against the front of the stage when they played their first spot and the dance floor was almost empty. John Lennon was holding his hand over his eyes, looking out and saying 'good evening, everybody, wherever you are.' They started playing and sounded so good, despite the lack of atmosphere and no lighting on the stage whatsoever apart from the normal houselights. It's hard to imagine now, with all the great music they produced in the following years, that they were a covers band in 1962. I remember them playing some Chuck Berry, Elvis, 'Sheila' by Tommy Roe and songs like 'Mr Moonlight' and 'A Taste of Honey', that made it onto albums later.

As the night went on, the hall became full and The Beatles rocked the place. Other things I recall from the dressing room are standing next to George Harrison and Paul McCartney and a couple of the Outlaws. They were all sitting down playing big semi-acoustic guitars doing some Chet Atkins-style country picking. The Outlaw was, I think, Ritchie Blackmore of Deep Purple fame and the bass player was Chas Hodges from Chas and Dave. I remember John Lennon being asleep at one point on a long table in a corner of the room.

George was mainly quiet and just having conversations with one or two people. Paul and Ringo, however, were very lively. Paul was very chatty and Ringo was quite loud and funny. Every time someone offered Ringo a ciggie, he would take the whole packet off them and offer everyone else one. I remember sitting on a table next to Paul while he was writing out a set list and inviting suggestions from others about what songs to sing. There were no other Beatles involved in this, though. Somebody said 'A Picture of You' by Joe Brown but Paul dismissed it, saying it had become old hat. I can also remember standing on the steps at the side of the stage with Paul and my older brother, watching Mike Berry and the Outlaws on stage. How I wish I had a camera with me that night to capture some of those moments. At least I managed to get all their autographs, which I still have to this day.

ST JAMES CHURCH HALL
23 NOVEMBER 1962, PADDINGTON, LONDON, UK

I WAS THERE: GORDON VALENTINE

I met them twice. One time we applied to the BBC for an audition. There was a show coming up for talent new to television. The audition was on Friday. It was at St James Church Hall in Gloucester Terrace. We rode down by train and put the amps and guitars in the guard's van. It was very pleasant. On the way down, I was reading about this funny looking group called The Beatles in the *New Musical Express*. I'd heard 'Love Me Do' and it was different. We got two London cabs to put all the gear in and set off to Gloucester Terrace and when we pulled up Epstein's big white Jag was outside, although we didn't know it was his at the time. We walked in and ten feet away from us The Beatles were playing a Chuck Berry tune. Then they played 'Love Me Do'. I'd been playing guitar from about 1959, playing in all sorts of groups, and ended up with the Johnny Taylor Five. We'd seen groups come and go so it was no big deal to see The Beatles, who were going to be famous, there. We had a chat with them and we put our gear on the floor and set up. We did the audition and we got the show. And The Beatles didn't. It was a programme called *The 625 Show* from Bristol, a national programme compered by Jimmy Young. I think we had about 12 million viewers.

I WAS THERE: ALAN VAUGHAN

During 1962 a colleague and I, both from Stroud, attempted to break into the popular music business, having written a number of songs and performed for some years. We attended the same BBC TV audition as The Beatles. We were auditioned directly after The Beatles and chatted to them. We loaned George our Vox amplifier when his packed up.

CLUB DJANGO
6 DECEMBER 1962, QUEENS HOTEL, SOUTHPORT, UK

I WAS THERE: KEVIN FINLAYSON

The name of our band was The Diplomats. We were a Southport band. We specialized in the Buddy Holly stuff. We used to do Beatles stuff and general rock 'n' roll. We used to do a lot in Southport, and travel around a lot. We played with Freddie and the Dreamers, Billy J Kramer, Gerry and the Pacemakers, Sounds Incorporated. We were busy, out five or six nights a week. That's all we did for five or six years. We used to play at Belle Vue on Monday nights, when Jimmy Savile was the DJ. He used to have pink hair. We played with The Beatles at the Queens Django Club on a Thursday night, before they had any hits or anything. Paul's bass amp had gone off, and he came over to ask to borrow an amp. Ringo came over too, to look at my kit. I had an American kit, a Ludwig. I said, 'Of course you can borrow the amp.' We had a little natter and Ringo said he liked that kit. I said I thought they (The Beatles) would go a long way and he said 'well, I don't know about that.' So I was right, wasn't I? Because he's worth £190m – approximately! I wonder if he remembers that? I obviously influenced him because a few months after, I think they were on *Scene at 6.30*, and he had the drum kit there, the same kit.

CAVERN CLUB
7 DECEMBER 1962, LIVERPOOL, UK

I WAS THERE: RON WATSON

There was another club in Liverpool called the Iron Door which is where the Searchers made their name. The Cavern was the principal venue, but they played all over Merseyside as they got more popular and more well known. And Epstein wanted to move them around a bit. They started playing on the outskirts. And then they did their first nationwide tour and then basically that was it. They essentially left Liverpool. At that stage, for people like me, that was almost the end of the era. They were never the same. When they started putting on those round collar suits and had those rather silly photographs sipping out of Coke bottles, this was not The Beatles we knew. But it was probably necessary for a commercial and acceptance point of view.

We were very fortunate. You saw them develop. You saw them change, particularly after Epstein took over. But you also saw them as a rock 'n' roll band that were literally unbeatable. There were lots of bands on Merseyside who were extremely good. But The Beatles – with probably one exception, The Big Three – wiped the floor with most of them. When they came back from Hamburg, they were more professional, they were more distinctive. They learnt a lot out there. People were pleased they were doing as well as they did but we all knew they'd gone. They were just not the same sort of band. You had all these thousands of people screaming and you think 'what is all this about?'

I was over in the States a few years ago and did a radio phone in which went across Michigan, Ohio and all these places. This lady rang and said she'd seen The Beatles at Shea Stadium in New York in 1965, and I said 'well actually you didn't'. If you saw Elvis in Las Vegas in 1976, you did but it wasn't the same Elvis that was on the Louisiana Hayride in 1955, '56. It was a different product. Unless you saw them at the Star Club in Hamburg or the Cavern in Liverpool or other venues in '61, '62, you never really saw The Beatles as a band.

Kingsize Taylor and the Dominoes made an album out in Hamburg for Polydor. It was the best album of the era by a Merseybeat group. And The Beatles' Star Club in Hamburg tracks were recorded by Kingsize Taylor. The quality's poor and the performance is pretty sloppy, because it was New Year's Eve and I think they were blind drunk. There's no recording that captures what it was like to be there during that period. It's a great shame.

In January 1963 The Beatles embark on a short tour of Scotland.

 # THE TWO RED SHOES
3 JANUARY 1963, ELGIN, UK

I WAS THERE: ARTHUR MCKERRON

I was a rugby player. I played hooker. We used to go there every night after a game, or after training, and have a meal. It would have been a Thursday. The back café was part of the Two Red Shoes. You entered it from the front side, looking down towards the old library. We were sitting in the dining area downstairs, next to the kitchen. Mrs Bonici was there, the wife of the owner of the Two Red Shoes, and I said 'who's that playing upstairs tonight?' 'Oh,' she says, 'it's some group called The Beatles.' And I said, 'Oh, do you mind if I go upstairs?' Because you could go upstairs and through to the dance hall. 'Can I come and see who's up the stairs there?' And she said 'aye, up you go'.

I went up and there was just these four boys on the stand, on the platform. The place was deserted. One couple were more-or-less just walking or jiving around the hall, and three or four couples were at a wee higher level where they had seating and tables. And about wo of the table had folks sitting at them. And that was all that was in the place at that time. That would have been somewhere in the region of nine o'clock at night, because we were just finished our meal. At that time, nobody recognised them. The place was dead.

I WAS THERE: ADELINE REID

In the '60s, I was a student nurse training at Dr Gray's Hospital in Elgin. Along with another nurse student, I lived in a boarding house not far from the Two Red Shoes ballroom. The landlady was very genteel, a companion to a lady before getting married. She was aloof and did not tolerate bad manners. We were her girls and she was very protective of us. All boyfriends were given the once over for approval – or not! Next door was another boarding house whose owners were friends of Albert Bonici, the owner of the Two Red Shoes. All of the artists who appeared at the ballroom stayed there and it was an exciting time for us next door to meet with some of them.

However, along came The Beatles and seemingly their appearance at the Two Red Shoes did not go down too well. My friend Joan and I were unable to get tickets. If I remember rightly the cost was 4/6 (23p), quite an expense for us in those days. Regardless, next day when I was about to go to hospital for duty, The Beatles were hanging out of the window next door. I could have reached out and touched them. Their personalities were cheeky and outrageous, and not what we were used to. I thought they were fun. I was wearing a hideous outdoor nurse's uniform and they shouted comments at me. John Lennon asked me to take his pulse. My face went the colour of a tomato. At the house door appeared our landlady, who proceeded to reprimand them for their cheek. She did not approve of them talking to her girls in such a shocking manner! You can imagine the chat at the hospital, and especially a week later, when The Beatles became famous.

TOWN HALL
4 JANUARY 1963, DINGWALL, UK

I WAS THERE: FRASER GOW, AGE 18

I worked for the Milk Marketing Board. I had another two mates with me that day. One was James Burgess. He had muscular dystrophy and he was in a wheelchair. And the other was James Gordon. The venue was the local town hall in Dingwall. It wasn't used that often. It was one of the halls that was donated by Carnegie. He donated it to the town. There's an upstairs and a downstairs. You could probably get a couple of hundred into it if they were dancing. It would be now and again that a special band would come up. We always went up the road to what they called the Pavilion in Strathpeffer, where they held dances every Friday and Saturday night. That was the 'in' place for going dancing but we thought 'well, we'll go and see what these guys are like.' I reckon there was about 20 of us there in total in a great big hall. It was just pretty empty. They were quite a loud band and in an empty hall it was probably making it worse. More echo than anything else, you know? Because there wasn't the crowd to dull the noise. They were a bit of a rock band. We thought, 'Och no, we can't be arsed with this,' so the three of us went away up to the local dance further up the road. The other venue used to run free buses to their venue, so we went off to see the local band which was the Melotones. I think The Beatles cut their losses and stopped playing, and the ones behind us got their money back. And about three weeks later they were the 'in thing'. They were off and running.

I WAS THERE: DOREEN DOUGLAS, AGE 18

I was a dance-mad teenager and, along with my late sister and friends, decided we would go to Dingwall to see for ourselves what all the fuss was about concerning this new pop group. I was never a fan of The Beatles and it took a lot to give up Strathpeffer Ballroom and the Melotones, but after some thought we decided we would give it a try. Along with the Melotones, I think there was also one of the Irish showbands, which was really fab. There was no contest. The Town Hall was almost empty and the few that were there, including my crowd, all shared a taxi and headed to the Strath. The Beatles were getting pennies thrown at them along with the jeers. Someone told me later that The Beatles had been seen in the bar at Strathpeffer Ballroom, sussing it out.

I WAS THERE: SARAH PURCHASE, AGE 18

I clearly remember them. It was a bit of a disaster as just a handful turned up. Myself and my friends were not impressed with them and left for Strathpeffer to see the group at the Pavilion. Ringo Starr was not there. The rest of them just sat around the stage making conversation with us and disappointed in the turn out.

I WAS THERE: BILLY SHANKS, AGE 17

They weren't very well known at that time. The word on the street was they were four lads from Liverpool. I didn't know anything about them. It didn't register that they had recorded 'Love Me Do', and the funny thing is that, when I went in the door to go in and go upstairs, the doorman said 'before you pay, go up and have a listen'. They were actually playing that song, 'Love Me Do', when I looked in the door and I thought 'no, no, it's not my type of music.' I walked out and went to the local village hall five miles away to hear the Melotones. I'm afraid I wasn't a very good judge of the music, because about six weeks later they were top of the charts and three months later they were worldwide and they changed the face of music. They were dressed very smart, all in black suits. Long hair, obviously, which hadn't hit the Highlands of Scotland by that time. We were still in short back and sides. I suppose some of the locals would say they looked scruffy. But they were tidy. A lot of the locals who came to the door decided 'no, that's not my style of music' and went to Strathpeffer. But the 19 that did stay talk about it to this day. One lad told me 'I pulled up outside the hall. I saw this green Volkswagen Beetle van with black beetles painted on the side and thought they were gypsies or tinkers or something.' And he thought, 'They can't be up to much. We're not going in there,' so they didn't even go into the hall because they saw The Beatles' van. The band was booked for £42 and the charge at the door was two shillings (10p), so they made quite a loss on the night. At the Caird Hall in Dundee later that year, half the people couldn't get into the hall. Unfortunately, Dingwall didn't look at it that way.

I WAS THERE: MARGARET PATERSON, AGE 17

I was almost 18 when I attended The Beatles dance in Dingwall. It was my first date with my late husband Tommy and I thought he had stood me up. The dance was almost over when the friend Tommy had given a message to remembered to tell me to go to the Strathpeffer gig, and that Tommy would meet me there. I sat on the stage all night chatting to The Beatles, and Paul in particular, who told me not to be upset as there were more fish in the sea than ever came out of it. He was lovely! They said, 'Where is everybody? This town is dead,' and I replied, 'Oh, no offence boys, but there is a great band on at the Strath and everybody is there and I'm going there soon. Why don't you come?' I am certain I saw them there but I met Tommy when I got there. I was married to my Tommy for over 30 years but he sadly died in a fishing accident. The Beatles were great. I organised the gig in Dingwall for the reunion of the 19 people who attended The Beatles performance and plaques were installed by Highland Council. One was placed at the stage and the second plaque was placed at the front door of the town hall. Many people come to have their photograph taken with that plaque.

I WAS THERE: HUGH PHILLIPS

I was in a five-piece band called Beat Unlimited. We'd been playing in the Hamilton area for a few years so we were quite well known in central Scotland at that point. We were playing up in Strathpeffer in the north of Scotland at the Spa Pavilion. It's quite a big, 600-person venue, and down the road two or three miles away The Beatles were playing in Dingwall Town Hall. The story was that no one had gone to see them because nobody knew them. They all came to Strathpeffer Pavilion, where we were playing.

MY DAD WAS THERE: JULIE KELLY

I was not at the Beatles concert in Dingwall but my dad, Dot McDonald, was, he being the caretaker in the Town Hall. His comments? 'A bunch of laddies making an awful noise!' And he said there was hardly anyone there, since everyone was at the Pavilion in Strathpeffer. Little did he, or anyone else, know what was to transpire. If I had known then what I know now I would have had him get their autographs.

MUSEUM HALL
5 JANUARY 1963, BRIDGE OF ALLAN, UK

I WAS THERE: ANDI LOTHIAN

I had heard 'Love Me Do' when it was released in November and really thought that would be a big hit, but it only got to 18 so there was no interest in The Beatles at that point. I had The Beatles in tandem with another promoter from the north of Scotland, a man called Albert Bonici, in January 1963. And that was just for town hall dances, which wasn't successful. They played in the north of Scotland. The Two Red Shoes ballroom in Elgin was one. The Town Hall in Dingle, where there was only 16 people and they all left and went up to Strathpeffer for a competition at the time to hear the local band the Merry Macs, was another. And I ran the last night, which was a Saturday night in a place called Bridge of Allan, near Stirling. There was a hundred people there – 96 drunk young farmers and four women – so the place was just a rammie. I had only one doorman with me so I was doing a lot of the bouncing as well.

The Beatles went on, did their stint and a penny hit Paul's guitar and chipped it. I was quite despondent about it because we had lost money on the event. It was the only time that a dance promoter had got the use of the Bridge of Allan borough museum hall, which was reserved for weddings and funerals and young farmers events. I had got it on the premise that there was no damage, and a lovely chandelier in the middle of the ballroom was almost wrecked so I think it was probably the one and only public dance that occurred in that era in the hall and it was The Beatles. They still talk about that. They stayed in the Royal, just up the road in the Bridge of Allan. About five years ago, my wife and I just happened to pop in for lunch. Unbeknown, the waiter said 'do you know who stayed in this hotel?' and we said 'no' and he said 'The Beatles.' We said 'nooo!' So it was a big event!

For the last quarter an hour of the dance, I went up and sat in the balcony and they announced that they were going to play three numbers, all of which had been recorded and were likely to be their next releases. I was sitting up there quite despondent and the music just shattered: 'She loves you, yeah yeah yeah…' and it just hit me like no other music had. I'm a musician. You know, 'I wanna hold your hand…', and I just realised the significance of the music. Outside of The Beatles and George Martin, I was one of the first people to hear those songs they had recorded.

On the Sunday, I phoned Albert Bonici and said, 'You know, Albert, although we've lost money, we need to get these guys back. They're going to be fantastic.' And he said, 'Well, I quite like them too.' And I said, 'No, I mean we really have to get them back. We have to get them back before any of these songs come out because they're all going to be huge.'

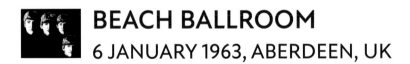

BEACH BALLROOM
6 JANUARY 1963, ABERDEEN, UK

I WAS THERE: HAMY HARWOOD

I played in a local group called the Strollers from 1959 to 1965. We were the supporting band at the Beach Ballroom for Dusty Springfield, Joe Brown and other bands at various towns across the North East of Scotland. The main music shop where all the groups in Aberdeen went was Forbes in George Street, managed by Harry Lord. I went to Forbes to meet the rest of our band and they were talking to some guys in the shop. I asked who they were and George, my rhythm guitarist, said they were The Beatles and were playing the Beach Ballroom the next day. I got talking to them and George Harrison was playing one of the guitars in the shop. George had a problem with his guitar and I think someone lent him a guitar for the following night. I'll always remember how dirty his fingernails were.

I WAS THERE: NORMAN SHEARER

My friends and I, who were in a local band called the Facells, saw these four scruffy-looking individuals falling out of their van the afternoon of the concert. I remember being surprised as I had heard 'Love Me Do' on Radio Luxembourg and thought it might be a girl group. The concert was terrific, but not for all of the audience. There are still silly rumours that they were booed off the stage but that is palpable nonsense. They were well received by the bulk of the audience and I still have a very clear picture in my mind of John Lennon standing on the stage with his guitar slung square across his body, belting out 'Johnny B Goode' and 'Roll Over Beethoven'. My impression was that they were great. Six weeks or so later, I was proved correct as they took off with 'Please Please Me'. My mate Ian was also there, sitting with his girlfriend near the front. He remembers that they finished with 'Love Me Do' and that the curtains were supposed to close. They didn't, and so they repeated the song whilst Paul was urging the technician to close the curtains. They finished and still the curtains didn't close so they sang it again and this time – success! That concert was an extraordinary night which I will never ever forget.

I WAS THERE: LIZ WILSON

My friends and I were regulars at the wonderful Beach Ballroom concerts for years, arriving early to queue and always managing to get a front row seat. I remember it being a freezing night and my friends and I huddling in the entrance, waiting for the doors to open. Whilst queueing, four scruffy-looking guys approached us to enter. Of course the door was locked as artists always used the back door to enter. Chatting to them, and explaining the situation, they were really nice. I loved listening to their funny accents. I'm sure they thought ours were too. While waiting for the attendants to unlock the door, we found out they were the act for the evening. Once they gained entry, we chatted excitedly about meeting the guys who were to perform, wondering if they were going to be any good. Little did we know what we were about to witness. When they came on stage – wow, what a transformation! Gone were the four scruffy guys and there stood The Beatles, wearing cute suits and identical Beatle haircuts. I cannot remember the opening number but the sound and their vocals were something I will never forget. I met The Beatles. I wish I had got their autographs!

I WAS THERE: MALCOLM STRACHAN

We'd formed a band in Aberdeen called The Playboys and we went to see quite a few gigs at the Beach Ballroom. The bands that came and played always chatted, but these guys were totally different. There was a definite aura about them. I'd seen them on a Granada TV special one teatime playing 'Love Me Do' and I remember thinking then 'they look really different', because of the fact that they all sang, and McCartney had his left-handed bass. We saw they were coming to Aberdeen and we thought 'we'll definitely go and see them'. They were totally different. Before that you relied on singers with backing groups – Shane Fenton and the Fentones, Mike Berry and the Outlaws, Johnny Kidd and the Pirates, Joe Brown and the Bruvvers. They were all good but The Beatles were just very different, as was the stuff they did – their own stuff and also Chuck Berry stuff, The Crickets. Paul McCartney did 'Till There Was You'.

It was really very, very good indeed. It wasn't a dance as such. It was a concert. Aberdeen City Council owned the Beach Ballroom, and in those days on a Sunday evening you couldn't have a dance. It wasn't allowed, and there was no alcohol licence either. It was a very good dance floor. They laid a tarpaulin out on the floor and put seats out, so you were actually sitting at a concert. When we arrived, we just went strolling in and upstairs to the coffee bar. There was hardly anybody there, but the four of them were just sitting there, having a cigarette and having a coffee. We stood and chatted and chatted for ages. It was good fun.

Paul McCartney was definitely the leader cum PR chap. He did most of the talking. He was very interested to know the kind of stuff that we liked, and tell us the kind of stuff that they liked. I didn't smoke, but they offered us cigarettes. They never stopped smoking. As they finished one, they lit another, especially Ringo Starr and George Harrison. They just smoked all the time. I talked to John Lennon about the Star Club in Hamburg and how hard they'd worked, because they'd work from nine in the evening until three in the morning. I said 'what was it like in the Star Club?' and he went 'it was just a converted gas chamber'. It went right over the top of my head and they all started laughing. They were in suits but it wasn't the round-necked ones. It was the ones with the ties and the proper collars. They were very smart.

There's been a load of urban myths that, when they actually played here they got the raspberry, that they got booed. That definitely did not happen. They went down very well. They really did. They did two sets. When they finished, John Lennon said, 'We're gonna play our new single 'Please Please Me'. It's out in a couple of weeks' time. Please go out and buy it.' They shot into that and we thought 'this sounds really good.' And that was the final number. Sitting chatting to those guys you definitely knew they were going to make it. They just had so much confidence. It was a fantastic evening. And so great to have actually met them.

I WAS THERE: BRIAN BEATTIE

It was a Sunday. I remember going with my mates. I'm sorry to say they didn't make much of an impression on us, or much of an impression on the crowd either. I'm just disappointed I don't have my ticket or any other memorabilia. It would be worth a fortune!

I WAS THERE: BILL COWIE, AGE 15

The Beehive Youth Club had a Wurlitzer juke box and on it was an exciting new record, 'Love Me Do' by The Beatles, which I played all the time when I was at the club. When I saw the advert in the *Evening Express* for the concert featuring the Johhny Scott Orchestra with special guest band The Beatles, I just had to go. Tickets were three shillings (15p) and it was an all-seated concert. I went with my brother Mike. The support band was the Johnny Scott Orchestra, the regular band. Their gear was all at the back of the stage so The Beatles had all theirs at the front. They were right in the front of stage.

We arrived early and had an opportunity to chat with The Beatles before the show about music, Hamburg and the Liverpool scene. We knocked on the stage door and were invited in to meet them. Back in those days, security didn't exist. If you were invited in, then fine. They were tuning their guitars and discussing their playlist. Being a musician myself, I was interested in their guitars. John played a Rickenbacker bought from a GI in Hamburg, George was using a Gretsch Country Gent on loan from Hessy's guitar shop in Liverpool as his own was in for repair, and Paul handed me his Hofner bass. I noticed their playlist, taped to Paul's guitar, only included two Lennon/McCartney songs – 'Love Me Do' and 'Please Please Me'. The rest were all classic rock 'n' roll. I requested Chuck Berry's 'Sweet Little Sixteen' as it was a favourite with my band.

The Beatles played two 45-minute sets. In the first section, they did a great selection of rock classics plus 'Love Me Do'. John dedicated the Chuck Berry song especially for the 'lads in the front row' – me and my brother! I could see how talented and destined for stardom they were. After the first set, we went back into the dressing room and talked about their favourite groups and singers. Tea and biscuits were served by a waitress in her old-style black and white council uniform and Paul offered us a cup of tea. John asked where in Aberdeen he could buy a guitar case. I suggested JT Forbes as they had a good selection of secondhand equipment, and I knew Harry Lloyd, the manager, would be helpful. I drew a map for them to go to the shop the following day.

During the second half of the show, they announced their new single 'Please Please Me'. The audience were enjoying their music very much by their applause and reaction. I could hear every song as there was no screaming. They were absolutely great. They were very polished and a great bunch of guys and the crowd loved them. It was obvious to me that they were something special and I knew that this band was going to go far. They just had that style, professionalism and charisma about them. I've seen a lot of good bands live and they were definitely the best.

There was a rumour that circulated about The Beatles being booed. That's not true. It never ever happened. They ran a bus service to the Beach Ballroom. The local Corporation bus transport did what they called a late bus on a Sunday down to the ballroom and there were several buses waiting outside. The timing of the concert and when it finished meant you were a bit touch and go to catch a bus, so some people got up and went to get on to catch the bus. There was a bit of confusion then as to what was happening, why these people were leaving. There certainly was no booing. During the break, when they went off after their first set, everybody thought that that's all they were getting – 45 minutes. And there was a sort of sigh of disappointment. But when the Johnny Scott Orchestra came on, they said that The Beatles would be back on again. Apparently, Brian Epstein asked them to break up their set and to do it in two 45-minute halves instead of doing it all in one.

As I was leaving I asked Tucker Donald, the resident Johnny Scott band singer, what he thought of them. He said 'they were okay' but he was not that impressed. I'm the luckiest guy in Scotland. To actually have The Beatles play a personal request for me.

I WAS THERE: KATHLEEN DONALD, AGE 15

My friend Pat Masson and I went to the concert that they used to have at the Beach Ballroom every Sunday. It was brilliant for dancing on a Saturday, but dancing wasn't allowed on a Sunday so they put chairs out and you were just there to watch the concert. I saw a few of the Sixties groups there that came up, such as Joe Brown and the Bruvvers and Shane Fenton. The Beatles were terrific. We stayed behind and went to their dressing room. John was my favourite, and Paul was Pat's favourite. There were quite a few folk there, but I knocked on the door and Paul answered it and we just asked if we could get their autographs. 'No problem.' They all came to the door and signed a piece of paper. It was quite exciting at the time. When I got married and left my parents' home, did my mother not have a clear out and throw away The Beatles autographs? Can you imagine? When I tackled her about it, she said, 'Oh, it was just a few names on a bit of paper.'

I WAS THERE: GAIL LAING (NEE FRASER), AGE 15

At the interval, I and others talked to them at the side of the stage where I got their individual autographs. I talked more to George Harrison because I thought he was nice looking. I kept those autographs until I got married in October 1967 and left the family home. A few years later, my mum moved house and, unfortunately, she must have thrown thc autograph book out. She probably thought it was rubbish. I wish I still had them, knowing the value of them. A lot of people didn't like them, but I personally did. I still have some 45s and EPs. But not many.

I WAS THERE: ALICE MCKAY, AGE 16

I first heard The Beatles singing 'Love Me Do' on Radio Luxembourg and was immediately captivated. When I read in our local newspaper that they were coming to Aberdeen and appearing at the Beach Ballroom, myself and three of my friends went to see them. Now the Beach Ballroom in Aberdeen was a very popular dance hall and on Sunday nights they ran concerts. Many other 60s stars appeared there – Joe Brown, Gerry and the Pacemakers, Eden Kane, Dusty Springfield and the Springfields, and others. When I told my friends I'd heard The Beatles on the radio and thought they were brilliant, three of them agreed to come with me to see what I was raving about. The fourth friend said, 'Yeugh! With a name like The Beatles, that's too much like creepy crawlies. I'm not going!' So off we went, the three of us. Boy, they were brilliant! They took the place by storm. We went backstage and met the boys and spoke to them and got their autographs, which I still have. They were just normal young lads then, very thick Liverpool accents and so down to earth. George Harrison was my idol. My friend who didn't come has certainly rued the day she didn't.

I WAS THERE: LOUISE SIMPSON, AGE 17

The Beach Ballroom held many concerts there on a Sunday and we were able to see many groups. I remember enjoying it. It was well received, and there were no boos as has been rumoured since. My friend and I were surprised to see Ringo Starr as we had seen him at Skegness Butlins holiday camp that summer. He was the drummer in the band there.

I WAS THERE: ALLAN SMART, AGE 18

I thought their performance was outstanding and to a large degree groundbreaking, but a proportion of the audience were not particularly impressed. In subsequent years I had the privilege of attending two further concerts, at the ABC in Blackpool in 1963, when the reception they received was unbelievable. Knowing The Beatles were performing there was the deciding factor in choosing to go on holiday to Blackpool. Seeing the Fab Four performing live on stage three times remains one of my happiest memories as a teenager.

I WAS THERE: JAMES STRACHAN

On Saturday 5th January 1963, my late friend Hughie Sutherland and I were at the Beach Ballroom for the dancing. During the band's break, Johnny Scott made an announcement that the following night's concert would be featuring an exciting group called The Beatles. He stated that the group had been getting rave plaudits during their time in Hamburg. After a bit of debating, we decided we would go to the concert. During the evening, we asked a number of people if they knew anything about The Beatles. The consistent answer was 'never heard of them'. We thought they might be a local group as, in the early '60s, Aberdeen had many local groups appearing in clubs and dance halls. The Beatles did not play on the main stage but on the dance floor to the left of the stage. They certainly played music you would have loved to dance to.

John Lennon came across as the lead man. The audience sat on chairs on the left side of dance floor, taking up about a third of the floor area. Early on, Hughie and I were convinced that the left-handed guitar player was a guy called Billy from Merkland Road who went to Old Aberdeen School. Twice when they were singing, the three guitarists turned round and pointed their guitars at Ringo, bringing a smile. Ringo looked a dour kind of guy. The audience cheered and applauded him smiling. At one point, John Lennon said that the next song they were about to sing would be released very soon. It was 'Please Please Me'. After 10pm John Lennon asked the audience to request any song they had played.

The late Donnie (Brian) Fraser requested 'A Shot of Rhythm and Blues', which they duly sang. At approximately 10.10pm, a number of girls left their seats to go and collect their coats. When he noticed the girls leaving their seats, John Lennon said over the microphone that he did not think they (The Beatles) were that bad. The girls came back and stood at back of the hall, making ready for a quick exit to catch the bus the council provided. Unknown to the band, the majority of the audience were getting ready to leave as soon as the concert was finished to catch the public bus home because the council laid on buses for both Saturday and Sunday. The buses took the passengers to Garthdee, Mastrick/Northfield and the Bridge of Don. You missed your bus at your peril; the drivers did not hang around and money to pay for a taxi was almost unthinkable. At the finish, The Beatles were given a warm cheer for their performance.

Hughie and I only had just over a mile to walk home. We finally agreed the left-handed guitarist could not have been Billy. We were not even sure Billy was a musician. How were we to know that the left-handed guitarist was to become Sir Paul McCartney? Several weeks later I met Hughie, who told me that group we had watched called The Beatles were No 1 in the pop charts. It still gives me pleasure telling people that I saw them live at the Beach Ballroom – to my wife's annoyance!

I WAS THERE: ELIZABETH WALKER

I was there that night with a friend. A group appeared every Sunday night so it was just another group to us. Rumour has it that they were booed off, but I can't remember that. It was a great night. Of course, 'Love Me Do' had come out in October 1962 and my husband remembered it was played on *Juke Box Jury* on BBC TV on Saturday night. It was voted a miss three to one by the panellists. One said 'The Beatles? What kind of name is that?'

MY MUM WAS THERE: WENDY CORMACK

My mum always spoke to the time she met them. She had gone to see them at the Beach Ballroom when she was 16 and spoke of them being booed off stage. She went backstage and met them and they said to her they would never come back to Aberdeen. They never did…

MY DAD WAS THERE: SHELDON JOLLY

My dad, James 'Jimmy' Jolly, had the resident band at the Beach Ballroom in the 1960s; he was the pianist and sort of the leader of the band. His band went on and did the first set, as was normal. The Beatles then went on and it was time for my dad's band to have dinner. Someone (probably, Fast Eddie, the sax player) was sent out to get fish and chips and a few cans from the Inversnecky Cafe. They got a first bite and a sip when the manager of the Beach Ballroom came flying through and said, 'Jim, you've got to get back out there. The crowd are throwing bottles at the band!' My dad and his band went back out and played a few standard numbers. When they finished and went back stage again, all the fish and chips and the beer were gone. Fast Eddie said, 'I'll never trust those scouse bastards again.'

I WAS THERE: ROBERT WILSON

I am told that the compere was Mr Alfred Wood. When it came to introducing the not then so famous four, the story goes that he invited those present to welcome not 'The Bee- tles' but 'the Bee-attles'. This account was given to me by two different people who, like me, were his work colleagues. Being much younger than Alfie Wood, as he was known to many, I never had the courage to ask him to confirm this blunder.

NEMS OFFICES
7 JANUARY 1963, LONDON, UK

I WAS THERE: ANDI LOTHIAN

So we flew down from Scotland unannounced to meet Brian Epstein on the Monday morning. We arrived at lunchtime and turned up in his office in London. He sat at his desk and he said 'so you think they're going to do well then?' 'Well, Brian, it's a bit more like we want to help you. The guys are really good and the weather was bad and so we'll take them back.' He said, 'Oh, you will?' We had paid them forty pounds a night and I said, 'the only thing is, Brian, we can't pay them forty pounds a night.' 'Oh you can't.' 'No we can't.' I said, 'We can pay them thirty pound a night.' And he said, 'Oh, you can?' And I said, 'Yes we can.' He said, 'Well, I tell you what. I know why you're here. I know, like you know, they're gonna be huge. So, despite the Bridge of Allan borough museum hall, despite that and everything else, they quite enjoyed their wee stint in Scotland. So, you can have them back but there's three conditions.' 'Oh. What are the three conditions?' 'Well, first of all, he said, 'it's none of your wee dance halls. You can have them back in October.'

And I'm thinking October. Well, probably all these three numbers will be out, they'll all be number one and they're going to be huge. We're getting a bit excited.

'Condition number one is it's going to have to be late in October just before they go to America. Condition number two is, because they're doing concerts in America, I'd like them to do concerts with you and with other promoters around that autumn period. So it's going to be concerts...' Well, we'd never promoted a concert at that point. And he said, 'The third condition is it's not your thirty pound a night.' 'It's not?' 'No.' 'It's not forty pound a night?' 'No.' And he held up four fingers and a thumb. I said, 'Fifty pounds a night?' He said, 'Five hundred pounds a night,' which is probably equivalent to ten grand a night now, and he said, 'OK, I'm going to leave the room for three minutes and I need your decision when I come back one way or the other.' And he just left the room.

Albert was flabbergasted. He said, 'Well, that's that then.' And I said, 'Albert, we've got to have them. We've got to pay this.' It wasn't much of a risk for me because I didn't have much money. Albert had the money. We came back, and much to Albert's chagrin at the time, we booked them. We got three nights in October.

I had left school when I was 17 and formed a jazz band. I was Scottish jazz band champion at 19, so my background was as a musician. One of the odd things about The Beatles was that boy bands came in and replaced traditional jazz and as jazz musicians we found ourselves supporting these kids instead of us being the main attraction. I saw the writing on the wall and I went in to promoting dances locally at the age of 20.

I was coming back late at night from dances and listening to Radio Luxembourg and I began to realise that in order to make a success of this, I had to endeavour to predict which releases were going to make it and which weren't. Because the managers wanted the bands exposed, but obviously they would endeavour to double the money even if the record was not a hit. I soon realised that I had a gift for picking the ones that were likely to be in the top ten at the time they were coming to Scotland. That was always my goal, to book them one month, two months, three months, four months ahead, judging how long it would take for that release to climb to its highest point. And it was either good luck or some bit of intuition. The fact that these two numbers hit me as being so brilliant was what made us take this huge risk of booking a completely unknown band at money way beyond they would have earned if the records hadn't done anything. But I was so certain they were going to be huge. They had two number one hits by the time they got to us in October that year. The third one had just been released and was going to go straight to number one. I put the tickets on sale in June and we sold out in Glasgow in a morning. It was pandemonium.

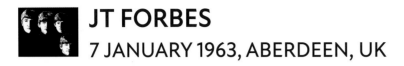

JT FORBES
7 JANUARY 1963, ABERDEEN, UK

I WAS THERE: BILL COWIE

After school the next day I went into JT Forbes and asked Harry if The Beatles had been in the shop. He said 'who? Those long-haired scruffy Liverpudlians?' He did sell John a case. The following year, as their fame spread, he changed his attitude and put up a banner declaring 'The Beatles shopped here'.

The Beatles second single, 'Please Please Me', is released in the UK on 11 January 1963.

THE EL RIO CLUB
26 JANUARY 1963, MACCLESFIELD, UK

I WAS THERE: PATRICIA HUGHES (NEE BENNETT), AGE 16

I was waiting outside for my friend. A car stopped alongside me and a broad Liverpudlian voice asked 'is this the El Rio, love?' Little did I know then that this was Paul actually speaking to me. When I recall this to my friends, most of them think I made it up. Very few people now remember the El Rio, although I had wonderful times there seeing lots of groups of the time.

I WAS THERE: DAVE JACKSON

The El Rio was in the Brocklehurst Memorial Hall. The main entrance was up a short flight of steps at the narrow end of the building. There was a lengthy delay to the expected start time as they had to travel from Stoke after an appearance at the Kings Hall. I was waiting with a friend who had to be home by 10.30, so she had to leave before the show started. The performance was something extra special – a very tight and perfectly performed set. There was a fantastic buzz in the hall, well worth the ticket price of five shillings. My daughter Lucy was born in 1974 and she and her friends are impressed that I saw The Beatles live.

I WAS THERE: KEN HOOPER, AGE 26

I used to go on the El Rio and one of the doormen used to let me in because he knew that I'd done a bit of boxing in the army. He was leaving and he said 'can you help us out?' And that's how I stepped in to do the job. I worked the door on the El Rio every week for a year or two. We had all sorts of groups every week. It was well supported, the El Rio. I was just doing a job because I was getting paid and I wanted extra money. I was paid £2, £3. I worked at the Parkside Hospital in the engineer shop. I was on the door when they came up the steps at the front. I think they had come from Stoke to Macclesfield and were going on to Manchester, like three places. They were just getting known, you see. They were queuing up down to the Water's Green pub. People couldn't get in. The boss, a Jewish bloke called Betesh, told us to keep letting them in. You couldn't move. You couldn't dance or anything. They were swinging on the rafters at the top. If you could get 200 people in there, there must have been 500. That's how bad it was. It was unsafe. You'd have never got away with it today.

I WAS THERE: BRENDA CLARKE

My recollections of that night are quite sketchy, probably because I was one of the very few people who wasn't actually that keen on The Beatles. My main memory is what a mess the room was at the end of the night. Part of the décor of the El Rio was ropes hung across the ceiling. So many people came that night that a lot ended up standing on tables and chairs to get a better view. Some of them hung onto the ropes as they were on the floor, and some of the tables and chairs were missing legs.

I WAS THERE: TONY CLARKE

Brenda and I met at the El Rio. I took an extra job there to help save for an engagement ring. There were usually three of us on the door; two of us were local and one from Manchester. The El Rio only served soft drinks so early doors was mainly girls, the lads not coming until the pubs closed when the place would be quite busy, 200-300 people. On the night The Beatles came, the numbers doubled and it was very busy right from the doors opening. They had brought in an extra doorman from Manchester so I was assigned to look after the group, showing them to the dressing room which was in the basement and, after they finished playing, taking the fans down three at a time to get autographs. The lads were very personable, chatty and modest bearing in mind the effect they had just had on the audience. The music really was fabulous and everyone there that night knew that this group was very special. As a thank you for looking after them, they gave me three lots of autographs, each signed by all of them. I gave two of them to really keen fans and put the other one somewhere safe. We've never seen it since and Brenda and I, who have now been married for 53 years, think it must have got lost in one of our many house moves.

I WAS THERE: ALAN LINGARD

I remember it well. My wife and I used to run a youth club at a Macclesfield church and the members had been asking us to organise a dance for them. They assured us that they would all be there and bring a load of mates. We went ahead and booked a local hall and laid on some music. Hardly anybody turned up. Where were they all? You've guessed. Down at the El Rio listening to this band from Liverpool that we had never heard of.

DOUGLAS
FEBRUARY 1963, ISLE OF MAN, UK

I WASN'T THERE: SANDRA LORD
The Beatles never performed on the Isle of Man but I well remember my father, who did all the bookings for the concerts on the Island in the Sixties for the now defunct Palace and Derby Castle Company, asking me what I and my friends thought about a group called The Beatles who had had a success with a record called 'Love Me Do'. I told Dad they were great and that he had to book them. He had been offered them for a one-night stand for £250 during the 1963 summer season and had to get permission from the Board of the company to book them. The Board told him – and he then told me – that they thought The Beatles were a one record wonder who wouldn't be around by the time of the 1963 summer season and that, anyway, they were too dear at £250. The rest is history!

PRINCESS THEATRE
FEBRUARY 1963, CLACTON-ON-SEA, UK

I WASN'T THERE: STEVE BASSAM
I was a school boy at Clacton Secondary Modern in the '60s and part of local folklore is that the notorious Entertainments Manager who ran the Princess Theatre, owned by Clacton Urban District Council, turned down the chance of having The Beatles perform the week before their first record hit the charts on the basis that they would be of 'little or any interest'. The CUDC was abolished and replaced by Tendring in the early '70s. They owned a good music venue in the Princess Theatre, and I recall watching Hawkwind there circa 1970 and possibly Quintessence. But they missed a trick with The Beatles.

MANEY HALL
1 FEBRUARY 1963, SUTTON COLDFIELD, UK

I WAS THERE: BRIAN COOK, AGE 20
A young lady where I worked told me about the show, saying this group is just making

the charts. I went with my pal Brian Trow and, as we did not drive, we got there by two buses. The problem was no buses ran in the area after 10pm. Consequently, we had to walk some ten miles home afterwards.

I WAS THERE: KEITH PADLEY, AGE 17

I attended Maney Hall Dance on the night The Beatles were there, travelling on my recently purchased Lambretta scooter (which I have still got). I met up with my pals there. I was in a small group called the Casual 5. We thought The Beatles were just another group at the time. I remember I had to get up to go to work next morning as a television engineer.

I WAS THERE: PAT BROWN

I saw The Beatles there but I can't remember too much about it, only that they were great and we were all a bit screamy! I went with my friend Elizabeth and shortly afterwards we saw them at the Hammersmith Odeon in London. We went down on a coach that was arranged by a youth club in Mere Green.

I WAS THERE: SHEILA BOLTON, AGE 16

My friend Janet and I saw The Beatles at Maney Hall. We were both 16. It was an arranged visit, as we had not been to Maney Hall before but we were very aware of The Beatles. We liked 'Love Me Do' better than 'Please Please Me'. I remember them singing 'I Saw Her Standing There'. I don't recollect it being very crowded as we could get right up to the stage and had plenty of room to dance. The Beatles seemed ordinary guys and very approachable.

We saw them again at the Plaza Handsworth and it was a very different story – it was packed and we said to ourselves how lucky we were to have seem them before they were very famous. It was a very vibrant time to be a teenager and we regularly went to pubs where live bands played. We saw Carl Wayne and the Vikings (The Move), Denny Laine and the Diplomats and many more. I also have the Rolling Stones' autographs as my friend was performing on the show *Ready Steady Go!*, miming 'All I Want For Christmas Is A Beatle'!

I WAS THERE: ANTHONY (TODGE) ROGERS

I was the vocalist in a rock band called Tony Brent and the Dakotas. I was also in a skiffle group with Chris Boughton and Allan Smith. Allan and I grew up together and bought our first guitars with our paper round money. The night The Beatles came to Maney Hall, I was there with Allan and we were ready for the girls, with hair greased down with Brylcreem and quiff pushed up in the front. Being in rock bands ourselves, we were more interested than most. We could have touched George Harrison. Paul stood next to George and then, of course, there was the great John Lennon. We were particularly interested in the small guitars they were playing. How could such a fantastic sound come out of such small guitars looking more like violins than the big heavy Burns and Fender guitars we were used to playing? We knew these kids had got something and, of course, not long after that they were known the four corners of the world with their fabulous music.

I WAS THERE: KAREL BEER, AGE 16

I was just 16. I went there on my own and paid my sixpence or whatever it was. The Beatles had arrived before the night got going and I remember asking someone, who was with the organisation and who had come in from where their Bedford or Commer van was parked, what the band were wearing, as if they were in their stage gear already. 'Jeans and leather jackets,' was the reply. They must have changed backstage into their early suits. I don't recall the Maney Hall show being full at all – I was right in front of the stage, but maybe I was not aware of how many people were behind me. What impressed me greatly was how tight they were and their repertoire, which included songs such as 'Please Mr Postman', 'Boys', '(You Really Got a) Hold on Me', 'Roll Over Beethoven' and, above all, 'Keep Your Hands Off My Baby', that George sang and which was a mere flip side of a Cookies single that I had. There was no screaming, just a really long set compared to what they would do on later package tours. After playing, they dashed off to another gig in Kings Heath.

On 2 February 1963, The Beatles embark upon a UK tour on a bill headed by Helen Shapiro, a female singer with two number one singles to her name.

GAUMONT THEATRE
2 FEBRUARY 1963, BRADFORD, UK

I WAS THERE: JOHN FIELDS

I was booked to see Helen Shapiro at Bradford Alhambra (aka Gaumont) and didn't even know that The Beatles were on the bill. They performed a few songs and then announced that they had just recorded this song and that folk would be able to buy it in a couple of weeks. They played this particular song, 'Love Me Do', and all the girls in the audience went wild. The audience didn't scream for Helen but The Beatles brought something different to the stage and the audience began shouting and then screamed and screamed for more at the end of their act. My friend Trevor and I looked at each other in amazement. 'What's happening?' he asked me. I was as clueless as him. We had never seen anything like it before. The excitement was overwhelming. Now we know it as the beginnings of Beatlemania!

I WAS THERE: ALAN LIGHTOWLERS, AGE 19

Myself and four friends were present at when The Beatles appeared with Helen Shapiro and others. We had tickets for the stalls and sat about six rows from the stage. We were all members of a local youth club and had a real interest in pop music and the charts. We attended a number of concerts at the Gaumont around this time. The Beatles had become known to us by virtue of their appearances on Granada TV's *People and Places*, ABC TV's *Thank Your Lucky Stars* and BBC Radio's *Saturday Club*. We attended the concert specifically to see The Beatles and were not disappointed. They appeared in the first half of the show and opened to a rapturous reception with the audience on their feet. Around six numbers were played and they closed with 'Please Please Me', which sent the audience wild. I can still picture in my mind Paul McCartney with his baby face and left-handed guitar.

   For the rest of the show, people were chanting for The Beatles to reappear which of course they didn't do. It was obvious to all of us that we had witnessed something very special and we all came away as firm Beatles fans. Inspired by seeing The Beatles at the Gaumont, and also by the film *Summer Holiday* featuring Cliff Richard and The Shadows, we decided to form our own group which we subsequently named The Atlantics. Four of us purchased guitars, amplifiers and drums and embarked on music lessons in Bradford. Once we had learned the basics, we commenced hours of practice to put together a portfolio of instrumentals. At a later date, we added a singer but the problem was he would only perform Buddy Holly songs. Nevertheless, we began to play at our local youth club dance nights, other youth clubs and some local pubs. For this we were normally paid £5 per night between the five of us, which paid for a couple of pints, a fish and chip supper and a contribution towards our hire purchase commitments on the equipment. It wasn't a lot of money but the group gave us access to girls and we were living the dream!

I WAS THERE: CHRISTINE MCCABE

We enjoyed The Beatles when they came to the Gaumont. I remember they weren't at the height of their fame then but we still stood on our seats.

ASTORIA BALLROOM
12 FEBRUARY 1963, OLDHAM, UK

I WAS THERE: MIKE DUNKERLEY, AGE 18

My father owned a manufacturing business in the centre of Oldham and I started work in the office there in early 1962. That September I started studying on a day release basis for the Ordinary National Certificate in business studies at Oldham

College of Commerce on Brunswick Street, which was later demolished to make way for the Oldham bypass. My classmates and I soon became friends – and more, in some cases – with the girls who were there full-time doing shorthand/typing courses. It was the beginning of the Swinging Sixties. The Astoria Ballroom had just opened and most of us were regular attendees at their Saturday Palais Nights. Discos had not been thought of in those days. A suit and tie were the required male dress wear and nobody was allowed in after 10pm. It was our high spot of the week.

The building had housed the Gaumont Cinema until it closed in about 1961. The owners then undertook much refurbishment with the top half of the building becoming a bowling alley and the bottom half the Astoria Ballroom. When the grand reopening took place in November 1962, free tickets were given to businesses around the Star Inn opposite, with the result that my father received one and gave it to me, so I was there on the opening night.

With so many pop groups being formed in those days, Tuesday nights became Teenbeat Special group night where groups from all round the country would appear. I cannot claim to have seen them all but remember seeing Gerry and the Pacemakers, Freddie Starr and the Midnighters, a Liverpool harmony group I really liked called The Chants and of course The Beatles. That night, dozens of us from the college aimed to meet up at the Astoria but when I arrived on the Number 9 bus from Royton there was a queue stretching right down King Street towards the Duke of Edinburgh pub, which was another landmark road junction. No tickets had been issued as all-ticket events were very rare in those days. My then girlfriend was almost at the front of the queue and had saved me a place so I just jumped in and we were amongst the first into the building.

I was so keen on this young lady, and enjoyed a brief romance with her, that I cannot remember her name, only that she lived on Walker Road in Chadderton. Half an hour later, there was pandemonium outside as the doors were shut, thus denying access to hundreds who were waiting to get in and couldn't. Helen Shapiro was on the bill but when The Beatles were on stage there was no chance of any dancing on the floor. There was just a mass of humanity, mainly girls, screaming at the group. To hear what The Beatles were singing was extremely difficult but I do recall hearing snatches of all the songs they tried to sing amongst the noise. What did impress me was how smart they looked. Whilst I never had a Beatle jacket, I went on to own, and still have, a number of tab collar button-down shirts and knitted ties.

When the show finished there was just time for a quick kiss and cuddle with my girlfriend before we rushed off to catch the last bus to our respective homes. I wonder what happened to my unnamed girlfriend from Walker Road and if she remembers witnessing this event? So yes – I was there!

I WAS THERE: ROY POTTS

The queue was long, going down King Street as far as the Duke of Edinburgh public house. Metal barriers were in place to keep the queues orderly. I arrived late and, as my mates Fred Winterbottom, David Wolstenholme and Roy Eccles were already in the queue, I jumped the barrier and joined them. We all gained admission to a packed crowd and a memorable performance.

THE RITZ
15 FEBRUARY 1963, KINGS HEATH, BIRMINGHAM, UK

I WAS THERE: NEIL REYNOLDS

I saw The Beatles live three times. I was knocked out by 'Love Me Do' so went to see them the first opportunity I got. 'Love Me Do' had been released only three to four months before and it was before they became really, really huge. A few of us from school went, including my best male mates and at least one girl, Sandra Oakley. The Ritz, Kings Heath and the Plaza at Old Hill were owned by the same woman, Ma Regan, and the acts would do an early show at one of the ballrooms and dash over to another and perform a second show while the group who had been on there first travelled in the opposite direction to swap over. The Ritz gig was the best because it was more intimate. There wasn't all the screaming that drowned them out at later gigs, and some watched them while others danced.

I WAS THERE: TONY LEE

One our friends had the job of ferrying the turns, including the Rolling Stones and The Beatles, between the Plaza in Handsworth and the Ritz in Kings Heath, which were both converted Birmingham cinemas, in his voluminous Humber Hawk. We were greatly impressed by his good fortune, particularly as he had never passed his driving test or obtained vehicle insurance. Consequently, we always refused to travel with him. he didn't have 'A Ticket to Ride'!

CARFAX ASSEMBLY ROOMS
16 FEBRUARY 1963, OXFORD, UK

I WAS THERE: NEIL ROBINSON

We were the support band to The Beatles at Carfax Assembly Rooms. Admission was six shillings (30p). Unusually, we were asked to set up in the afternoon. Guitarist Will

Jarvis, myself and our roadie took all the equipment to Carfax and unloaded and set up. John Lennon and Paul McCartney were there, so we set up our gear and actually played a few rock 'n' roll songs with the two of them. They asked us if there was anywhere nearby where they could eat and the four of us walked from the hall together. Originally Will suggested Browns in the covered market but it was decided to go to a Chinese in Ship Street. For some reason, and I have no idea why, I said I needed to go home and turned down the chance to eat with them. So Will, John and Paul went there to eat without me. A personal and rather unpleasant memory of the day is that after we had changed for the evening gig, we left our possessions in the changing rooms at the back of the hall. The only people in there were ourselves, The Beatles and their road manager. On returning after the gig, my jacket and wallet containing £17 (which was a lot of money in 1963) were missing. This was reported to the police. The jacket, minus wallet, was found the next day by the police by the side of the road leading into Basingstoke which, by co-incidence, was where The Beatles played next.

I WAS THERE: PAUL WEAVER (AKA PAUL FANE)

I was the drummer with the Madisons. I used to work in a men's outfitters in Queen Street and didn't finish work until about 5pm. So I had a routine of having a shave and getting myself ready when I got to the venue, in the hope that the rest of the group would set my equipment up. On this particular evening I had taken delivery of a brand new Ajax drum kit and the lads took the drums to the dance hall and set them up. I arrived and went to the Ladies, which was the only place there was any hot water. As I was shaving, I could hear all this drumming going on. A heck of a lot of pounding and drumming. I thought, 'This sounds a bit odd.' So, covered in shaving cream, I came out of the Ladies and walked into the dance hall to see Ringo Starr banging away on his drum kit and Paul McCartney banging away on mine! Now there was an unwritten understanding between musicians that you didn't interfere with each other's equipment. So I saw red and shouted at Paul McCartney to get off my drum kit. I don't know whether anyone had ever shouted at him in that way before. I think he was a bit taken aback. I was annoyed because I hadn't played the kit myself. It was a brand new set and, had he taken the trouble to look, he would have seen that all the drum skins were completely pristine and had never been played. Bellowing at Paul McCartney and telling him to get off my drum kit wasn't one of my finest hours. A couple of years later I saw the interview with John Lennon where he responded to the question 'Is Ringo Starr the best drummer in the world?' with 'He's not even the best drummer in The Beatles.' And I thought, 'That's quite true, actually.' Because Paul was a good drummer. It's just that he happened to be hammering away on my brand new kit!

GRANADA THEATRE
23 FEBRUARY 1963, MANSFIELD, UK

I WAS THERE: KATE DRAKES

I was one of the lucky people to see The Beatles at the Granada way before they were famous. Top of the bill should have been Johnny Kidd and The Pirates but they had an accident on the way to Mansfield and never turned up. Consequently, The Beatles played way more than they were going to – and we were hooked. They looked so different in their smart black collarless jackets and pudding basins haircuts. I don't remember screaming but they certainly gave me goosebumps. While waiting outside for my friend Carole, a lady of the night came up behind me and said 'get off my patch bitch!' I had no idea what she meant but moved very quickly! I wonder now – what was I wearing?

I WAS THERE: COLIN KIRK, AGE 19

I was at that show and have still got the programme, with Helen Shapiro top of a bill which also included The Red Price Band, The Honeys, Dave Allen, Danny Williams, The Kestrels and Kenny Lynch. The stalls cost six shillings and sixpence (33p), which was a lot of money for us then and they did shows at 6.30 and 8.30pm. I went with my workmates who were all in the building trade – myself, Malcolm and Lynne were plumbers working at the same firm, Malc's brother Colin was a bricklayer and Lynne's brother Brent was a plasterer. We went to the 8.30pm show, which gave us time to get home from work, get ready and meet at 6.30pm for a couple of pints in the Eclipse, the pub opposite the Granada in Westgate. It was very crowded outside the cinema with people waiting to get in for the second show and there were a lot of people who did not get tickets but were just there to soak up the atmosphere. When the audience from the first show came out it got very busy indeed. Watching The Beatles, you could hardly hear them singing with the girls screaming their heads off, but it was a great performance and we all agreed after that they would go far. It was a great period in music and they wrote such an amazing amount of songs which even today will get people up dancing, remembering the words. They shaped the music world that we have today. It was great to be there.

I WAS THERE: DES TURNER

I remember seeing The Beatles at the Granada cinema in Mansfield – converted to a stage – on two occasions in 1963 when I was, or should have been, studying for my 'O' levels. The first occasion was in February '63, in the very early days of 'Love Me Do' and 'Please Please Me' and The Beatles had only been booked as a support act to Helen Shapiro. Even so, their performance was rapturous and the crowd noise deafening.

I WAS THERE: BOB WILSON

The top turn was Helen Shapiro, but as for any details – well the mists of time have done a lot of fogging. As a teenager I use to go to most of the Granada shows with pals and they were always enjoyable and memorable. I would always go to the live groups and then see many of them later on *Top of the Pops*. Off the top of my head, I remember seeing The Beatles, Rolling Stones, Shadows, Manfred Mann, Tommy Roe, Bruce Channel, Del Shannon, The Kinks, Johnny Kidd, Joe Brown, Gene Vincent, Peter Jay, Billy Fury, Chris Montez, Dusty Springfield, Helen Shapiro, Frank Ifield – and a lot more!

GAUMONT THEATRE
26 FEBRUARY 1963, TAUNTON, UK

I WAS THERE: GEOFF CROSS

I was at the Gaumont Theatre – now the Mecca Bingo – and I had stalls tickets. They were not top of the bill. I'm sure that was Joe Brown, but I might be wrong. I was lucky because their second release had just hit the No 1 spot that week and when they came on the girls went mad. I can remember just hearing something but not that much which was a pity because I was a big fan. I do remember that the amplifiers were tiny compared with today and the PA was minimal.

Danny Williams topped the bill, replacing Helen Shapiro who had a heavy cold.

ODEON THEATRE
1 MARCH 1963, SOUTHPORT, UK

I WAS THERE: IAN LLOYD

I could not believe the screams. My father said, 'How can they hear? They can't hear what they're singing.' My Dad managed the Gaumont from 1956 right the way through. He put on all sorts of shows. My father was such a showman. I'll give him his due. He used to promote and do whatever he could to fill the place. And he did fill the place. The Gaumont's capacity was around 2,000 people. And Dad used to fill it every Saturday night. I met them the first time they played the Odeon. My father brought me backstage when they were supporting Helen Shapiro, and obviously they hadn't hit the big time then.

Ringo Starr had his arm in plaster and my sister Valerie sat on his knee, having a good old chat with him. He was really nice. John Lennon had his glasses on that were so thick you could probably see the moon with them. He was smoking. They were all smoking. He was quite a nice sort of bloke, but he wasn't particularly interested in us. He was obviously thinking about the show, where they went wrong. I think he was just having a bit of a post mortem after the gig, to see what they could improve on.

Paul McCartney was preening. I didn't get on with him. I thought he was a bit egotistical, the pretty boy 'look at me' one, which didn't go down well with my father.

George Harrison was the nicest of the lot. He was lovely, and really interested. He certainly made the effort. I said to George, 'I've got to get into this. What's the best advice you can give a young lad who wants to pick up a guitar and play?' He looked around the dressing room, which wasn't great quality. They weren't built for pop stars. They had the bare necessities, with mirrors with lamps round it, and this one was cold and damp. So George looked around the dressing room and he said, 'Well, if I were you I wouldn't bother.'

I WAS THERE: RON WATSON

I remember the Odeon show quite well because it was the local one and a relatively small venue. But the hype and the screaming had started by then. The Odeon one was actually quite raucous.

CITY HALL
2 MARCH 1963, SHEFFIELD, UK

I WAS THERE: BARBARA SYKES

My dad used to be a commissionaire at Sheffield City Hall. Me and our Carol used to go to all the concerts from school, sometimes in school uniform. They used to have seats on the stage at the City Hall, so we were actually sat on the seats on the stage when The Beatles were playing. My dad said, 'If you girls are sitting on the front you've got to behave yourselves. No screaming. No running to touch 'em. We'll put you there so that everybody else behaves.' But of course we screamed. And they'd turn round and sing to us. Carol was the sensible one, even though she was the younger one. She was the one who said 'don't scream. Dad told us not to scream!' and I said 'all right, Carol, I won't.' And then she'd be screaming alongside us.

They'd sing and then they'd have a break and we'd go in in the interval to go and meet them and get their autographs. Then we'd go back out. When we went in the back, I always got a kiss from them, or a photograph. But I never got a photograph with The Beatles. It'd always be 'come on girls, they're due to go back on stage.' But there was always one that was hanging back, that was the last one out, and I'd be going, 'Oh, come here, let's give you a kiss. Let me put my arm around you.' Carol would be going,

Clockwise from top left; Tony Lee knew that the guy who ferried The Beatles across Kings Heath hadn't passed driving his test; Kate Drakes saw the Fab Four in Mansfield; Geoff Cross can't remember who topped the bill in Taunton; Bryan Ivan Wyatt (second right) discovered The Beatles on a trip to Liverpool in 1962; Anthea Craig got the boys' autographs at Margate thanks to her dad, Jack Green; June Freeman had never heard of The Beatles when she went to see them; Barbara Sykes saw The Beatles at Sheffield's City Hall and ignored instructions not to scream.

Clockwise from top left: Wendy Driffield's cousin got the Beatles' autographs for her; John Kightley worked Northampton ABC the night The Beatles played; Julie Causebrook and her friend didn't let not having a ticket stop her from going to see The Beatles; Susan Hutchinson with her father, who was none too happy with John Lennon; Norman Scott met The Beatles in Leyton (two photos); Pauline Lever was at Northampton in March 1963.

'Come on Barbara, we'll get in trouble.'

I had The Beatles' autographs on my arm. And I covered it in a plastic bag when I went in the bath so I didn't get my arm wet because I wanted to go to school the next day and show everyone at school 'oh, I've met The Beatles'. I got their autographs in my autograph book as well which, sadly, I sold not long ago. But we did meet 'em. I remember John Lennon asked my dad if he could take me out, and my dad said, 'No you can't. Come on, girls. Get their autographs. Come on. Let's have you out of here.'

I remember that we used to go in at the stage door at City Hall. We used to knock on the door and say 'Dad, it's me' and he'd let us in. As we got there this time, there were crowds of girls around the door and we eventually did get to the door – banged on the door – 'Dad! Dad! Dad! It's me!' Then all the girls were banging on the door – 'Dad! Dad! It's me!' As they were shutting the door, they shut the door on Paul McCartney and they opened the door again and dragged him in. But the girls didn't realise it was one of The Beatles. They thought it was the police holding them back. They used to hold them back and we used to walk through. We were pretty lucky girls, I'll tell ya! It was absolutely fantastic.

When you came out your ears would be ringing. You couldn't hear what they were singing because they were all screaming. It were wonderful. We were lucky to have a dad that got us in. We used to catch the bus into Sheffield city centre, 'town' as we'd call it. We'd come out of school, get on the bus and we'd start on the bus. 'Crikey I wonder what it's going to be like?' You'd get all giddy and excited. And I think that's what it was. And it built up and built up. And then they came on and they always had somebody else on besides The Beatles. It was Helen Shapiro. And the person compering the show would be going 'we're gonna have The Beatles on in a bit. Who'd you like best?' And they'd say their names and we'd all scream at the ones we liked. And I think it built up from there. 'Who's coming on next? Who do you like best? Do you like George?' And he'd say each name and all the girls would scream at which one they liked best. When we were sat there on the stage it was so difficult not to get giddy and scream, and especially when they turned round and they looked at you. 'Oh God, he's looking at me.' Somebody had made a beetle, like a kid's crawling beetle, and they threw it on the stage to them. And one of The Beatles picked it up, brought it over and gave it to me. That was quite exciting. And I've still got it in the loft somewhere. Next day, going to school with The Beatles' autographs on my arm? Well, it were all right, that.

ROYAL HALL
8 MARCH 1963, HARROGATE, UK

I WAS THERE: WENDY DRIFFIELD (NEE FROST), AGE 15

My cousin Trevor Stannard was there. He was 19 years old. He went backstage afterwards and there were a few guys trying to hold back the girl fans fighting to get into The Beatles dressing room so he helped the guys push the girls back and was invited to meet the group. Paul and John greeted him but were busy working on a song but George and Ringo chatted to him for a while. He asked them what they thought of Harrogate and they said it was OK but there were too many old ladies and tea shops! He knew I would want their autographs and George tore a piece of cardboard off a box in the room and they all wrote their names. I've still got it and I never collected any other autographs – it would have been downhill after that! We went together to see them perform in York not long after. My cousin was Beatle mad at the time – he had the hair, the jackets and the boots!

I WAS THERE: BRIAN INGRAM, AGE 17

I attended that night at the Royal Hall. It was a fantastic night and an unbelievable experience. Half of us danced and the other half gathered around the stage and just watched.

I WAS THERE: BRYAN IVAN WYATT

In 1962 I was 16 and living in Wetherby, North Yorkshire when I went to stay with an aunt in Liverpool. One evening she made my cousin, who was three years older than me, take me to a place called The Cavern, where I came face-to-face with a group called The Beatles. To say I was bowled over would be an understatement. When I returned to Yorkshire, I asked everybody at the youth club if they had heard of this group but no one had. I began buying the *New Musical Express* hoping to read about them.

Then, in January '63, a friend, who was the girlfriend of the lead singer of a group called the Apaches, told me they were booked to appear with The Beatles at the Royal Hall in Harrogate in March. She got me a ticket. During the evening, my friend came looking for me and took me backstage where I met the Fab Four. I loved their accents, especially George's, but I was somewhat taken aback by Lennon's swearing. Every other word was the 'f' word. They autographed my programme (which I sold in 1978 for £1,200 when I was hard up, and which I bitterly regret). I can remember watching their performance. They were not drowned out by screaming, as happened at their concerts later that year and in '64.

I saw them three times when they appeared at the Odeon in Leeds. The first occasion was on 5th June 1963 and there was very little noise when they were performing. At the second concert, there was noise but you could still hear them. But by the third concert the noise was deafening and you could not hear a thing. For that last concert, my friends and I queued outside the Odeon for 36 hours to get tickets.

On 28th June 1963, The Beatles also played at a dance at the Queens Hall in Leeds, the old tram sheds. I attended with a girl called Shirley, the same girl I took to the June 5th concert. A makeshift stage had been built against a wall made from scaffolding poles and planks. The stage was about shoulder height. When they came on, Shirley and I rushed to the stage. I curved my arm around George's ankle and he looked down and said 'you again'. He had remembered me from Harrogate four months before. I still cherish those days and the fun I had.

I WAS THERE: JANET SUTHERLAND

I was twelve years and one month old. The Beatles had just erupted. It was quite amazing, like a tsunami of adoration. The evening was so full of screaming girls surging forward, trying to get closer to the stage. It was electrifying, a bit overwhelming and very exciting. And they were the support act!

I WAS THERE: NORMAN HUMPHREYS

My family moved from Aintree to Maghull soon after the war, where the Albany Cinema, one of the first Merseyside cinemas built after the war, would later play host to one of the very few charity events the Fab Four gave during their career, a fundraising event for the local St John's Ambulance Brigade on 15th October 1961. They were tenth on the bill on a show compered by none other than comedian Ken Dodd. When the St John's Ambulance Brigade were later looking for better accommodation, my father, using his contacts in the Liverpool shipping industry, obtained a derelict wooden barge that was languishing in one of the disused docks (where Everton's new football stadium is being built) and the cadets pulled it seven miles up the Leeds-Liverpool canal, where it was moored and used as their HQ for many years.

I was a student at Birkenhead Technical College in 1961 and '62, with no lectures on Wednesday afternoons. I would often take the original 'Ferry cross the Mersey' back to the pier head. The student fare was tuppence in old money (1p) and I'd spend time at the Cavern Club enjoying the lunchtime sessions. The walk up to Matthew Street from the pier head was a very short stroll and the entrance fee for the whole lunchtime session was one shilling (5p). I remember seeing many of the groups that subsequently made it big on the back of the Beatles' success, including The Big Three and The Merseybeats, but I must be one of the few people never to have seen The Beatles at the Cavern during my Wednesday visits.

Bob Wooler was the Cavern's compere and DJ. I had an early interest in photography, so I made a simple request to Bob for me to be able to take photographs, not just looking towards the stage but also from the cramped band room at the side. I managed to get shots of bands from the stage side, and remember on one occasion getting in the way as Aaron Williams of The Merseybeats wanted to get on stage and being told in no uncertain terms to get out of the way – no 'f' words were needed in those days, just a gentle shove!

After my student days, it was time to get a job and I found myself working at the Cairn Hotel in Harrogate, just up the road from the Royal Hall. My then girlfriend and I bought tickets to see The Beatles when they were playing there on 8th March 1963. We paid ten shillings and sixpence (52.5p) each to watch them play. How I managed to find the money for a ten and six ticket on my £6 a week wage remains a mystery to me. The Beatles played two slots and, during the interval, the audience were invited backstage to meet the lads and get their autographs. All I had with me was a copy of the Liverpool tide tables which my father used to give to his customers at Christmas. I got the boys' autographs and kept them safely for several years until we moved back up to north-west of England, when I managed to lose the booklet during the house move.

Many years later, I found out that The Beatles had recorded 'From Me To You' and 'Thank You Girl' at Abbey Road Studios just three days before. My daughter and her family later lived near Abbey Road and I must be one of several grandfathers who have insisted on walking over the famous zebra crossing when visiting so that I could show my granddaughters the photograph sometime in the future.

I was working at the George Hotel in Stamford in Lincolnshire in the summer of 1965. A chap came into the hotel to ask if we were still serving lunch. On being told that we were, he drove his van into the hotel's inner courtyard and out stepped the four Beatles. The hotel has a smaller room to the right of the restaurant entrance and it was in this area that they had their lunch. Staff took the precaution of drawing the curtains to give them some privacy, but they were in and out and continuing on their journey within 30 to 40 minutes. I don't think news of their stay was widely known. I can't remember it being reported in the local newspaper. Sadly, it was my day off so I didn't witness this myself. The table was still there in June 2023 when I visited. It's the window table on the left as you walk in to the small extension to the restaurant. If only I'd been there and got their autographs on that visit, it would've made up for the Harrogate set I lost in the house move.

RIALTO THEATRE
13 MARCH 1963, YORK, UK

I WAS THERE: DUNCAN CURRY, AGE 17

I saw them in March 1963 and then again in November 1963. The first time John Lennon didn't turn up – he had a throat infection – so there was just three of them. I'd been used to watching Cliff Richard and the Shadows and Elvis Presley and all that.

We'd just gone to see Chris Montez and Tommy Roe, who were flavour of the month in those days and were topping the bill. Groups playing and singing were something new. Before that it was singers with their own backing groups, like Cliff Richard and the Shadows. The Beatles closed the first half of the first show. The three of them came on and it was instant impact. Everyone knew how good they were. They were dressed in black with the Beatle collars. I didn't know much about them. McCartney sang that song from *The Music Man*, 'Till There Was You', and I thought 'what on earth was that? I've never heard anything like that before.' It was fantastic.

Two weeks later they were on television and everybody in England knew about them. They were on a Bill Grundy show called *People and Places* just after that. And then they got a show on the radio on Monday nights called *Pop Go The Beatles*, so they just kept getting more and more publicity. Although there was only the three of them that night, they got through it perfectly well. I knew they were going to be big. I certainly knew they were going to be big by the time I saw them in November.

I WAS THERE: JOHN PAUL ROBERTS, AGE 15

I always used to go with my friend Ron. I had only just left school. The firm that I worked for at the time was a chartered accountants and we used to do the accounts for the Rialto and the Clifton Bingo at the time, when Mr Prendergast had it. And the chap used to go quite regularly there to do all the cashing up and the ticket sales and everything. It was about 9/6 to get in, in them days. I remember seeing them twice – the four of them. I also saw the show where George was missing. There was only three once because George Harrison didn't come – he had a bad cold or throat. I don't know whether somebody actually stood in to play the guitar.

John Lennon was absent for the March 1963 show in York.

EMBASSY THEATRE
17 MARCH 1963, PETERBOROUGH, UK

I WAS THERE: PETER HALL, AGE 15

I saw The Beatles perform at the Embassy. The concert I saw featured Chris Montez and Tommy Roe. The evening was opened by a local band called the Dynatones, whose bass player was Colin Hodgkinson, who still lives locally. I went alone, although I later discovered that my future wife was also there. They played 'Love Me Do' and finished with 'Twist and Shout' and I still have a copy of the tour programme.

ABC CINEMA
20 MARCH 1963, ROMFORD, UK

I WAS THERE: DEE BESLEY

I was there with my best friend Sheila to see Chris Montez and couldn't understand what all the screaming was for. I found it a bit embarrassing. The Beatles were playing second fiddle to Tommy Roe and Chris Montez. I had not heard of The Beatles. It must have been shortly before the group's popularity skyrocketed, and I've always said it is my claim to fame that I saw The Beatles before they were famous!

I WAS THERE: MALCOLM PAUL, AGE 16

I first heard the sound of The Beatles at a party at Heaton Way youth club in Romford, Essex on the Saturday immediately before Christmas in 1962. I had not previously heard of them but the record being played, 'Love Me Do', sounded very distinctive and quite different from anything else I had heard. It immediately aroused my interest and some days later I bought it at Wells Music Stores in Romford with one of those record tokens which were very much favoured as Christmas presents at that time. I was born in October 1946 and had therefore only recently turned 16 years of age. That said, my interest in pop music was already well established, although access to recorded music on the radio in those days was very much restricted by the Musicians Union and the record companies who feared its impact on their members and their profits.

I very much favoured American music. 'All Shook Up' by Elvis Presley was my first ever purchase and others such as the Everly Brothers, Ricky Nelson, Del Shannon, Brenda Lee, Roy Orbison and, most notably, Buddy Holly – still a lifelong favourite – were played unremittingly on my Dansette Major record player. This was all to change over the early months and the big freeze of 1963. 'Love Me Do' was only modestly successful in the UK charts, but sufficiently so as to provide a platform for the group on radio and television, particularly the former, during which the powerful individual personalities within the group began to emerge to an increasingly wide audience.

The first time I was able to see them live was in March 1963 at the ABC cinema in Romford. They were on a tour headlined by Tommy Roe and Chris Montez, two Americans who had had huge UK hits with 'Sheila' and 'Let's Dance' respectively the previous autumn. The Beatles had been signed up as a supporting act prior to their increasing success and popularity, not least enhanced by their release of 'Please Please Me' at the beginning of the tour.

Six of us took the bus into Romford for the 9pm performance clutching our 12/6 tickets, all of us already big fans of the group from their radio performances of many of the numbers that were to appear within days on their first LP, *Please Please Me*. The

Beatles did not disappoint and performed most of the tracks that were to become so familiar, culminating in 'Twist and Shout', with John Lennon at his loudest and best. They generated great excitement and it was the first time that I sensed, not least from the audience reaction, that they were going to be something more than a short term phenomenon.

Sadly, signed as a supporting act, their performance closed the first half of the show and created somewhat of an anti-climax for the audience and the two Americans that shared the second half. As we went home on top of the bus, I recall quite clearly an ongoing discussion amongst us about which one was Lennon and which one was McCartney (I got it wrong on that occasion!), suggesting that their songwriting talents were already registering with people. The release of the *Please Please Me* album finally marked their arrival as a remarkable new talent. Even my parents and those of my friends took to their music and their humour and personalities as they became regulars on radio and television. Everybody seemed to buy the album – not a cheap purchase at 32 shillings for most people in those days.

I WAS THERE: ALAN SNOWSELL

I saw The Beatles at the ABC Romford. They were supporting the Tommy Roe/Chris Montez tour together with The Viscounts, Debbie Lee, Tony Marsh and the Terry Young 6. They had released 'Love Me Do' to reasonable reviews but were not top of the bill. The thing I remember about them was that they were very professional but not necessarily going to be listened to more than 50 years later!

I WAS THERE: JULIE CRUICKSHANK

My parents and neighbours in George Street, Romford – where we lived – told me that Ringo's step grandmother lived in George Street and that The Beatles stayed at her house after the concert.

The Beatles first album, **Please Please Me***, is released on 22 March 1963.*

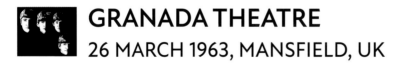

GRANADA THEATRE
26 MARCH 1963, MANSFIELD, UK

I WAS THERE: BARRY ANCILL

Approximately two weeks after The Beatles appeared in Mansfield at the Granada on the Helen Shapiro package, they were back as part of the Chris Montez/Tommy Roe tour and on a cold Tuesday night myself and an old mate of mine, Donald Walker, were there. The bill also included Bill Black's Combo, a band who worked with Elvis. The Beatles on that cold night were third on the bill to the two American stars but The Beatles totally upstaged them, making them look third rate with the crowd going wild. It was rumoured that, with The Beatles unable to get out of the theatre, a certain Mansfield lad called Shane Fenton (alias Alvin Stardust) bought them fish and chips. It's a night I will never forget.

About three months later, Donald and I were travelling to London in the middle of the night. It was midweek and we used to help my brother-in-law in his removals business. He pulled into Watford Gap services southbound on the M1 and said he was going to have a sleep. We jumped out of the wagon and somebody shouted 'The Beatles are in the Grill and Griddle northbound!' We legged it over and – sure enough – there they were, sat at the bar and returning from recording *Pop Go The Beatles*, which I had listened to on the radio the previous teatime before we set off.

I WAS THERE: JUNE FREEMAN, AGE 18

My friend Anita and I went to most of the shows at the Granada in Mansfield. We were 18 and had gone to see Chris Montez and Tommy Roe. I had never heard of The Beatles but, boy, when they came on, I knew they were going to make a big impact on the music world. They were the last act on the first half and were fantastic. Girls were screaming and shouting. We didn't want them to leave the stage. The second half was an anticlimax really and I although I enjoyed the rest of the show, I fell for The Beatles that night and especially Paul, although he didn't replace Cliff Richard in my affections! I still have the programme from that night. We saw a lot of the top acts at the Granada. I remember one concert when Gene Vincent was in the audience and because he hadn't got a work permit to perform on stage he sang from there. Those were the days.

I WAS THERE: DES TURNER

The second occasion that I saw them was a month later, in March '63. This time they were supporting Chris Montez, and I think Tommy Roe was also on the bill. By now they were hugely popular and the audience noise was even louder, so much so that I couldn't hear all the words of the songs, but could only pick them out by the rhythm of the drums and guitars. On both occasions they were well worth seeing, but it's a pity I couldn't hear the music. Even in those early days, the freshness of their music and their charisma shone through, and it's something I will always remember, and be pleased to tell the grandchildren about – who is Olly Murrs anyway? Who could have imagined the global phenomenon they would become?

I WAS THERE: ELAINE SMITH

We were at the show when they were a support act to Helen Shapiro. We heard everything and thoroughly enjoyed the show. But The Beatles were at the Granada again as support act to Chris Montez and due to their popularity Chris Montez exchanged places on the running order with The Beatles and gave them top billing. There was screaming and shouting but we still enjoyed it, as did my younger sister who we took with us. We thoroughly enjoyed that show as well and we are both so very proud to be able to say that we saw the Fab Four live in Mansfield – twice!

ABC THEATRE
27 MARCH 1963, NORTHAMPTON, UK

I WAS THERE: JULIE CAUSEBROOK, AGE 14

For a short time, like most people of my age, I had a frenzy over The Beatles. Paul McCartney was my favourite. I was a pupil at Spencer Secondary Modern School for Girls and can remember that the first time The Beatles came to Northampton I couldn't get a ticket to get in to see them, due mainly to not being prepared and not having saved up enough pocket money for a ticket (they were like gold dust). But my best friend Glennis Blenco and I went down to the Savoy Cinema to try to see them arrive.

The word was that they would be arriving by helicopter and everyone was excited and on the lookout for something to happen. A crowd mingled outside the cinema but we saw nothing. We were told later that they were smuggled in the back way to the cinema through one of the factories in St Michael's Road. We were on the lookout, but didn't see them. But as I was walking up Abington Street towards the cinema, a guy who was being chased by a horde of screaming girls was running away from the cinema. He ran into me outside the Wedgewood restaurant and cake shop and grabbed me by the shoulders to stop me falling over. He apologised for nearly knocking me down, said he had to go and then ran into the Wedgewood to escape the girls. I then realised it was Tommy Roe. Meeting him briefly somehow made up for not seeing Paul McCartney on that occasion. Tommy seemed a really lovely guy and so polite. He must have escaped from the pack of girls, because I never read anything in the *Chron & Echo* to say different.

I WAS THERE: ROGER FRISBY

A mate had a spare ticket because he had finished with his girl and so I went instead of her. It was on a Thursday night and we went for a drink before the show in the Bantam Cock next to the cinema. In early 1963, people were aware of the group but not the individuals, and unknown to us they were drinking in the back room, so when we left we were mobbed by girls asking which Beatle we were. We had to say that we not John or Paul. I think we missed a great chance to enjoy ourselves but no matter!

We had seats in the balcony and I had the records they had already released, so their set was familiar but live they were better than anything we had ever seen. They could sing for a start and harmonise as well. Groups didn't do that. They were on after Chris Montez and before Tommy Roe, both of whom were good, and I suspect that most people went to see Tommy Roe who had a current hit with 'The Folk Singer' rather than The Beatles, but The Beatles must have made an impression.

The year before, we used to run dances in our youth club and were looking for different groups to the Northampton ones so we went to see a local chap who booked acts for mainly working men clubs, He gave us a list of groups he was currently booking. They were generally London-based, groups like Nero and the Gladiators and Neil Christian and the Crusaders, each at around £125 each. We asked if there was anyone cheaper. We were advised that groups from Liverpool were becoming popular and also cheaper – The Searchers, Gerry and the Pacemakers – and a group called The Beatles could be had for about £50. We normally paid about £5 to £7 and thought we would lose a fortune on these unknown groups so we declined!

I WAS THERE: JOHN HARRIS

I was there with friends from Northampton Technical College, all aged 17 or 18, for the *Please Please Me* tour. As far as I was concerned, 'Love Me Do', although not a number one in the charts, represented the breakthrough in British pop in the same way that 'Hound Dog' had marked the start of the rock 'n' roll era seven years earlier. The music of The Beatles and the other Mersey and Brit groups expressed the new optimism of the post-war years. We were happy because we believed we could change the world. We could hardly hear The Beatles because of the predominance of 13 and 14-year-old girls in the audience who screamed throughout their performance, but the material was so familiar that it didn't matter. Chris Montez left the biggest impression, with his all-action performance. My parents, being in their sixties, were indifferent to my musical tastes, but most parents didn't think it would last. Having said that, those with a passion for music in general seemed impressed and interested in The Beatles music and I think many parents were at least fascinated.

I WAS THERE: PETE SPENCER, AGE 13

I went to both concerts with my sister Diane, who was 16. I wasn't too bothered about going – I was just getting interested in folk and blues music, and Bob Dylan in particular. But my mother's friend owned a shop in Weston Favell and she'd been given two tickets in return for putting up a poster in the shop window so she passed them on to my mother to give to us. It was the first pop concert I'd been to, apart from seeing Tommy Steele at Skegness a few years earlier. As far as I remember the first show was more about Chris Montez, who had had a hit with 'Let's Dance', with a few screams when The Beatles played.

I WAS THERE: CAROL NEEDHAM, AGE 16

I got the tickets the day they were released, but didn't have to queue. I just went in and got them about midday. My friend and I were in the front row. The Beatles were the last act before the interval. I wasn't impressed. George had black teeth and I was much more interested in seeing Tommy Roe who headed the bill. In all honesty I don't remember Chris Montez. Tommy Roe caught my eye and winked at me and that was the highlight of the show as far as I was concerned. When The Beatles returned later in the year, people queued outside the ABC all night to get tickets. I didn't bother with this performance but did go to many other live concerts at the ABC over the next few years, much to my parents' disgust. We would often walk the four miles home so that we could calm down, although this often made matters worse as it made us much later home than if we had caught a bus.

I WAS THERE: DI NEWBERRY (NEE BENSON), AGE 13

I was lucky enough to be at both concerts at the ABC in Northampton. The first one I went to primarily to see Chris Montez and Tommy Roe, but was well impressed with The Beatles then. I even managed to get Paul and George's autographs after the show at the stage door.

I WAS THERE: GISELA OAKES, AGE 14

I attended Notre Dame High School in Abington Street in Northampton and was due to go on a school Mediterranean cruise in March of 1963. When we heard The Beatles were coming to town on 27 March, I cancelled my place on the cruise and my friend Christine and I bought tickets for the first performance at 6.30pm. We played truant from school and spent the day waiting at the stage door behind the ABC Cinema, hoping for a glimpse of The Beatles, who were supporting Chris Montez and Tommy Roe – but to no avail.

The Beatles weren't as popular then as they became a few months later, so we very much enjoyed their short time on the stage as there wasn't too much screaming. But it was over far too quickly as there were six other acts and two performances per night. After the concert, Christine and I again took up our positions at the stage door. Our waiting was rewarded when George Harrison – my favourite! – and Paul McCartney emerged and we walked down Abington Street with them as far as the Gayeway

Nightclub, which was down a short alleyway at the top of Abington Street, opposite what is now the Radio Northampton building. It was very surreal, and being only 14 years old (nearly 15!), we were incredibly embarrassed and tongue-tied. I had a pack of Maltesers and offered them to George and Paul and we all shared the pack. I kept the wrapper – which was white then – and the pen they used to write their autographs until I sold my Beatles and Stones memorabilia at Bonhams in 2009.

Unfortunately, there was no sign of John and Ringo. I think John had a girlfriend from Northampton at the time so he was meeting her. We did know her name at one time but I cannot recollect it now. Knowing someone from Northampton probably explains how they were familiar with the Gayeway Nightclub. They seemed to know where they were heading as if they had been there before. Friends and I also went to see The Beatles seven months later at their 6.30pm performance at the ABC in November, but they had become so popular by then it was difficult to hear the music above the screaming.

I WAS THERE: PAULINE LEVER, AGE 12

I would try to emulate everything my sister did, so I became a Beatles fan because my sister liked them. I liked George because my sister did, although I really did think he was the cutest. I had to sit next to my mum. I think I spent a lot of time just watching the fans and they fascinated me. My sister, always the more ladylike of the two of us, was horrified by the screaming. They sang 'A Taste of Honey', which I really liked, and 'Please Mr Postman'. I remember 'Please Please Me' because The Beatles shook their heads throughout. At the end, my mum grabbed my hand and led me back to the coach. My sister took her own time getting back to the bus.

I WAS THERE: KEITH SHURVILLE, AGE 14

I was getting into the music scene and liked Tommy Roe's 'The Folk Singer' and obviously had heard Chris Montez's 'Let's Dance' and The Beatles' 'Love Me Do'. On seeing that they were all appearing in Northampton, I persuaded my parents to let me and a friend go to the ABC and purchase tickets. It was after I bought the tickets that 'Please Please Me' was released, and so I was the envy of my friends when I disclosed that I had tickets to see The Beatles. I travelled from home in Earls Barton with a friend. The experience was unbelievable, with screaming girls only intent on the seeing The Beatles. Yet my main lasting memory of the whole event was Chris Montez singing 'You're the One'.

I WAS THERE: DIANE STRATFORD, AGE 11

I went to the show with my 7-year-old brother and my grandma and granddad. The tickets had been given to my granddad as he knew the manager at the theatre and they hadn't sold them all! I remember thinking they were certainly different to anything I had ever seen before and, lo and behold, several months later they were a household name. How I have wished over the years I had stopped to speak and get their autographs. I have been a lifelong fan. Grandma and Grandad thought they were too loud.

I WAS THERE: JOHN KIGHTLEY

For many years I worked with the touring producer Owen Price who always seemed to give me the job of controlling the mic leads – no remotes then – for the scores of stars that performed there over the years, something one couldn't do for the groups because they all played with mic stands and the mass of amplifiers either side of the stage. There was always good behaviour from the groups. They spent much time at the back of the stage strumming guitars, etc. and contrary to many rumours at the time, the girl fans were not allowed back stage. Can you imagine the chaos if they had? There was a lot of screaming and shouting that greeted the lads just before the interval.

ABC CINEMA
28 MARCH 1963, EXETER, UK

I WAS THERE: CHRIS GALE

They were supporting Chris Montez and Tommy Roe and I thought, 'they'll probably go places.' They came to the stage door, which they used to do at the ABC in those days. I got their autographs, and a few others, in a book. I married young, about 19 or 20, and when we got a flat and I moved out, I left all this stuff in my bedroom along with a lot of old records. When I eventually got a house, I said to my mother, 'I'll take all that stuff away that's in my bedroom.' She said 'what stuff's that?' I said, 'All the old records and books and everything.' She said, 'Oh, I ditched that old stuff.' I said, 'Mother, that's my youth you've just thrown away.' She just binned it. Whether the bin men realised what it was and they got lucky or it just went to the tip, I don't know.

ODEON CINEMA
30 MAY 1963, MANCHESTER, UK

I WAS THERE: DAVE WALLACE

We managed to get tickets for the Roy Orbison and Beatles show in 1963. It was an amazing show. Gerry Marsden of Gerry and the Pacemakers sang 'You'll Never Walk

Alone', later recording it. Orbison came on and soared through his repertoire. You could hear a pin drop. Then it was absolute bedlam as The Beatles did their stuff, though you couldn't hear a thing due to the screaming. I reminded Gerry of it years later, when we were invited backstage with Little and Large at the Grand Theatre in Blackpool, and he pretended it wasn't him!

DE MONTFORT HALL
31 MARCH 1963, LEICESTER, UK

I WAS THERE: GERALDINE HOPES (NÉE BEADLE), AGE 13

This was my very first concert. I adored Chris Montez's and Tommy Roe's songs, but I fell in love with the music of the support band on the tour – The Beatles! The seats were simply wooden chairs all on the same level, and if one was in the seats furthest away from the stage, one had to stand to get any sight of the stage whatsoever. So, with De Mont having sold around 50 to 60 per cent of their tickets, and the expensive seats nearer the stage being only half full, they were soon filled by the audience from the cheap seats.

It was an amazing concert and probably only one of a few Beatles concerts attended by so few people. By the time of The Beatles' second concert at the De Mont, in December 1963, I was unable to get a ticket – people had camped out at the Town Hall box office overnight, and all tickets had been sold. Disappointed as I was, I felt that I'd had the privilege of seeing them before they became famous, and it is one of my favourite memories.

I WAS THERE: ALAN DUTTON

We started to queue at around 10pm. I was with my then girlfriend, who later became my wife, and one of her friends was with us. The ticket office was in the council offices on Charles Street, but the queue was already around to the back of Lewis's in Fox Lane. At around 3am, the police decided to consolidate the queue and moved everybody up. What was a fairly orderly crowd suddenly became a mad dash and then an almighty crush. We finished up outside Halfords – the crush was that bad I heard a cracking, and the shop window went in. Fortunately, no one was hurt.

The show itself was amazing. The noise from the audience was horrific, but the atmosphere was like nothing I have experienced before or even after. A memory to last a lifetime. I also remember Tommy Roe and Chris Montez on the bill and an American girl group, the name of which I can't remember.

I WAS THERE: GLENISE LEE

I have forgotten the boyfriend(s) who paid for the tickets, but I do remember three evenings spent at the city's De Montfort Hall. I went with a boy in late March 1963 to see Cliff Richard and the hall was full, sold out. The girls were screaming. The following week, 31 March 1963, we went to see The Beatles and the hall was not full. Tickets were still available. There was some screaming. It's because of the lower noise level, when the boys on stage could make themselves and their songs heard, that I remember hearing a heckler. After one song, after the applause and screaming had subsided to the level that my dad would have called 'still far too loud for comfort', a heckler from the audience shouted something that John Lennon didn't like. John crossed to the front of the stage, glared down at the audience and said, 'The last time I saw a mouth that big, it had a hook in it!'

My boyfriend struggled to get tickets for The Beatles' concert on 1st December 1963. We had to fight through crowds of shrieking fans to get into the concert. We were near to the coach that was delivering the band. Later, I realised I'd lost a button from my winter coat in the scrum. Screaming? The roof was lifted! After the concert, I found my button. Metal, the size of a half crown, it had been flattened by the coach. I treasured that button for years.

PAVILION GARDENS BALLROOM
6 APRIL 1963, BUXTON, UK

I WAS THERE: SUSAN HUTCHINSON (NEE BRUNT), AGE 21

I was living in the Grove Hotel. My parents were the managers. On one of the occasions when The Beatles came to perform at the Pavilion Gardens, they wanted to stay at the Grove Hotel overnight. But having booked in at around 4pm and using all the facilities in the rooms, they decided to go back to Liverpool after their performance. My father, who was not a meek and mild man, said they must pay for the use of the rooms as they would need cleaning, etc. before they could be relet. John Lennon said to my father, 'Don't you know who we are? We are The Beatles.' To which my father answered, 'I don't care if you are the bloody cockroaches – get out!' Needless to say, no one knew how famous they would become and what a pity I didn't get an autograph. Bed and breakfast at the time was £1 5s (£1.25). Perhaps they couldn't afford it.

LEYTON SUPER BATHS
8 APRIL 1963, LONDON, UK

I WAS THERE: NORMAN SCOTT

I was quite a successful DJ for a good number of years. I started off in my local youth club in Chingford, Essex. I saw an advert one day in the *New Musical Express* that a guy was looking for DJs for clubs and it turned out the guy actually lived in Chingford. His name was Ron King and he owned an entertainment agency called Galaxy Entertainments. I think the biggest group he had signed to him was Amen Corner. I went for an audition and got a job as a DJ. And what this guy used to do was find church halls that you could hire, and he hired the same halls the same day every week. He had about five or six different halls all over the place and we'd go along and we had to set up all the DJ equipment.

One of the halls Ron King hired was a place called Leyton Superbaths. It was an indoor swimming pool but they only used it as a swimming pool in the summer period. In the winter they boarded the swimming pool area over and it was a dance hall. It had a big stage and I DJd there, and every so often we'd have bands on. The Beatles had their first two records – 'Love Me Do' and 'Please Please Me' – out, and they were moving on to bigger venues like theatres. But Brian Epstein kept them to their contracts to finish off doing the few remaining dance halls that they'd been booked for, and one of those was the Leyton Baths. I wasn't DJing that particular night, it was just a bands night, but because I worked there I just walked anywhere I liked. And, of course, The Beatles weren't as big then as they became but nevertheless it was a sell-out. It was packed out.

I went round to see them and they said they'd like a drink. I can't remember if the Baths sold alcohol, but there wasn't a bar behind the backstage so I went across to the pub opposite and I brought back four bottles of beer for them. Then we found out we'd got no glasses so they drank the beers out of the cups. I've got a picture of them with cups in their hand but it's not got tea in them. It's beer. We got on really, really well because they liked the same music as I did. I was a big rock 'n' roll fan in those days – Bill Haley and Little Richard and Jerry Lee Lewis – and they were into those. Then it was almost time for them to go on stage.

I asked them if I could take a photo of them. John Lennon said, 'Yes, that's no problem. I'll line the guys up. Once we line up, I'll count to three and you take the photo.' So that's what he arranged. But Paul McCartney had been about to clean his teeth and he'd still got the tube of toothpaste in his hand. John counted to three but John, being the fool that he was, went 'one – two – THREE!' Well we all jumped, including Paul McCartney and, as he jumped, Paul squeezed the toothpaste tube and a whole stream of toothpaste shot out and went all down his trouser leg. He wiped the toothpaste off but there was a big white stain on his trousers and Ringo Starr said, 'You'd better cover that up, Paul, because nobody will believe it's toothpaste'. And off they went. They did a whole set of cover versions, and obviously 'Love Me Do' and 'Please Please Me'. And I think it was the very first time they played 'From Me To You', because they announced it was their new single.

'From Me To You', the third Beatles single, is released on 11 April 1963.

CO-OP HALL
11 APRIL 1963, MIDDLETON, UK

I WAS THERE: MICHAEL WILSON, AGE 18

I was there with some friends. We were members of a pop group called The Confederates that worked the North West scene in the Sixties. I had just turned 18 a few days before the Beatles gig, which was on a Thursday night, and we were able to squeeze this gig in around the bookings we had on the Friday and Saturday. They were very smart with good musical equipment and also very loud. But they had to be loud to be heard over all the young teenage girls constantly screaming. I remember one or two of the audience coming over faint and having to be attended to. The Beatles had a great rapport with the audience, cracking the subtle jokes they were famous for, being scousers, although I think many jokes fell on deaf ears through a lack of understanding. They were very professional throughout their set. They played for a good hour and managed to escape the building but with some difficulty.

The Confederates were relatively successful, but not successful enough to turn professional. We played most of the Manchester clubs and working men's clubs that were going at the time, occasionally playing in Liverpool and Stockport, where we became very friendly with The Hollies. If we were free, we would go to one of their gigs and heckle them mercilessly, and they did the same with us. We had an old Bedford van that used get covered in lipstick after every gig. Getting it off the windscreen was a nightmare. We occasionally played at Belle Vue's Top Ten Club, when Jimmy Savile was the resident DJ (but enough said about that). Those were great days, never to be repeated. Modern kids will never ever get the entertainment that we created for ourselves.

I WAS THERE: JANICE HEWERDINE, AGE 15

I went with my friend Susan. The Beatles were brilliant. I remember lots of the girls screaming.

I WAS THERE: HELEN BARKER

I was there with four of my friends. Tickets were 7/6d and we bought them from Central Records in Middleton. Barry Chaytow was the promoter, who I went to work for twelve months later. I don't remember lots of screaming going on where you couldn't hear the music, but a photograph of the crowd was published in the newspaper at the time. Going off the looks on our faces we were all in awe of what we were watching. I still have John Lennon's image in my mind, as he was my favourite. I am so glad I went to see them just as they were coming famous, as it was an unforgettable experience. My husband had the chance to see them in Blackpool, but couldn't afford the price of the ticket. He has always been gutted that he never saw them as he is a huge fan!

I WASN'T THERE: BARBARA THORNLEY

I was too young to go but I remember my mum sewing two dresses, for my eldest sister and for one of my cousins. The fabric had a Beatles print.

I WAS THERE: JEAN NAWAZ (NEE KENNEDY), AGE 15

I went with my friend Jacqueline Hamer. I was too shy to ask for their autograph.

I WAS THERE: PAULINE HEALEY

I wasn't that impressed. I only went because I got a free ticket and to keep my friend company. I was more of an Elvis fan.

I WAS THERE: WAYNE DOCKSEY

I was just a teenager then, about 12 years old. All my school friends were going down and I remember going down there and standing outside the Ashton Arms. There used to be a roundabout in Middleton then, and the hall was across the road. There were probably 30 or 40 kids outside. We all knew one another, because Middleton was not a big place in those days. It was more like a village than the town it is now. I remember all the kids and all the shouting, wanting to get in. And we were singing their hit of the time. We didn't get in to see them. We saw a van pull up and people getting out but we were too far away. There were too many crowds of people for us to see what was going on. It was a big event in Middleton. Five doors down from where I lived on Gladstone Street, there was a young girl who was going out with one of Herman's Hermits. It was the beginning of the pop scene.

I WAS THERE: BARRY CHAYTOW

I worked in the clothing business during the day, making school uniforms. One of our customers, who was in Middleton, suggested to me one day that we should get involved in the music business. This was completely out of the blue. The singer Bobby Vee was appearing in Manchester at the time. I said, 'I know nothing about the music business. Why would I want to get involved?' But he said he knew one or two people who were running some groups around and so I said I would look at it. He got in touch with a couple of people with local bands and I found a venue in Middleton, which was the Co-op Hall, and contacted them to see if I could hire it out. We did it, and we made some money that night, so I thought I would try and continue doing it.

A little bit later, people were talking about The Beatles and wondering how we could get in touch with them. I rang up Brian Epstein, explained who I was and said, 'Can I come and see you?' and that I wanted to book the Beatles. He said, 'Yes, come along.' Two minutes later, I was down the East Lancs Road and off to see Brian. I explained what I wanted to do and that I wanted to book them and he said, 'Well, if you want to book The Beatles, you've got to book all my other artists as well,' which I did. I started off with other people like Billy J Kramer and Gerry and the pacemakers, and then I used to work with The Hollies and everybody who was a recording artist in those days – people like the Searchers and Jet Harris.

I paid The Beatles £110 for one hour. They did two half-hour sessions. I was paying groups £10, £15, £20. The week after, I was paying people like The Hollies, who were really big at the time, but obviously not as big as The Beatles, £10. So £110 was a lot. But we still made money on the night. People were prepared to just pay any price at all to get them.

I worked with them four or five times. I used to run the Imperial Ballroom in Nelson too. That was a massive place and I put The Beatles on there. When I said to the manager there, 'I've got a group I'd like to put on in a few weeks,' he said 'who are they?' I said 'The Beatles'. He said, 'I've never heard of them,' I said, 'Well, you will do as they're going to be great.' Because, obviously, had to push all the artists I was working with. I will try them anyway. That was a massive night. There were about 3,000 people inside that night.

The Imp in Nelson was every Saturday night. And I regularly used to run a place in Leigh, at the Co-op, and in Nantwich. Leigh and Middleton were more-or-less midweek. We used to meet up on the motorway sometimes on the M1. Everyone used to meet up on the M1 after gigs, at one or two in the morning.

I had to organise security at Middleton and I had a couple of bouncers on the night, but they weren't really needed. Everything went fine. It was a really great night with no trouble, no problems. Of course, they became big very, very quick. One minute nobody had heard of them and the next day they were in America and doing everything else. I had so many contracts with them and Brian honoured the contracts, but later I just couldn't have booked them at the price that they wanted.

BRIDGE HOTEL
15 APRIL 1963, TENBURY WELLS, UK

I WAS THERE: PHILIP BURLEY

My late wife was living in the town and I was in lodgings there. My late father-in-law was one of the organising committee and Maureen always claimed that it was her idea that they were booked. She got their autographs. I'm hanging on to her autograph book for the kids' inheritance!

MAJESTIC BALLROOM
17 APRIL 1963, LUTON, UK

I WAS THERE: MARGARET SENIOR

Elvis and Cliff Richard records were more popular in the charts. But posters suddenly appeared in a side street in the town advertising 'One night spectacular featuring The Beatles.' I remember friends saying, 'What a funny name for a group. They can't be great if they're in a small cinema.' We'd just been to see The Tremeloes playing live at St Albans in a big theatre. They couldn't compare with The Beatles. The opinion was they were a band for the girls. None of the boys that I knew liked them.

IMPERIAL THEATRE
11 MAY 1963, NELSON, UK

I WAS THERE: CHRISTINE BALDWIN (NEE WHITTAKER), AGE 17

I was working at the Borough Building Society on Parker Lane in Burnley, the building now occupied by Contact Burnley. My friend Pam's boyfriend, David, had a cousin called Bill who was playing in a supporting group. Bill showed me through to the backstage but there was nobody about. I knocked on the dressing room door and Paul McCartney answered. He took my autograph book into the dressing room where all four Beatles signed it. I still have the autographs.

Three guitars and a drum set pound out another number from the Top Twenty. If you were a "square," then you just wouldn't understand what all the fuss was about and were probably thinking that your entrance money could have been spent on something better. The amplifiers might have been too loud and the lyrics might have been distorted, but the teenagers in this photograph were having the time of their lives.

Clockwise from top left: Barry Chaytow promoted The Beatles at Middleton's Co-op Hall; newspaper cutting showing Helen Barker in the crowd at Middleton's Co-op Hall; Jack and the soon to be Pam Strutt were at Brighton Hippodrome; Jill and Alan Snowsell were both Fab Four fans; Malcolm Mosley was at Romford Odeon; Roger Grigg was at Birmingham Town Hall when Roy Orbison was no longer the headliner; Jan Bounden went to the Cavern and also saw The Beatles at Norwich's Grosvenor Rooms.

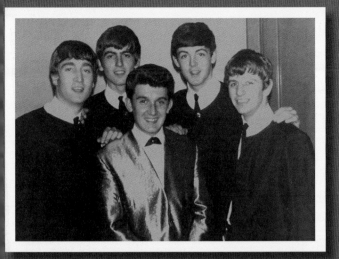

SUNDAY NEXT, 14th July   At 6 and 8.30 p.m.

JOAN REGAN
AND SUPPORTING ARTISTES

Reserved 8/6, 7/-, 5/6   Unreserved 3/-

• MARGATE'S MOST FABULOUS SEASON ATTRACTION •

DANCING WATERS
WINTER GARDENS SUN LOUNGE

DAILY (inc. SUNDAY) From 10.15 a.m. - 2.15 p.m. - 7 p.m.
(Last Performances Commence Mornings 11.45 Afternoons 4.30 and
Evenings 9.15.)

Admission Adults 2/-, Children 1/-

WINTER GARDENS MARGATE
General Manager & Licensee: J. D. GREEN, F.I.M.E.

★ Programme

MONDAY, 8th JULY & Week
6.30 TWICE NIGHTLY 8.45

1 OVERTURE
   BERT WALLER and the
   WINTER GARDENS ORCHESTRA

2 PAN YUE JEN TROUPE

3 DON CROCKETT

4 DEAN ROGERS

5 DEREK ROY

6 THE DAKOTAS

7 BILLY J. KRAMER

INTERVAL

HEATS EVERY
THURSDAY
at 11.15 a.m.
MISS
MARGATE
£1,000
NATIONAL
BATHING
BEAUTY
CONTEST
THE OVAL
if Fine and Sunny
or
WINTER
GARDENS
if wet or dull

8 DEREK ROY introduces
   THE LANA SISTERS

9 DEREK ROY

10 THE BEATLES

"GOD SAVE THE QUEEN"

Stage Manager ... ... GEORGE FAGG
Chief Electrician ... ... KEN AUSTEN

The Management reserve the right to make alteration in the programme
which may be rendered necessary by illness or other unavoidable causes

COMMENCING TUESDAY, 16th JULY at 8 p.m. AND THEREAFTER MONDAY, FRIDAY & SATURDAY at 8 p.m.—TUESDAY, WEDNESDAY, & THURSDAY, 6.30 & 8.45 p.m.

NORMAN VAUGHAN IN "THE NORMAN VAUGHAN SHOW"
WITH

JOE (Mr. PIANO) **HENDERSON** ★ **LENNY THE LION** with Terry Hall
BOB & MARION KONYOT - GILL & TERRY - ANNA DAWSON - THE 10 SWINGING LOVELIES
BERT WALLER AND HIS ORCHESTRA

RESERVED SEATS 8/6, 7/-, 5/6   UNRESERVED 3/-   CHILDREN UNDER FOURTEEN 2/6   TO ALL PARTS AT 6.30 PERFORMANCES

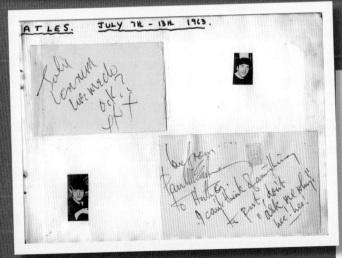

Clockwise from top left: Garth Cawood almost stole the spotlight from The Beatles in his silver jacket; Sue Flanagan saw The Beatles three times in Birmingham and was devastated to learn that John was married; Anthea Craig got the boys' autographs at Margate; Diane Alger (in the glasses) stood on her seat to see the boys; Jenny Wilkin (right) and her sister Trish got front row tickets for one of the Margate shows in July 1963; Anthea Craig's Beatles autographs; programme for The Beatles' week in Margate.

GROSVENOR ROOMS
17 MAY 1963, NORWICH, UK

I WAS THERE: JAN BOUNDEN (NEE BIRD), AGE 14

I got their autographs. I remember walking there. I went with school friends, one a girl called Jenny who I went to school with, and a friend of hers whose name I can't remember, but I think she got the tickets. They were 7/6 (38p). We might even have got them on the door. I still have my ticket and the flyer, which has got their autographs on the back. I got Paul and John and George's autographs addressed specially to me.

It was a place called the Grosvenor, which doesn't exist anymore, on Prince of Wales Road, quite near Thorpe Station. They used to have lots of groups there but that was the only time I ever went. At the time, everybody seemed to like the Rolling Stones or Elvis Presley or Cliff Richard and I didn't really like any of those. I liked Billy Fury. And then along came The Beatles and I did like their music.

The three of us were standing right against the stage and I can remember the wooden stage not being particularly tall. It only came up to my knees. We were right against the stage when The Beatles were on stage. I was to the left of the stage and George Harrison was nearest me, and then Paul. You wouldn't have known they were going to become as famous as what they did.

The *Daily Mail* had published a photograph of the four of them walking down Oxford Street and I wrote to the *Daily Mail* and they sent me the photograph. I took that to the Grosvenor and after the performance I went round to the side gate. There were some very tall iron gates but you could see through these gates and there was a white van that The Beatles had come in. They were in the van and I remember calling their names. Eventually John, George and Paul came out of the van and signed this *Daily Mail* photograph I'd got. It says 'to Jan love from John, George and Paul.' I've got all four signatures on the flyer, but the photograph is only addressed to me by those three. I didn't see Ringo. Paul also signed on my wrist and I went home and covered his autograph with cellophane. When I went to school on the Monday, three days later, with my signature of Paul still wrapped up, I was quite famous. I didn't wash it for about a fortnight. And I wouldn't ever sell the autographs because it's just memories. My memories.

I WAS THERE: SANDRA HAWES, AGE 16

I went with a girlfriend from school called Lorna Hannant. Her uncle was the manager of the Grosvenor. He asked her would she like to go and she asked me. A night out! So she took me with her. We liked them and it was nice to see them. I can remember it was only a little stage they were on, and we stood right in front of them. I think we both liked George at the time. But on the night, her uncle asked if we wanted to go backstage and meet them and get their autographs and we said 'no', we didn't think we wanted to do that. I don't think we were really that struck, to be quite honest. So we missed out on the chance of getting their autographs. I'd have been thousands in now!

The Beatles embark on a further UK tour headlined by Roy Orbison, but audience reaction is such that the Big O is soon demoted to second place on the bill.

EMPIRE THEATRE
26 MAY 1963, LIVERPOOL, UK

I WAS THERE: RON WATSON

Roy Orbison was the headliner at the Empire show and they did a short 30-minute set. Don't get me wrong. They were OK and that was a bit quieter than the Southport Odeon show. But from 1963 onwards, they were a different band. It was after that that their huge ability as songwriters came to the fore. There was never evidence of that in the early years. The songwriting side of it was not evident in those early days. When you started listening to the albums, and the songwriting talent came out, you started appreciating the hidden treasure.

GAUMONT CINEMA
28 MAY 1963, WORCESTER, UK

I WAS THERE: SUE INNIS (NEE ROBINSON), AGE 18

I went with a girl friend who was a year older whose name I cannot recall. I had heard of The Beatles on Radio Luxembourg in the winter of 1962, whilst I was away nursing in Northampton. I kept telling everyone how good they were but they didn't seem to know anything about them, so I congratulate myself on being the first to spot their potential. Not long after, they had their first hit and everyone wanted the record, and all the lads wanted the Beatle jackets and the longer hair, which parents objected to.

It was manic seeing them. I was sitting in the second row, but I was disappointed as I could not hear them for the screaming. Several young girls were escorted out because they were overcome and felt faint. The little I did manage to hear was great. They made a great sound and played all their hits. I didn't join the throng to see them leave the theatre as it was mayhem. But it was very memorable.

I WAS THERE: SANDRA LONGMIRE, AGE 14

Having first read about The Beatles in some teenage magazine, it was decided that Paul McCartney was the most beautiful boy in the world! There was great excitement when we found out that The Beatles were appearing at our local Gaumont. My friend Mary's mom went and queued to get us tickets on the front row for 12/6 (63p). There were two performances in those days and we went to what was called 'the first house'. We had decided not to scream as Paul would then notice us. The naivety of being only 14 years old! After the show, where Roy Orbison was actually top of the bill, we waited outside for autographs. They were becoming quite famous by then and it would not have been safe for them to come out and face the mob.

We handed our autograph books in and they came out duly signed, but to this day I am never sure if they are genuine as I believe both Neil Aspinall and Mal Evans, who worked for The Beatles, were very good at faking their signatures. They did however talk to us through the dressing room windows. I remember George just gazing out of the window at all the crowd. He must have felt trapped. One of the girls who lived close by went home and got him a hard-boiled egg. I wonder if she remembers that? Paul was also using a cine camera at the time and he was filming us all screaming. I often wonder what happened to that piece of footage. To conclude the evening, I remember my mother and little brother appearing, not to take me home but to join in! Much to my embarrassment, my mum started shouting for Ringo!

RIALTO THEATRE
29 MAY 1963, YORK, UK

I WAS THERE: JOHN PAUL ROBERTS, AGE 15

They used to do two sessions. They did the half past six and half past eight shows. Roy Orbison was the main one on. They finished the first half. And when we knew they were on, I used to get the front seats. I used to get the front seats within the first half an hour for most of the groups that were there – The Beatles, Gerry and the Pacemakers, Little Richard, Gene Vincent and all those. I've got all of the programmes for them. I liked the late '50s – Little Richard Gene Vincent. Jerry Lee Lewis. And then it was the American groups like Tommy Roe, Chris Montez and all those lot. The Beatles stood out. It was a different sound. The audience was screaming, going mad. We were at the front so you could hear them a bit. We always went to the second show. After everyone else went round to the back door to try and get autographs, we went up to the stage and stood just in front of the stage. The roadies came on and were talking all the equipment down and the group were just there talking and walking about.

GRANADA THEATRE
1 JUNE 1963, TOOTING, LONDON, UK

I WAS THERE: SEAN SMITH

I saw them on a package show at the Tooting Granada. They opened with 'Please Please Me'. John didn't play the harmonica but picked out the intro on guitar instead. I next saw them at The Beatles Christmas Show at the then Finsbury Park Astoria, which was a variety show and which was good enough for me to go again the following year. At all three shows, there was the usual barrage of screaming but I could always hear the music and it was excellent, which was not surprising given their apprenticeship in Hamburg. They were a very special talent but I think all their good stuff petered out in 1964. In my honest opinion, their best album was the first. *Please Please Me* was recorded in 12 hours when they all had streaming colds. They asked to postpone the recording and were refused. Perhaps for this reason it has all the best aspects of a live performance.

HIPPODROME
2 JUNE 1963, BRIGHTON, UK

I WAS THERE: MELANIE JACOBS, AGE 14

I saw them a few times but one concert in 1963 sticks out. We knew tickets would go fast but went on sale on a school day. It didn't occur to us to skip school – we wouldn't have dared. We were at grammar school and terrified of getting told off. Parents didn't approve of The Beatles then. They thought they were scruffy and distracted us from school work. They were correct there! They refused to get tickets for us, although after a year or two they changed their minds a bit as they thought the Rolling Stones were appalling and The Beatles were then quite preferable!

My grandma, bless her, went and queued for tickets for myself and my three closest friends as a surprise. We were so thrilled. So off we went, four young teenagers, by ourselves on the bus and so excited. We didn't hear a thing at the concert of course, as we just screamed and screamed. I'm not even sure why. In those days, parents didn't mind you going somewhere by yourself so long as you were home on time by the

10.30pm curfew and didn't get run over or make them stay up late!

Roy Orbison was on the bill. We had front row seats for that show but we didn't want to see poor Roy. He came on with his trademark sunglasses. We thought he was blind and I'm ashamed to say we sat poking our tongues out, making funny faces as we thought 'get off! You're boring and you can't see us anyway.' There's nothing quite so insensitive as a group of 14-year-olds, and it was only years later we found out that he had sensitivity to the light and wasn't blind. By then we were old enough to know better and I confess to feeling a little ashamed!

I WAS THERE: JACK STRUTT, AGE 20

Together with my future wife, Pam, I saw them at Brighton Hippodrome when they first appeared in the town. The tour had started out with the Big O, Roy Orbison, topping the bill after huge success with songs such as 'Only the Lonely', 'Crying', 'In Dreams' and 'Falling'. However, by the time the tour reached Brighton, what became known as Beatlemania was taking hold and the boys effectively topped the bill. Also on the bill that night were Gerry and The Pacemakers, balladeer David Macbeth, one hit wonder Louise Cordet and Tony Marsh, acting as compere. Pam was 17, so this was one of our early dates. It would be back to work next day but this was too good an opportunity to miss. We had booked to see the show not because The Beatles were in town but primarily to see Roy Orbison who was – and still is – my favourite male pop singer. His songs never date. When we arrived in Middle Street for the second house, it was bedlam. The teenage girls who had come to see The Beatles were already in a state of high excitement and it promised to be a memorable evening.

I imagine Roy may have been somewhat apprehensive before going on stage, given that the vast majority of the audience were there to see The Beatles. But any fears he may have had were soon dispelled – he had a walkover. He just stood at the microphone with his black guitar and dark glasses without hardly moving, except to pull out his harmonica for 'Candy Man'. I don't know how long his act was scheduled to last but my memory is of sustained cheering at Roy's performance and I'm sure he carried on for a long encore.

At this stage of the tour The Beatles were closing the show and, as elsewhere, the Hippodrome audience went berserk. I don't recall hearing too much of the music because of the screaming girls. The atmosphere was something I had never experienced before at a pop concert and I'm so glad I didn't miss it. My only regret is that I didn't retain the tickets or programme for the show.

I WAS THERE: KAREN TYRRELL

When I was 14 and on holiday in Torquay, I met a girl from Liverpool and she gave me The Beatles' home addresses. They had just made their first record so I wrote to both George and Ringo. I have two short letters from Louise Harrison and a note from Ringo in reply. I got to visit and stay with that girl in Liverpool the following year and went to the Cavern one lunchtime when the Merseybeats were playing. I have a large collection of Beatles memorabilia of newspaper cuttings, photos, magazines and tickets.

I saw The Beatles live three times, at the Brighton Hippodrome when we were seven rows from the front, at the Fairfield Halls in Croydon when we were in the Royal Box(!), and one of *Christmas Show* nights at Finsbury Park. As my friends and I were all in the typing class at school, we had the whole class typing out cardboard flyers for months which read 'CALLING ALL BEATLE FANS! PLEASE DON'T SCREAM AT THE BEATLES!'. We went along the whole massive queue on the day and gave out hundreds of them. I like to think they worked - to an extent!

TOWN HALL
4 JUNE 1963, BIRMINGHAM, UK

I WAS THERE: ROGER GRIGG

In my early twenties I used to see most of the big acts when they came to Birmingham. When we bought the tickets for this show it was to see the headliner, Roy Orbison. The Beatles were only a support act and were just becoming really popular. But by the time we went to see the show, The Beatles were huge. Roy Orbison stood down to become the support act to The Beatles, going on stage before them. After the performance we could understand why. As soon as The Beatles came on stage the audience exploded. The teenage girls in the audience screamed throughout the performance. We could barely hear The Beatles above the audience noise, but it was a fantastic experience and one I'll never forget.

I WAS THERE: TONY NEWSON

Roy Orbison was the big name then, but he was dropped down the order and came on before The Beatles, who were put on as top of the bill. But Roy was so great. The audience were all screaming for The Beatles all the way through until Roy Orbison came on. He shut them up and then they were all screaming for him to stay on, even knowing that The Beatles were going to follow him. That's how good Roy Orbison was. I knew what to expect from The Beatles but it was the one and only time I saw Roy Orbison and I'd been a fan going back to 'Only The Lonely' when I was leaving school. He definitely lived up to expectations. The Beatles I saw this time were the 'scrubbed up' version.

I WAS THERE: NEIL REYNOLDS

I saw them supporting Roy Orbison. He'd got such a great voice. The audience were totally respectful so you could hear every note. That wasn't the only contrast – the Big O had a great voice but no stage presence and hardly moved. The Beatles were the complete opposite, jumping about and very animated.

I WAS THERE: SUE FLANAGAN

The show at the Town Hall was quite tame compared to the others I saw. I saw Roy Orbison too, but The Beatles were all everyone wanted to see. I had already bought *Please Please Me*. In my diary I wrote, *'Saw Beatles at Town Hall. Absolutely great, fab and all the rest. Love them all. JL especially.'*

ODEON THEATRE
5 JUNE 1963, LEEDS, UK

I WAS THERE: SUSAN BROWN

I managed to see The Beatles twice at the Odeon in Leeds. The first time was at the Roy Orbison concert in 1963, just when The Beatles were rising to the top. My friend and I got seats for the early performance but were a couple of rows from the back in the stalls. We were there almost as soon as the doors were opened and had only been seated for a short time when we heard a few 'murmurings' and turned round to see Ringo walking along the back row just behind us. He had nipped out to a local sweet shop, and Paul was walking down the aisle at the far side. They both then disappeared through the door next to the stage. Oh, that I'd thought to get their autographs.

The programme stated that Roy Orbison and The Beatles were both due to play in the second half, with Gerry and the Pacemakers closing the first half, but Roy closed the first half. It was just a brilliant concert.

I WAS THERE: JENNY MASKELL

When we saw them the first time in Leeds, Roy Orbison was top of the bill and they were supporting him. But they went very quickly from first appearing on television to being a phenomenon. How long did it take? Six months. A year, maybe. They were so different from anything that had come before and it was at the right time as well. People had been watching Cliff Richard, Billy Fury and there was just something different about The Beatles. It was just their clothes, their hair. Just everything about them, really.

CITY HALL
8 JUNE 1963, NEWCASTLE-UPON-TYNE, UK

I WAS THERE: BRIAN SWALES

I saw The Beatles live once and went to The Cavern once – but not at the same time! I really can't remember if it was 1962 or 1963 when a friend who played the drums and who knew a local group called The Denmen, asked if I wanted to join them for a visit to The Cavern. They were hoping to meet Bob Wooler, the Cavern's compere, to get a booking there. We went in the group's canvas-topped Land Rover, travelling overnight to Liverpool – not a comfortable journey bouncing around in the back by any stretch of the imagination! Arriving early next morning we found a transport café and had a wonderful greasy breakfast. Later in the day, the Land Rover was parked up somewhere in Liverpool so we could visit a music shop and, like a fool, I left my wallet in a coat in the back. We returned to find the Land Rover had been ransacked and my wallet with all my money in was gone. A 10/- note and a £1 note… I was devastated. In the early evening, we had a drink in The Grapes, a pub opposite The Cavern which The Beatles used to frequent. The Cavern was packed, and I think the groups that were on that night were The Big Three, Earl Preston and the TT's and Faron's Flamingos.

I only saw The Beatles live once, at Newcastle City Hall. In those days, my close friends and I didn't really like them. We thought they were just for young screaming girls; we were there to see Roy Orbison! At least one of Roy's hits had violins on it and we wondered if his live performance would include the strings. We were quite surprised when he came on stage with three female violinists stage left and leads coming from their violins – I assume they were amplified. The only thing I remember about The Beatles' performance is the screaming girls… it was deafening! I had always thought that The Beatles were second on the bill to Roy that night, but they topped the bill.

Later that year, The Beatles made their first visit to my home town of Stockton-on-Tees. It was Friday November 22nd. We still weren't fans of The Beatles. I was on a bus, on my way to a friend's house to play records, and the bus was full of young girls full of excitement on their way to the Globe Theatre. I was glad to get off. During the evening, as my friend and I were playing records in the front room, his mother came in and said a news flash had come on the TV saying that President Kennedy had been shot. We just looked at each other in disbelief.

After playing the Globe in Stockton and Newcastle City Hall the following night, they stayed at the Eden Arms Hotel in Rushyford. (Several years ago, a sheet of headed notepaper from the hotel and containing all their autographs sold for £4,465 at auction at Christie's.) On the Sunday morning, the group's hired Austin

Princess failed to start. The AA were called but were unable to get the car going. A replacement car was hired from Minories in Newcastle and the boys were at last on their way to their next gig at Hull. By now, many fans were in the hotel's car park and the AA man struggled to get away. The hotel manager was reported to have said, 'This Beatlemania makes me sick…'.

In the 1980s, I worked with a chap called Brian Hanton who originated from Liverpool. One day I was in WH Smiths and looked at a book about The Beatles. There was a picture of The Quarrymen, showing John Lennon, Paul McCartney and one or two others. The name on the bass drum was Colin Hanton. When I next went into work, I mentioned the photograph to Brian and jokingly said, 'Is Colin Hanton any relation?' I was very surprised when he said, 'Yes, he's my brother. I remember when John and Paul used to come to my mother's house to practice.' I have read several accounts as to why Colin left The Quarrymen, but Brian told me his brother was the only one who was working at the time. He was an apprentice upholsterer, and perhaps he thought that was a better option than being the drummer in a local group!

KING GEORGE'S HALL
9 JUNE 1963, BLACKBURN, UK

I WAS THERE: ERNIE ROBINSON, AGE 19

My wife-to-be and I booked tickets to go and see Roy Orbison, who was top of the bill, not The Beatles, who were just a support act. Gerry and the Pacemakers were on the same bill. Margaret seems to think Cilla Black was too, but I don't remember that. was. But everybody was more excited about The Beatles than Roy Orbison. Now I really didn't know anything about them. They were just a name as far as we were concerned. But obviously other members of the audience must have already heard about them because people were stood on the chairs and screaming. We were surprised at the number of screaming girls and people standing on their chairs. We were looking at one another and thinking 'what's all this about?' After all the enthusiasm, the screaming and the standing on chairs and the clapping, Roy Orbison seemed an anti-climax. So we saw them before they were really, really famous. Or they might already have been famous and it passed us by, because we were thinking we were going to see Roy Orbison!

I WAS THERE: MARGARET ROBINSON, AGE 18

They weren't the main act that night. They were the supporting act for Roy Orbison and all the girls were getting carried out, fainting. It was a really good show.

THE PAVILION
10 JUNE 1963, BATH, UK

I WAS THERE: LLYN HARRINGTON

My crowd never went to see them, preferring to spend our cash on booze. Later that evening, at kicking out time, a group of northern blokes asked us for directions and we spent some time taking the piss out of one another's accents. The next day we were surprised to see in the local paper a photo of these blokes who were in fact The Beatles and friends!

CITY HALL
15 JUNE 1963, SALISBURY, UK

I WAS THERE: JOHN RATTUE

I went to the concert with the lady who became my wife in September 1963 and. We took with us our three bridesmaids, who were in Salisbury for the purpose of having their dress fittings. If I recall correctly, John Lennon had appeared on *Juke Box Jury* earlier in the evening and was flown to Old Sarum airfield to appear at the gig.

I WAS THERE: JEAN DEVINE, AGE 14

I couldn't hear a thing. It was just screaming – screaming, screaming, screaming all the way through from the audience so you didn't hear them at all playing. I must have gone with a school friend but I really can't remember which one it was. It was my very first concert. And what a great way to start!

ODEON CINEMA
16 JUNE 1963, ROMFORD, UK

I WAS THERE: MALCOLM MOSLEY, AGE 12

I was in the first year of the senior school and developing a great love of pop music. I used to catch the 252 bus from Romford to my school in Collier Row. On my way home, I used to sit upstairs at the front on the right-hand side with my friends. The bus travelled down South Street towards Romford Station and the Romford Odeon was about 50 yards on the right-hand side before the station. As the Odeon came into view, we could see advertised The Beatles' name in big letters and I used to wish to be able to see them. To this day, I still regret not having seen The Beatles perform.

I WAS THERE: DENISE BENNETT, AGE 14

My friend Marilyn and I went. My mother bought the tickets. I was wearing a Beatle jacket with no collar that my mum had made me in dark brown corduroy. Dad dropped us off. We had front row seats in the wings. Four girls who were sat behind us had made Paul a 21st birthday card as it was his birthday that week and I believe they got to go back stage after the show to hand it to him. We had all screamed throughout the whole performance. And after the show, my friend and I – along with many others – went around to the back door and screamed at anyone who poked their heads out of an upper window!

I WAS THERE: ALAN SNOWSELL

By the time I saw The Beatles in June they were stars and topping the bill at the Odeon, Romford. It was quite a line up as it also featured Gerry and the Pacemakers and Billy J Kramer and the Dakotas, with the Viscounts as support. After a long forgotten argument with my dad, he did not give me the money for the gig in advance so on the day I simply turned up at the theatre for the early show in the hope of getting a spare cheap ticket. I remember seeing a green Ford Classic arrive at the side of the theatre and Paul McCartney climbing out and rushing into the side entrance pursued by screaming fans. I wandered into the theatre more in hope than anything and was surprised to be able to purchase a standing ticket for four shillings and sixpence (23p). This actually afforded me a better view as I was raised above the seated audience and it also cut out a lot of the screaming. I should have kept the ticket!

I WAS THERE: JILL SNOWSELL (NEE GOODALE)

I went to the ABC in Romford in March 1963 to see the Tommy Roe and Chris Montez tour but have no recollection of The Beatles at all. I then went to the Odeon in June and remember an incredible evening. I got off the bus and met up with my friend Christine Chetland. As we passed Romford Station, there was a girl standing there who had been to the earlier performance. She was talking to friends with an expression of wonderment on her face and using her finger to demonstrate the round collars on The Beatles' suit jackets and to describe their hair!

The *Romford Times* published a photograph on its front page of The Beatles all looking down at the fans from a narrow brick balcony at the side of the Odeon before the first performance began. I still have the first Beatles LP I bought. I wrote all over the back: 'Paul is fab, smash, smart, cracking, gear.' 'Paul is fabulous, swinging, marv.' 'Paul is great.' 'The Beatles are gear, fantab.'

I WAS THERE: HAZEL BARHAM, AGE 14

We did nothing but scream the whole way through and I wonder now if we ever really heard them singing. I can remember also being hauled off The Beatles' car. screaming, by a policeman.

I WAS THERE: RICHARD TOLBART

I was too young to go but I remember seeing an article in the *Romford Recorder* about how they stopped in Chadwell Heath High Street to buy cigarettes. I was disappointed I hadn't been there to meet them because that's where I lived and it's amazing such a small moment in time would make the local paper.

I WAS THERE: MALCOLM PAUL

They seemed to tour relentlessly. Having seen them in March, it was a welcome diversion to see them again in June as I was in the midst of taking my GCE 'O' levels. This time they topped the bill and closed the show, but with some very adequate supporting acts in the form of Gerry and the Pacemakers and Billy J Kramer and the Dakotas, all of whom had emerged from Merseyside on the coat tails of The Beatles – and their songwriting skills.

ODEON CINEMA
21 JUNE 1963, GUILDFORD, UK

I WAS THERE: JEAN JONES, AGE 26

I was lucky enough to get hold of two tickets to see The Beatles with my best friend Mary Davies. We were both married to men from the most northerly part of North Wales, a mere spitting distance from the wonderful Liverpool, but our husbands weren't interested in a night of screaming women when the snooker hall and beer beckoned. There were other artists on the bill that night but we were not remotely interested in them. We were both in love with The Beatles and that was all. My favourite Beatle then (and now) was Paul. He had such a cheeky face on him. Mary was smitten with John. They were all so smartly dressed in beautiful dark, fitted suits. What I most recall about that evening was John – with the greatest of humour – picking up several pairs of women's undies from the stage and thanking the ladies most profusely for their generous gifts. Fortunately, we were sat just too far from the front to make it worth the risk of throwing a pair of our best bloomers. I'll never forget the ringing in my ears from all the screaming, which lasted until the next day. We felt we were too old to scream at 26 – we had a bit of a squeak though, and clapped a lot. A Fab night, one I'll never forget and I feel so privileged to have seen them.

I WAS THERE: MAUREEN ROGERS

My memories of seeing them live are of young girls going up to the stage, crying and holding their hands out, calling their names and passing them flowers. The atmosphere in the hall was electric. It sounded like everyone was going mad with excitement, me included. I was so excited I could not reach the loo in time.

I WAS THERE: INGRID FERBERT

I was upstairs in the gallery. They were wearing their famous Beatle suits. My friend who got the tickets was called Angela Reardon and we were at school together. She actually lived next door to John Lennon in St George's Hill.

TOWN HALL
22 JUNE 1963, ABERGAVENNY, UK

I WAS THERE: AVELINE JAMES

At the time we didn't realise it was any big thing. We were just all excited. There was a promoter chap called Eddie Tattersall and thanks to him we saw Lulu and The Dave Clark Five. We were very fortunate to see as many people as we did. Several of my friends were not permitted to go as parents were quite strict in those days. But I thought The Beatles were pretty squeaky clean and I think my parents thought the same. It might have been a different story if I'd wanted to go and see the Rolling Stones.

The tickets sold out fairly quickly. An old boyfriend of mine keeps telling me that he was the one who bought me the ticket but I don't remember that. We had been to the football ground in the afternoon to see John Lennon arrive in a helicopter. John had been at another event beforehand and then had to get here for the evening. The helicopter landed at the Abergavenny Thursdays football ground. My mother came along. She had my younger brother and my niece in a pram and I think she was more excited at seeing the helicopter land than some of the teenagers were.

It was mayhem in the evening. There were quite a lot of males in the audience but it was the women, the girls, that were the screaming fans there. It was absolutely jam packed. The evening went in a blur of joy – and screaming! I'm in a photograph taken at the Town Hall. You can see me stood right in front of Paul McCartney. A chap I was at school with many years ago was a big railway fanatic. When one of the photographers in town died, he went to the auction and bought a lot of his memorabilia including a lot of his old films. He just happened to find these photographs of The Beatles that the photographer had taken on the night. He had them printed off and lots of people bought them. It was just strange how the memories of that evening came to life again.

My father had the Esso garage on the Hereford Road at the time and the day after the concert The Beatles pulled into the garage for petrol. Dad came to tell me that Paul and John had come in for petrol so I had the great pleasure of meeting them briefly and getting their autographs. Some years later, I let my young brother take them to school to show his friends. Unfortunately, they did not come back home with him and to this day I do not know who took them. My brother has to live that down every time we get together. Still – good memories! My favourite was and always will be Paul McCartney.

I WAS THERE: KEITH COLLETT

Eddie Tattersall was the main man that brought The Beatles and many other groups like The Hollies to the Town Hall. I had suits made to measure at the local Burtons shop for The Beatles and The Hollies concerts. They were great. I would like to go back to those days!

ASTORIA BALLROOM
25 JUNE 1963, MIDDLESBROUGH, UK

I WAS THERE: GORDON VALENTINE

They were getting bigger and bigger. We heard they were coming to the Astoria Ballroom in Wilson Street in Middlesbrough so we went along and saw the manager and said 'do you need a support band?' He said yes and so on the afternoon a few of us were there carrying in the Vox amps, the drums and all that. The Beatles just walked in. They were incredibly scruffy. Ringo Starr had a jumper on with big holes in the elbows. I asked Paul McCartney 'are you getting enough work?' and he said 'yes'. Anytime I see any of the boys from the group now, they always take the mickey out of me for saying that! The Beatles came on and you couldn't hear them for screaming. But they were just very nice blokes, very pleasant fellahs. We thought 'just another band.' My God, they changed the world.

QUEENS'S HALL
28 JUNE 1963, LEEDS, UK

I WAS THERE: GARTH CAWOOD

Eventually I was booked to do another compering job. Acker Bilk was top of the bill but The Beatles had just broke and so they had to reverse the running order. Acker still went down an absolute bomb but he didn't close the show. The Beatles had to close the show. I met them a few times. The picture of me with The Beatles was taken in Leeds at the Acker Bilk show.

I WAS THERE: JENNY MASKELL

I was about 14, 15, 16 when it was all going on. My mother was only 18 years older than me and she was interested in them as well. She came with me. We did it as a family. I went to an all-girls school and when they were on a television programme called *Calendar* in 1962, all the girls were talking about seeing them on it. We found out that they were based at the Cavern in Liverpool. Then we heard that they were supporting Acker Bilk in Leeds. I remember this tram shed place. There were no seats. Everybody was stood around. I could have touched The Beatles from where I was standing. And Acker Bilk's 'Stranger on the Shore' was 'top of the pops' at that time so he was obviously the starring act. It was a mixed audience of jazz fans who'd gone to see Acker Bilk and people like us who'd gone to see The Beatles. We actually went into The Beatles dressing room. They were still walking about and fairly accessible at that time, and Paul and Ringo walked out when we were just sort of hovering about beforehand. The friend I was with asked Paul McCartney for his autograph. I don't know whether she's still got it.

I WAS THERE: BILLY WALKER

When I saw The Beatles originally at the Odeon in Leeds, they just played a five song spot, so you didn't get to see the real Beatles. When I went to see them at the end of June at the Queen's Hall, it was a stand-up occasion. The Queen's Hall was an old tram shed and an ad hoc arrangement for a venue. Acker Bilk was also on the bill, but I wasn't interested in Acker Bilk, so I didn't stay around for the rest of the show. I was watching John Lennon most of the time because I was learning the guitar and I wanted to know how they played these songs. When The Beatles came on, to be introduced by Garth Cawood, they played two spots and they played different songs in each session.

Garth introduced them individually. This was amazing, because nobody had introduced The Beatles individually before. He said, 'Ladies and gentlemen, Ringo Starr.' Ringo tottered on and sat down at the drums. He then said 'George Harrison' and George, very knock-kneed and very shy, walked on. There was no screaming. This was a university-type audience. He said 'Paul McCartney' and Paul came on and waved and smiled. And then Garth said, 'Ladies and gentlemen, the leader of The Beatles – John Lennon!' John walked on stage, squinted his eyes and said 'where's the microphone?' and then 'one, two, three, four…' and they went into 'Money (That's What I Want)'. They went through the whole *Please Please Me* album in the two sessions. They did 'You've Really Got a Hold On Me' and John sang lead on about 85 per cent of the songs. It was like John Lennon and his backing group. John introduced Paul singing 'A Taste of Honey', but this was like the Engelbert Humperdinck of The Beatles beginning, there and then. Paul did 'Till There Was You' and you could hear every sound. There was no Beatlemania at this point. Beatlemania had not arrived.

REGAL THEATRE
30 JUNE 1963, GREAT YARMOUTH, UK

I WAS THERE: PAULINE PORTER, AGE 15

It was totally amazing. It's so far back I just can't remember. They were top of the bill. I went with girlfriends from school. I was living in Gorleston. You're totally star struck. I don't think I heard any of the music at all. Because there was so much noise going on. The theatre? You wouldn't have got another person in there. It was absolutely packed. And you never heard any of the music. It was just permanent screaming. Paul was my favourite. It was a big deal at the time. Oh my God. I saw The Beatles!

THE RITZ
5 JULY 1963, BIRMINGHAM, UK

I WAS THERE: SUE FLANAGAN, AGE 17

My friend and I worked in Birmingham town centre. I had no time to get home and back so went straight from work. I asked someone what bus to catch, found the stop and got chatting to another girl in the bus queue. I asked her where the Ritz was in Kings Heath and she said 'are you going to see The Beatles?' 'Yes, we are,' we replied. 'Are you a member?' 'No,' we said. 'Well, you won't get in but if you save me and my friend a place in the queue, we will sign you in.' Deal done.

The queue wasn't too bad but we were early. The girl from the bus queue arrived, we let them in and into the dance hall we ran. The stage was just a raised wooden platform and I sat on the left end and waited. On they came and guess who was at the feet of Paul McCartney? Yes – me! He smiled at me and I very gently reached out and held his foot encased in a Beatle boot. My hand stayed there for a little while. Paul sang I don't know what song but I was in heaven. The Redcaps played next and as Ringo's drums were being taken to the door, they caught up in the dress I was wearing. What a night. Only Dave Walker, the singer from the Redcaps, told me, 'You do know John is married, don't you?' Well, I was devastated.

THE PLAZA
5 JULY 1963, BIRMINGHAM, UK

I WAS THERE: MAGGIE BELL

The Plaza was situated in Rookery Road, Handsworth and, along with another venue called the Ritz, belonged to Ma and Pa Ryan. My husband Michael was employed there as a barman and told me about all the groups that played there. When I asked him about The Beatles, he said he 'thought they were quite good'.

SQUIRES GATE AIRPORT
7 JULY 1963, BLACKPOOL, UK

I WAS THERE: DERRILL CARR

The Beatles first came to Blackpool in July 1963 to appear live at the ABC Theatre in Blackpool. Along with thousands of other people, I was at Blackpool's Squires Gate Airport when their plane landed there, trying to get a glimpse of them. I could only see them from a distance as they were quickly escorted to a car waiting on the runway and taken away. I then went straight to the ABC Theatre, but there were thousands of people outside blocking all the roads and surrounding area. I never got to see The Beatles play live. Blackpool concert tickets for the Beatles were like gold dust and very expensive.

The Beatles appear at the Winter Gardens in the seaside resort of Margate, Kent, playing two houses a night for six consecutive nights.

WINTER GARDENS
8 – 13 JULY 1963, MARGATE, UK

I WAS THERE: ANTHEA CRAIG (NEE GREEN)

Jack Green, the Entertainments Manager of the Winter Gardens, was my father and it was he who was responsible for booking The Beatles for the week from 8th July 1963 – twice nightly! He had the foresight to make the booking in January of that year, just before they really took off. I was born and raised in Margate until sadly my parents divorced and I moved to London with my mother. However, I was allowed to take some time off school and take two friends from school to see The Beatles. I suddenly became very popular! My father arranged seats for us quite near the front and we screamed ourselves hoarse. It seems a shame now that we didn't listen to them singing. At the interval, my father took the three of us back stage to meet The Beatles and get their autographs. I asked them to use a name of one of their songs in the autograph. George was my favourite and I so hoped he would use 'with love from me to you' – which he did. John and Paul were also happy to comply, but Ringo was rather grumpy and did not. At that time, it was rumoured that John was married so I asked him straight out if he was married. He looked a bit non plussed but he said yes. It was a wonderful experience that I often look back on. Incidentally, I took a set of autographs back to a school friend who could not attend and she got about £3,500 for them about ten years ago. I could never sell mine!

I WAS THERE: JENNY WILKIN, AGE 13

I emigrated to Canada in 1974 but grew up in Margate from 1960 to 1967 and attended one of their concerts in 1963. My father was the Deputy Town Clerk of Margate. He died of a massive heart attack at the age of 49 in 1963, leaving my mother (then aged 39) and three daughters. My older sister had already moved out on her own to Sussex, leaving me and my nine-year-old sister Trish in Margate with my mother. As a kind gesture Jack Green, entertainment manager for the Winter Gardens and a colleague of my father, gave my sister and me front row tickets, together with back stage passes to meet The Beatles at intermission. The concert was an overwhelming experience, with hundreds of fans screaming and crying hysterically from start to finish.

At intermission, my sister and I were collected and ushered backstage – to the rage of devoted fans in the audience! We were taken to The Beatles' dressing room where we were greeted by Paul McCartney who was very friendly and welcoming. George was friendly but shy and did not interact much. Ringo was quite sullen and basically ignored us and John sat with a towel over his head the whole time so we could not even see his face! I am sure they were not thrilled to have to accommodate two 'children' during their break, but they were not rude to us. We left after our 15 minutes with them with autographs in our autograph books and signed photos – all of which were lost over the years – and boasting rites with our peers.

I WAS THERE: ROZANNE DUNCAN, AGE 17

I was working in my first job at David Greig, Westbrook. Engaged to be married, I took a part-time job as a programme seller at the Winter Gardens so when I was asked by the supervisor how many shifts I would work, I naturally said 'all of them'. All twelve concerts were a double bill with Billy J Kramer and the Dakotas, and at one of the shows I was told to get some more programmes to sell during the interval. Not knowing the layout backstage, I entered the stage door and instead of going down the stairs leading to behind the stage, I started going up and guess who was coming down? Billy J Kramer! Just imagine my embarrassment.

A comedian whose name I've forgotten had the unenviable slot immediately after the intermission of holding the audience at bay whilst waiting for our idols to take the stage. He was so funny and he held the audience completely in his hands by doing a skit about Christine Keeler.

The amazing music that followed couldn't be heard for the screams of the audience and at every performance the balconies seemed to be moving as the fans jumped up and down – it was quite frightening! I'll never forget that amazing week. I saw all twelve concerts and got paid for the privilege.

I WAS THERE: DIANE ALGER, AGE 20

I first heard of The Beatles in Dreamland Ballroom. The DJ played 'Love Me Do' and we were all spellbound. The DJ had to play it seven or eight times after that as we were all blown away with the sound. I remember the show I saw as if it was yesterday. We were all shouting and screaming and, being short, I stood on my seat because I couldn't see them on the stage very well. The next thing that happened was that everyone else was standing on their seats. I wondered why John Lennon was squinting with his eyes half shut. It wasn't until years later that I read about the fact that he needed glasses and could only see the front row beyond the stage. A few of us stayed after the show in the hope of getting The Beatles autographs, but we were told that they had gone. I shall never forget that night.

I WAS THERE: TONY CARPENTER

I went twice to see the show. On the Wednesday evening, the ticket cost three shillings and sixpence (18p) and I bought a seat in the auditorium. On the Saturday evening, there were still some seats available and I went with a schoolmate, Nobby Marcroft, whose parents had a small hotel opposite the venue, in Fort Crescent. This time the ticket price was seven shillings and sixpence (37p) and I bought a seat in the right-hand balcony looking at the stage. The place was really rocking. It was the first time I had seen dancing in the aisles. Over the week, momentum had gathered in the district and the school bus was very animated in the mornings – the girls were having heated discussion as to their favourite Beatle. I recall that Paul seemed to come out at the head of the list!

I WAS THERE: WENDY HOLLETT, AGE 17

In July 1963, my 21-year-old brother Vincent asked me if I wanted to see The Beatles at the Winter Gardens in Margate, as he had two tickets. The tickets cost 8/6 (43p). At the time, I liked Cliff Richard and the Shadows but I said yes! Before the night that we were going to see them, we went to the theatre just to stand outside and listen. A couple were coming out of the theatre and said 'you can go inside as there's no one at the door', so we went in and saw them for a few minutes for free.

On the night, we walked into the Winter Gardens and noticed that they had built a wooden rostrum at the back. As soon as The Beatles came on, the noise was deafening, with girls screaming. I was young too but I didn't like the screaming. I wouldn't have minded if it was after a song had finished, but not during the performance. They were also banging their feet on the rostrum. My brother and I were knocked out by The Beatles but we went there to listen to the music and I could never understand what all the screaming was about. After the concert, my brother and I went round to the back of the theatre and caught The Beatles getting into a blue car. Ringo wound down the window and he signed my book. I then asked Ringo if I could have John's autograph and he passed my book to John. John signed it and passed it back to me and said 'here you are, luv' and he went off with my pen. I didn't mind! It was such a good evening. I went back again at the end of the week for 3/6 (38p).

I WAS THERE: JANET PILCHER (NEE FURBY), AGE 21

I went with my friend. I don't remember much except that I moved from my seat to get a better view, leaning against the radiator situated by the entrance to the toilets and joining in the screaming. I can still see them on the stage in my head but I can't remember what happened afterwards. I was probably traumatised by what I'd seen. What a night.

I WAS THERE: TONY LAMPERT, AGE 17

My father had died in a car accident a few months before. We were living in Sandwich and, after Dad died, we had to move so I went to stay with my grandmother in Ramsgate, which is where I had originally grown up. I renewed an old friendship and, with his friends, started to go to pop concerts. There were many in Margate at that time and during 1963 we literally had an invasion of chart stars coming to the town, either to the Dreamland Ballroom or to the Winter Gardens. The first band I remember seeing was Brian Poole and The Tremeloes and I was then hooked on seeing live bands. And not small local bands, but the big names that kept appearing almost week after week.

To understand the impact of The Beatles, you have to look at the music that had been in the charts up to that time, and why it changed so dramatically. We'd had a diet of Cliff and The Shadows, Adam Faith, Billy Fury, Helen Shapiro, etc. All good pop music of the early Sixties but a bit bland. I remember listening to 'Love Me Do' on the radio and not liking it much, although DJs were starting to mention The Beatles because they sounded different. Then they appeared on TV singing 'Please Please Me' and it was like a bolt of lightning. I love pop music and this song performed by them was out of this world at the time – instantly catchy, very melodic, beautifully sung and so exciting to watch. Also, they were witty, intelligent and able to handle themselves in interviews. Then they came to Margate.

The *Please Please Me* album had been released and tracks were being played everywhere – in the clubs, on the radio. People couldn't get enough of the new sound.

The Winter Gardens show happened in July, as the *Please Please Me* album captured the nation, so we got The Beatles at full throttle. In the Winter Gardens there are the main seats at the front, some raised seats at the back and some balconies. I sat somewhere in the middle, maybe a dozen or so rows back, in those front seats. I can't remember who I was with but I had a good view of the stage. Apparently, it was a variety show but I have no memory of anything else and The Beatles closed the show. I imagine it was just the excitement of seeing them that excludes everything else.

My most distinct memory is of John Lennon singing 'Twist and Shout', which closed the act. He was directly in front of me and, as he jumped up and came down again, his hair lifted up and down. It's a funny thing, but that's what I remember most vividly. Oh, and the girls screaming. I remember looking around and being amazed at how they just screamed and screamed and screamed. I think we know now why girls did that, because they couldn't have been listening to the band. I think the boys went for the music but the girls for the sex appeal. Those girls were absolutely hysterical. It was quite an experience. I think Paul McCartney said he eventually broke up the band because he couldn't stand those girls screaming so much and because it meant he couldn't hear himself any more. Looking back, I should have bought a programme but didn't. I did eventually get a programme the following year when I went to the *New Musical Express* Pollwinner's Concert at the Empire Pool in Wembley, where they topped the bill along with Cliff Richard. I still have it.

I WAS THERE: DAVID NORMAN, AGE 19

It wasn't until about 1963 that listening to our pop songs became a regular feature. Before that it was mainly coffee bar juke boxes. Or, if you were lucky, a rock 'n' roll social hall. One such 'hall' offered this for us teens twice a week. There was a sign to the effect of 'no alcohol or high heel shoes allowed'. I had previously been to the Winter Gardens to see top name artists including, one Christmas Eve, the Marty Wilde Christmas package show which was all rock 'n' roll. I loved it.

So when The Beatles started to achieve their fame, starting with 'Love Me Do', I wasn't totally committed to this 'new wave' of music. The same applied to my buddies at that time. We were still into Gene Vincent, Marty Wilde, Cliff and Elvis. That night, we went as a party. For my own point of view, it wasn't just to go see a band called The Beatles but for the promise of a good evening out. It was obvious, as soon as we walked into the Winter Gardens hall, that something special was about to happen. I remember a feeling of almost tension amongst the audience already there. It was fairly obvious that the majority of the audience were teenage girls and I felt almost as if it was their music that was about to be played. Which, in a way, it was. The music scene was changing fast with still a mix of beat ballads and one or two rock 'n' roll songs in the charts. But groups such as The Beatles, Billy J Kramer and the Dakotas and Brian Poole and the Tremeloes were beginning to be the start of the new pop trend.

Billy J Kramer and the Dakotas finished their act to loud applause and screams, and I remember the curtains pulling back and there they stood. The Beatles – four fresh faced youths, perfectly groomed in matching suits and each with luxuriant mops of hair. They didn't at that moment quite match up to my expectations, or maybe I was still making comparisons with the rock 'n' roll stars which I still listened to. They launched into their first number – a Chuck Berry song. They sang nine songs. And what before had been deafening screams from the audience now rose to produce an almost constant bombardment of sound. I remember leaving after the concert and thinking that I had just seen something special. It put a new perspective on the singers and groups which previously I had held in such high esteem. The music scene changed that night. Although it wasn't until sometime later, when The Beatles started to achieve national prestige and international fame, that I realised just why and how that evening had been so special.

I WAS THERE: MARION SIMPSON

I saw them with my friend Jenny. She went backstage to meet them and I didn't. We had front row seats, possibly on the Thursday. I mostly remember all the girls screaming. I didn't scream as I wanted to listen to them. I remember hanging around outside a lot hoping to see them but only saw Billy J Kramer's band. Sadly, my memorabilia got thrown away when I lived overseas and my parents cleared out their attic when they moved. I had so many magazines, plus the programme.

I WAS THERE: BARRY SOLLY, AGE 12

I consider it an absolute privilege to have seen them in my home town at the Winter Gardens. Because it was never a concert venue. It was a ballroom. You've got concrete pillars all over the place. It's all flat. A couple of balconies. But it was a ballroom. We hadn't got a television. We got all the magazines. We'd seen pictures of them in the *New Musical Express* and the *Record Mirror*. We'd heard them on the radio. We listened to *Pick of the Pops* with Alan Freeman on a Sunday teatime. And we become aware of all this different style of music, of music changing. I was very lucky. Mum took me to the Winter Gardens and all the stars of the day were there.

In 1963, Gerry and the Pacemakers had the first national number one of the beat boom era. And then at the beginning of June we had Jet Harris and Tony Meehan at the Winter Gardens. And they had been at number one with 'Diamonds' and had a hit with 'Scarlett O'Hara'. We sat there in awe looking at them. I remember when we came out of the Winter Gardens, we saw a poster and I said to my mum, 'Look that's that new group they've got coming called The Beatles.' Straight away she went and booked up. And it was the anticipation – even now it tingles me to think of it – the anticipation of seeing them live. And then we were aware that they were going to be there for the week. All the stars of the day stayed in a big hotel in nearby Birchington, and it became clear that they'd be in the area and we would see them on the night of the concert.

We went to see them on the second night, the later show. In those days it was more of a variety show, so you got a comedian, a juggler, probably an acrobatic troupe, an impressionist, a lower grade comedian and a compere. And then the top stars. There was usually a good support act that would finish the first half. In this case it was Billy J Kramer and The Dakotas. It was tremendous to see them because they'd suddenly become popular and we'd all heard of them and they were there on stage, standing there in their suits and ties and shirts – so smart. And these songs that we'd heard on the radio. And then, all of a sudden, everyone realised that in the second half The Beatles would be there. And there were a couple of acts after the interval. I think it was the comedian.

And then Derek Roy, who was the compere, came out and said his bit and everyone just started shouting and screaming. And he said 'right that's it – no more. The Beatles!' And the curtains went back and all hell was let loose. They stood there and they sang their songs. You could hardly hear them, but it was the sheer excitement and the anticipation that The Beatles were going to be there. It was tremendous.

Bear in mind this was before 'She Loves You' was released, before 'I Want To Hold Your Hand' at the end of the year. They'd only had 'Please Please Me' and 'From Me To You', and they were singing all these other songs. They sang what is still my favourite Beatles song, although it was geared more towards the female fan, 'Thank You Girl'. They sang that as an encore. Twice.

There's nothing like the beat music of that era. Nothing like it at all. On the night, we were well aware something big was happening in the music industry. Even then I thought 'how lucky we are. We're going to see The Beatles' and all of a sudden they were there.

For sheer excitement nothing comes close to seeing The Beatles live. We were lucky enough to see them right there at the beginning, when everyone wanted to see them. No one really knew what they were all about. As the years went on, I loved The Beatles for what they were then, from '63 to about '64, '65. Once they got into psychedelia – *Rubber Soul* and *Magical Mystery Tour* – I really wasn't into that. I just prefer them for what they were. Three guitars and a drum set, singing beat music live. So much happened in 1963. We were just coming out of an horrendous winter. People had just about got over the war and had a bit of money in their pockets, buying televisions, cars, things like that. Plus of course it was Margate in the Swinging Sixties, with tremendous summer times on the beaches. And then all of a sudden the music changed and the youngsters had got something to cling on to. A year later, in 1964, it went a bit haywire with the Mods and Rockers. But 1963 was the catalyst for the next few years, music-wise. Fate dealt me a great hand. I was there.

I WAS THERE: WENDY STILWELL, AGE 17

I went with my friend Margaret but we never heard them because of the screaming! We both got their autographs. They were signed in their dressing room whilst we waited outside. I sold mine in the 1970s for about £30 through the *Exchange & Mart*. Margaret sold hers recently for £2,500. I should have waited!

I WAS THERE: LINDA PLANT, AGE 15

We were all still at school. You just waited for the next single to come out. 'Please Please Me' had come out about six months before. It was something different. There was all this big Merseybeat sound. They bigged it up if it was from Liverpool, because all the groups were coming from Liverpool. You got the Swinging Blue Jeans, and you got Gerry and the Pacemakers, Billy J Kramer. They were all under Epstein's umbrella. For us down on the south coast, it seemed all the entertainment was either in Liverpool or London. When I was growing up down there, it was wonderful because nobody went on package holidays. It was always Ramsgate and Margate and loads from London came down on holiday. We lived on the very edge of the south east coast. But nobody ever came there to play gigs. Everybody either finished their tours in London or, when they came down to Margate or Ramsgate, it was like the queen visiting. We might as well as lived out in the wilds of Norfolk.

And you'd have to get on a train for two hours to get to London. There wasn't the transport available, so when you got these big groups coming down to our little coastal town it was a huge event. One day Dad came home and he said, 'I've managed to get two tickets to see The Beatles.'. That was like manna from heaven. He must have paid top price, which was eleven shillings for two tickets. I took the boy next door. Of course, in those days you caught the bus and you got dropped off outside the Winter Gardens, where there were all these people and we went off and saw the concert.

Billy J Kramer was on the same bill. It really was fantastic. You'd got the balconies and the girls were screaming over the top of them. You see photos of girls in the 1960s, crying in the audience? That's how it was. We'd all got short bobbed hair. We were fashionable for our era. When you got these four lads coming on stage – well, the roof went off. We were amongst the first proper teenagers. But it was so innocent. We were still in ankle socks at 15, 16. I think tights had just started to be invented. If you went out with a fellah, there was no naughties going on. Everything was so innocent. You didn't sleep with anybody until you were married, athough the Pill had come into being.

I always call it Miss Marple time, with the midwives going around on their bikes. That's how it was. All very nice. During the war years and just after, anybody in their teenage years were mini-versions of Mum and Dad in fashion. They were dressed like Mum and Dad. And then you had the Fifties and Bill Haley and Tommy Steele. They were the real first pop stars. Then you got Cliff Richard in the late '50s and then you got skiffle and Lonnie Donegan. But then, as the Sixties came into being, you got a lot of the fashion designers coming through like Mary Quant and people like Vidal Sassoon and the haircuts. And these all gelled together and you had a totally different type of teenager coming through. You had Jean Shrimpton and the short dresses and the mini skirts. And then you had the Mini motor car, and that all suddenly became very trendy. So from the Fifties, where everybody dressed like Mum and Dad, and where you had the Teddy boys and the quiffs and the hair, suddenly you had a new era in the Sixties. And it's never been like that ever since. You haven't had that great change. When you look at long-legged girls today, in their mini skirts and their long hair, we were exactly the same in the Sixties. The music, the hairdressing, the fashion designers all helped to make it different from what had gone on ten years earlier, and twenty and thirty years before that. You've still got girls in bikinis today that you started to have in the Sixties. I wish I was back there!

After Margate, The Beatles play shows in Blackpool and Rhyl and then commence another week-long residency in the seaside resort of Weston-super-Mare.

ODEON THEATRE
22 – 27 JULY 1963, WESTON-SUPER-MARE, UK

I WAS THERE: DES HENLY, AGE 16

I was in a band called The Iveys. That night we had been playing a gig a few miles out of town at Rossholm School for Girls at Brent Knoll. After our gig we made our way back to Weston. I was on my Triumph Tiger Cub motor bike with Bob on the back, Remo was on his Vespa scooter with his brother. Mario's Dad had managed to get all of our gear on the back seat of his Rover 90. Riding into Weston, we were astonished to see thousands of highly excited people surrounding the Odeon cinema. Then it clicked that The Beatles were in town and had just performed their first night of a week-long series of concerts at the Odeon. Although they were the biggest band around in 1963, they had not yet reached the extraordinary heights for which they were destined, hence their week of concerts in Weston-Super-Mare. It was obvious from the crowds that The

Beatles hadn't yet left the Odeon so we parked up to savour the moment.

After five minutes, the hubbub from the crowd turned into a roar as a white 15cwt Thames van backed up to the exit opposite the Bristol and Exeter pub. The Beatles were about to exit the building. Their long-time friend and driver, Neil Aspinall, was at the wheel and was gingerly reversing the vehicle through the crowd, trying to position it so that The Beatles could jump straight into the back from the stage door. Not an easy manoeuvre given the frantic crowd. The Fab Four burst through the exit and dived into the van, still finding time for a smile and a wave to their fans. The back door slammed shut and they were away. We jumped on our bikes and followed in hot pursuit.

We soon realised they were hopelessly lost and were going around in circles and getting nowhere. On their second excursion into Wadham Street the van stopped. They must have seen us following them as one of the back doors opened. George Harrison's head appeared and he asked me in his unmistakable Liverpool accent, 'Can you tell us the way to the Royal Pier Hotel please?' Trying not to show my excitement at this unexpected encounter, I said 'sure, follow us'. We headed off with The Beatles in tow until we reached the hotel and, still grasping the moment, followed them inside. However, we felt a little awkward standing in the reception with them. Not knowing what to do, we turned and said goodnight. John Lennon looked at us. 'Thanks very much lads – goodnight!' Still excited, I thought that was the end of our Beatles experience, but it was only the beginning!

We had booked our tickets for the second night's concert months before. I knew one of the Odeon's managers and that night he asked me 'was that you on the motor bike last night?' I said 'yes' and he said, 'We just can't get The Beatles away after the show. The crowds are far too big. So we've made a plan. We are going to use decoy vans at one of the other exits. If you can be backstage each night, we will decide which one we intend to use at the last minute. You can be there waiting with your bikes to guide them to their hotel.' We jumped at the offer, and for the rest of the week became The Beatles official outriders!

One night, The Beatles spilled out of the designated exit. We were waiting for them but the van didn't appear. There we were on the pavement with the Fab Four, with thousands of screaming fans just around the corner looking for them. Any second, we expected someone to shout 'THERE THEY ARE! and for us to be engulfed. George said what I thought was 'let's get the car'. It so happened that, that week, George had put his Mark 10 Jag in for a service at Victoria Garage which had an entrance directly opposite the exit being used that evening. Mike Millington, one of our team, was a mechanic there and held the keys to Victoria Garage.

We all ran across the raised grass plantation to get to the garage's entrance on Alexandra Parade. On the way, John Lennon fell over with a curse. I helped him up and we carried on running, genuinely frightened we would be spotted by the mob at any moment. We entered the garage, Mike took the band to George's car and they all looked bemused. There we were with the four Beatles, still in their Beatle jackets and Cuban-heeled shoes, with their ties firmly in place, standing in a dimly-lit garage in Weston-super-Mare. It was surreal!

George said, 'What the hell are we doing here?' I replied, 'You said 'let's get the car' George.' 'I said cab not car.' But they all jumped in George's car and we escorted them home safe and sound. Being backstage with them for the next four nights, we had many conversations and ended up on first name terms. When some of my friends realised we were in such a privileged position, they naturally tried to take advantage of this and get closer themselves. We delivered many love letters, along with fluffy toys and other presents.

On one occasion, as I handed Paul McCartney a love letter with hearts all over it, the sender had asked me to tell him exactly which seat she would be sat in that night. 'Paul, this is from a girl with blonde hair who will be blowing you kisses from the third row.' John, coming down the stairs from the dressing room, overheard me and said 'girls? Where are the girls?' 'I thought you were married?' I said. Being just 16, I was taken aback by his response. 'So what?' Until he followed up his comment with a broad grin.

Every night we spent at least 15 or 20 minutes alone with The Beatles waiting for our exit instructions. There was many a conversation, and many memories: John Lennon composing on a piano backstage (composing what, I wonder?); being told off by all four of them because the brake light on my motorbike wasn't working and having to promise to get it fixed; a long and animated conversation with George about his love of cars, particularly his Mark 10 Jag; the time their van stopped at traffic lights, girls recognising them and screaming, only for Ringo to grin at me, pointing vigorously to his chest and assuring me that the girls were screaming for him not me. And lastly, backstage at the Odeon, I watched every performance from the wings and was never more chuffed than when Paul glanced at me and gave a wink of recognition.

I WAS THERE: PETE BROWNETT, AGE 15

As a very young and naïve 15-year-old, I was just starting my job as an apprentice photographer and was helping out on the assignment of taking a set of photographs of The Beatles when they visited the town. I was allowed to take one photograph in amongst the set that was taken. It was my birthday three days after the shoot and I managed to get the 32/6 (£1.75) needed to buy the latest album, which took some doing as Weston-super-Mare was closed on a Thursday. But determination prevailed. Armed with the album, and a considerable amount of pride, I proceeded to get autographs from all members of the group. I was an awestruck teenager but clearly remember discovering that the four of them were down to earth human beings with a wonderful outlook on life and respect for their roots. This made a lasting impression on me and gave me a philosophy by which I have lived and worked ever since.

I WAS THERE: ANN BAXTER, AGE 13

My best friend Judy and I lived and breathed for pop music. We danced for hours around my red Dansette record player to Cliff and the Shadows. Elvis, The Tornados, Frank Ifield and Susan Maughan. But nothing prepared us for the sounds of John, Paul, George and Ringo. Imagine our excitement when we read in the local newspaper that The Beatles were billed to appear at the Odeon Cinema. We rushed to buy our tickets for the performance on 23 July 1963. We could talk of nothing else.

Finally, the day came and we caught the bus to the Odeon. Considering that The Beatles were already making quite a sir, the queue wasn't too long but the buzz of excitement was unmistakable. We took our seats and sat through a supporting cast of Tommy Quickly, Gary and Lee, Dan Thompson and Tommy Wallis. The other group appearing was Gerry and the Pacemakers. The odd scream could be heard as Gerry Marsden sang 'How Do You Do It?' and then 'I Like It'. But the screams were deafening as the time came for The Beatles to be announced. They ran on stage and the audience erupted. It was wonderful. We just had to join in with the screaming and singing. I'd been a rather reserved young lady until that point but I couldn't contain myself. The boys sang 'I Saw Her Standing There', 'Love Me Do', 'Please Please Me', 'From Me To You' and 'Twist and Shout' along with other tracks from my treasured copy of *With The Beatles*, and we enjoyed every moment. Afterwards, we waited at the stage door but they'd left by another exit. We couldn't leave things like that.

We found out they were staying at the Royal Pier Hotel at Anchor Head and the next day, armed with our autograph books, cameras and my *Beatles Monthly* magazine, Judy and I caught the bus to the hotel. Just as we got off the bus right outside the hotel, we caught sight of Gerry Marsden in the foyer. I rushed across with my camera and snapped a magnificent photograph with my Brownie 127 and he also gave us an autograph. A few other fans were hanging about with us, but nothing was happening. Judy and I decided to wander to the back of the hotel. How lucky could we be?

We could hear the voices of John, Paul, George and Ringo and a transistor radio playing on a balcony about ten feet above our heads. So near and yet so far, but nothing was going to deter me now. Judy gave me a leg up and somehow my head just about reached the balcony and I was able to see the boys with their wives and girlfriends. They were so friendly at what must have been a great invasion of their privacy. With just a head showing through the railings, and hanging on for dear life, our autograph books and magazines were passed round and autographed. John even asked my name and if I hadn't been perched so precariously, I would have swooned. I walked all the way home clutching the autographs on my *Beatles Monthly* magazine and my autograph book. I will always treasure the one that says 'To Anne, love John Lennon'. I was invited, along with some other Beatles fans, to tell our story on TV on the sad occasion of the fire at the Royal Pier Hotel in Weston-super-Mare some years late. The hotel was virtually burnt to the ground and we were invited to talk about our experiences as the hotel was smouldering.

I WAS THERE: SYLVIE BROOMHALL

I was working in a salon called Lloyd and Osbourne which had a wig room at the top of the building, a ladies salon in the middle and a gents salon on the ground floor. It was a really exciting time and I went to see The Beatles at the Odeon, but it was even better when they came into the gents salon one day to have their famous hair cut. We in the wig room went mad with excitement and wanted to go down to the salon but our boss wouldn't let us. I wish I had swept the floor and saved the famous hair! My son and friends are so envious when I tell them all about that time.

I WAS THERE: LESLEY WELLS, AGE 10

I remember everyone was screaming so much. As I was only ten years old at the time I had to go with my mother. She had to put her hands over her ears for all the noise that was going on around her. I can remember where we sat in the stalls. Funny how you remember things so many years ago.

I WAS THERE: CHRISTINE PIERCE, AGE 15

The Odeon auditorium was lovely and big, with a large stage. The Beatles were grouped in the centre, with Ringo behind Paul, George and John on a podium. I wish I could remember how they sounded because it's extraordinary, recalling now, how small the single amps – one for each guitar – were and how sparse the stage was, especially compared to how things are today. When I bought my ticket, they were the new 'buzz' and it had been easy to get a front row seat.

When I arrived for the concert, only a short time later, they were the new 'rave' and so the house was packed and the screaming had begun, so they weren't that easy to hear. I particularly remember tins of sweets flying through the air. Someone had reported that one of them liked toffees, which were dangerous enough being thrown individually – both for them and for us in the front row. But some of the girls decided to throw tins, one of which caught Paul on the bone above his left eye. I can imagine what kind of language that would provoke now but, after recoiling and still playing, he clearly mouthed to no one in particular 'I wanna go home'. The old Jack Vowles riding stables had the pleasure of their company during their visit. I remember being furious because my mum – of all people – saw them riding near our house!

I WAS THERE: DAVID VENN

I went with my future wife to see them on the Thursday during their week's stay in Weston. We were driving home in my little 1938 Morris 8 Tourer and as we passed the Royal Pier Hotel, we saw The Beatles pouring out of the back of a white van outside the front entrance. We pulled up and, grabbing the programme for the show, I ran across and managed to get Paul and George to sign it. I approached Ringo but a roadie grabbed him around the waist from behind and pulled him into the door and into the hotel. I have no recollection of John being there, only the other three. I would love to have got all four of them to sign.

I WAS THERE: JANET VOCKINS

I went with my future husband (since divorced) who had a local rock group in Swindon, and some of the band. It was a lovely evening – lots of screaming. Our parents didn't think they would last. After all, they wore jackets without a collar!

BREAN SANDS
27 JULY 1963, WESTON-SUPER-MARE, UK

I WAS THERE: MARK TILLEY, AGE 17

I met them on the beach at Brean when they were clowning about taking a very famous picture of them playing leapfrog. I was down on the beach with my mother and family. I said 'I wonder what they're doing down there?' because I could see there were two or three people with cameras and The Beatles were at Weston at the time. They'd come out to Brean to take photographs. I didn't actually like them at the time, being very much a Buddy Holly fan, although I have since come to enjoy them.

I was wearing one of these great big straw hats which was about two foot across. And they took the mickey out of me a bit and one of them put it on. I can't remember if they actually had a photograph taken with my hat, but I got it back. They weren't rotten. They didn't take it away from me. But they were clowning about. I can't remember which one put it on. I know I got three of their autographs. The hat's gone. It was one of my mother's hats for the beach. One of these straw type hats with a very wide brim, almost like a Mexican-type hat. People say of those photographs, 'Oh, it's at Weston.' No it's not – it was at Brean. And I know – because I was there!

Clockwise from top left: Ann Baxter saw The Beatles at Weston-super-Mare and got their autographs; David Venn got Paul and George's autographs in Weston; Brenda Pirozzolo was annoyed by all the screaming girls; Mike Winters had a poster from the Southport show he saw; Sylvie Broomhall was working in the hairdressing salon in Weston when The Beatles came in to get their hair cut; Christine Pierce remembers tins of sweets flying through the air towards the stage; Janet Vockins' parents were shocked that The Beatles wore collarless shirts.

Clockwise from top left: Alan Forrester saw The Beatles in Kirkcaldy; Fraser Elder drew a batch of caricatures of The Beatles and signed personal copies for the boys; Linda Groom thought that John would notice her if she didn't scream – he didn't; Roger Frisby pretended to be Brian Epstein; Margaret Cole's parents thought she was mad to go and see The Beatles; Colin Little had a Beatles suit made; Jackie Goodfellow queued overnight for tickets.

QUEEN'S THEATRE
4 AUGUST 1963, BLACKPOOL, UK

I WAS THERE: STEVE GOMERSALL, AGE 14

The Beatles were the first band I ever saw. There were four of us went from school. We were all from Blackpool and attended Tyldesley Secondary Modern School. Basically, The Beatles took over our lives when they hit. 'Love Me Do' got to 17 in November 1962 and that didn't really register that highly with most of us, but when 'Please Please Me' hit number one the whole school – the girls and the boys – we'd just never been influenced to such an extent. The girls wanted to be with The Beatles. And we wanted to be The Beatles. We loved the the fact that they were northern lads who had an incredibly dry sarcastic sense of humour and that they thought nothing of authority.

I was always a music freak from being a child. My parents bought me the Shadows first album in '61. My grandmother was a wardrobe mistress at the Grand Theatre and the Opera House and I got Tommy Steele's autograph. I've still got his 78s to this day. My friends and I were obsessed. We were potty about music. And in those days Blackpool got everybody.

The Beatles were a phenomenon. They were the punks of their era when they came along and you compared them to Bobby Vee and all those kinds of characters. Plus they wrote every single they had a hit with, which was unprecedented. We thought, 'These are real and they're ours. They're knocking the Americans out of the hit parade.' We were obsessed with the fashions as well. I remember buying a pair of Beatles boots from Stead and Simpsons for 72/6 (£3.63). I had bought a Beatles suit, not the rounded collars but the first ones they wore for the publicity shots for 'Please Please Me'. They had velvet collars and velvet cuffs. I remember another kid in Blackpool being very, very annoyed because I'd beaten him to it. But it was this insane kind of dedication really. I suppose kids still have it now for Boyzone and stuff like that.

But we'd never seen anything like that, because before that it was distant heroes – Chuck Berry, Little Richard, Elvis Presley and the like. They were people we couldn't identify with because we'd never seen them, only seen rare black and white footage of them. So The Beatles were 'what is this?' And even the Stones initially were never in the same bracket as The Beatles. The Beatles were gods. Marianne Faithfull said that when she was with Mick Jagger, Paul McCartney used to go round to see them and Mick Jagger was the pupil and McCartney was the teacher. And they could play. That was another thing. And they were innovators. George Harrison had a 12-string Rickenbacker before anybody else. They were using tone pedals before anyone else. And sitars, for God's sake. They were outstanding. Their energy was incredible. And they didn't take themselves seriously either. They were fearless.

I went to see them the first opportunity I got. Unfortunately, like a lot of people's experience, we didn't hear much of the band because of the screaming and the poor amplification. But it was an incredible atmosphere and when it finished, girls were like vultures, swooping round the place trying to get a view of them, wondering whether they were going to come out and try to escape. I don't know how they got out of the building because the girls were circling the building.

So we put our collars up at the back and ran down this back alley. We couldn't resist running like lunatics. The girls started following us because they didn't know who the hell we were. We went around a couple of corners and eventually stopped and turned around and started laughing. And the vitriol that came out of their mouths when they found we weren't their treasured boys – oh dear, oh dear, they didn't like that at all! We were buzzing for ages afterwards.

I WAS THERE: JOHN MOORHOUSE, AGE 17

Me and my mate were working for the local Co-op grocery department while his sister was a secretary. The noise was certainly hard going. I remember the girl who was sat next to me being on the verge of losing herself and turning to me and saying 'aren't they great?' Their last song, which just about brought the house down, was 'Twist and Shout'. I'm fairly certain it was an all-Liverpool show with the likes of Cilla Black and The Fourmost. Although late getting home, we made it to work on time. When we were waiting to go into the theatre, a girl was selling programmes. David put me off buying one. He said, 'I'm not buying one at that price. They are nearly as dear as the seats.'

In early August 1963 The Beatles fly to the Channel Islands.

 # SPRINGFIELD BALLROOM
6, 7, 9 & 10 AUGUST 1963, JERSEY, UK

I WAS THERE: CAROL CHARLTON, AGE 17

I had to plead with my parents to let me go. I stood right at the front of the stage, in line with Paul McCartney, who was my favourite. The place was packed. The Beatles were brilliant and the time went very quickly. It seemed unreal that I was actually seeing them live. I was lucky to go backstage at the end of the evening and sit on Paul McCartney's knee while getting all their autographs! It was a really memorable night. I became an avid fan – my mum made me a black collarless corduroy jacket like theirs and I had my hair cut in a similar style and collected every conceivable article and fan club magazine, all the LPs, etc. I still have most of it. My dad was a taxi driver up at the airport who was asked to take The Beatles to Swansons Hotel when they arrived. He said he would take their luggage but not them as he didn't want his car damaged with screaming fans surrounding his car. I didn't know this until he came home and mentioned it. I was horrified! Fancy missing out on the opportunity to say that The Beatles travelled in my dad's taxi. Can you imagine how envious my friends would have been?

I WAS THERE: JOHN HENWOOD, AGE 17

I was 16 and had just started work when 'Love Me Do' exploded into our world. 'Please Please Me' and 'From Me To You' had been released by the time they arrived in Jersey. 'She Loves You' was soon to follow and they may have previewed it at Springfield. They did a lot of other artists' material at that time and, as a fan of Chuck Berry I'm not sure I altogether approved of all of it, but there's no denying they did it really well.

I was one of the lucky individuals who saw The Beatles at the Springfield Ballroom although to refer to the venue as a 'ballroom' was conferring a status on it that it didn't deserve. Springfield was what we would today call an event venue and it hosted everything from trade fairs to livestock shows and, yes, it did from time-to-time act as a concert hall. In truth it was a bit of a dump and, although one or two tears of nostalgia might have been shed, few objected to its demolition some years later. Today it's a sports venue and grandstand overlooking Jersey's principal football pitch – our little (very little) Wembley.

Those were the days when headliners still toured minor venues playing to audiences counted in hundreds rather than thousands. Indeed, a thousand Beatles fans squeezed into Springfield would have broken all fire regulations and even the somewhat sketchy health and safety rules of the day. I'd guess the audience on the night I saw them was around 500. To say I remember it really well would be to stretch the truth, but I was probably wearing my pale blue Prince of Wales check suit, with very tight trousers and what my mother called a bum freezer jacket, because the style was to cut the jacket – no vents – just below the waist. I probably had a faux hanky in my top pocket – just four peaks of white cotton showing with, inside the pocket, a piece of card stapled to the fabric. My car – a white Triumph Herald convertible – was parked outside and I thought I was pretty cool.

It was pretty crowded inside but there was just about room to dance. Not that many girls wanted to dance. They preferred to squeeze in front of the low stage and just swoon at their idols. I certainly don't recall the screaming and near hysteria that was to mark some of The Beatles' later gigs. I worked for Channel Television as a trainee, drafted in to do everything from making the tea to pushing a TV camera round the studio floor. It was a really privileged opportunity and I worked in the industry for the next 38 years. Channel Television had a connection through common shareholdings with EMI and when we started doing a local pop programme, *Now Look Hear*, EMI made available artists signed to their labels. I was at that time training as a sound recordist and went as part of a crew to EMI's headquarters in Manchester Square, London to film a series of interviews with their artistes. I can't recall whether it was there, or in Jersey, but we did an interview with The Beatles. Many years later, when Channel Television was about to celebrate 50 years of broadcasting, they hunted high and low for that film without success. They called me and asked if I knew what had happened to it. Well, I don't know for sure, but there was a time when the film library was running short of space and someone – I know who it was, but won't name him – took the view that a lot of old material was no longer of any value and it was dumped. I'm fairly sure The Beatles interview, along with countless others with pop stars of the day plus irreplaceable scenes of Jersey and Guernsey in the 1960s, was destroyed. A little tragedy.

I WAS THERE: SUSAN BLYDE

They were lounging outside Springfield Hall. I and two others were waiting for a cab. There were three of us. The cab pulled up and as we were getting in the band asked if they could squeeze in. We all set off to St Helier. They were being very normal, and we all chatted about music.

I WAS THERE: BRENDA PIROZZOLO (NEE EVANS), AGE 13

I was one of the many young girls that attended that event. I managed to be standing right in the front of the stage. They were fabulous but the girls behind me were really annoying as all they did was scream and they didn't listen to the music. I went with my friend Janet Langlois, who is unfortunately no longer with us, and at the end of the evening we were told we could get autographs if we went to the side of the Springfield opposite La Coie Hotel. We queued up outside the door and some guy took my *Beatles* magazine up to the Fab Four and they signed it for me.

'She Loves You' is released as a single in the UK on 23 August 1963.

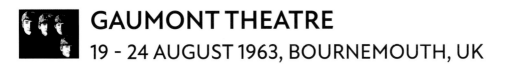

GAUMONT THEATRE
19 - 24 AUGUST 1963, BOURNEMOUTH, UK

I WAS THERE: ALEX OLDHAM

The Beatles were booked for a week at the Gaumont in Bournemouth before Beatlemania struck. They performed every night, plus matinees on Wednesday and

Saturday. On the first day they were there, I was walking towards the stage door and the man on the gate opened it for me to walk through. I've often wondered why; whether it was because I had a Beatle haircut and wore the fashionable clothes or, which is quite likely, whether it was because I resembled Tommy Quickly who was also on the bill. Anyway, as a result of this I saw every performance that week from the wings because he continued to open the gate for me every time I approached it. He was an older chap and I think we all looked the same to him. As a result I met most of the musicians playing and also George and Paul. They knew I was only a fan but didn't care. Paul was messing about on the drums one afternoon when I stopped to watch him and he openly chatted to me as he would. George I met only briefly but he was friendly also. They were such happy days. A couple of years later, The Byrds played there and I saw them from the wings of the stage by using the same technique to gain entry!

The Beatles were staying just a few doors away from the Gaumont, in the Palace Court Hotel. They were there for the whole week and it was in the ballroom of the hotel that the iconic cover photo for *With The Beatles* was taken.

A few months later, in November, I saw The Beatles twice at Bournemouth's Winter Gardens – once on the bill with Helen Shapiro and once when they headlined. I queued all night for tickets for that show and we were in the second row. It was where I first heard John do his infamous 'rattle your jewellery' joke. Beatlemania was such an exciting time. I'd live it all over again if I could.

IMPERIAL HOTEL
25 AUGUST 1963, BLACKPOOL, UK

I WAS THERE: DERRILL CARR

I met Brian Epstein, manager of The Beatles, several times during 1963 to 1965 as I waited patiently outside the ABC, Queens and Opera House stage doors in Blackpool for The Beatles to come out after their shows. Brian kept a low profile but was happy to sign autographs and chat to the fans while The Beatles were taken out through other exits. I got his autograph in July 1963. I found out that The Beatles always stayed at the Imperial Hotel in Blackpool whenever they had a concert. The Imperial was the best hotel in Blackpool and also hosted the Conservative and Labour Party annual conferences. I knew the Imperial Hotel well. I had been there many times collecting footballers' autographs as all the big teams stayed there. I went to the Imperial several times in July and August 1963 when The Beatles were appearing at the ABC and the Queens Theatre in Blackpool. On one occasion in August 1963, I remember it was pouring down with rain. I was the only person standing outside the entrance to the hotel and I was soaked. A doorman took pity and told me to wait at the back of the Imperial Hotel where he said I would definitely see The Beatles. I thought it was a wind up but decided to give it a go. After a couple of hours, a taxi appeared, a back door of the hotel opened and out came The Beatles. I was the only person there and fortunately it had stopped raining. I rushed over and they all signed their autographs on a sheet of paper and chatted to me before getting in the car. They were all waving as they drove away. They were four normal guys laughing and joking with each other, whose lives had changed forever and perhaps fame was not all it was cracked up to be. (I sold the original autograph for £1,000 many years ago.)

At the end of August 1963, The Beatles begin another week-long residency, this time in the seaside resort of Southport.

ODEON THEATRE
26 – 31 AUGUST 1963, SOUTHPORT, UK

I WAS THERE: THERESE HOWARD, AGE 13

When The Beatles were still living in their Liverpool homes, we got all the gossip, but after 'Please Please Me' gave them fame and launched Beatlemania they moved to London, leaving their Liverpool fans behind. When they came back to Southport, they were top of the bill and supported by great Merseybeat groups like The Big Three and, of course, Gerry and The Pacemakers. What a great concert! I had not been to The Cavern at that time, being only 13 years old, but older family members and neighbours were talking excitedly about this group called The Beatles, and I already loved the music. So when my friend's older brother offered to take us to this concert, we didn't hesitate. They lived across the road to me so we often shared games and bought records between us. My parents allowed me out at night if accompanied by older friends and family. I remember feeling really excited and totally absorbed in the music. Gerry sang 'How Do You Do It?', which had already reached number one in the hit parade. He then introduced The Beatles and the crowd went wild. I don't remember too much screaming at that first concert – I also saw them at the Liverpool Empire in 1965 – so we could hear their wonderful unique sound clearly. Most of the songs they sang were their early hits – 'Please Please Me', 'Love Me Do', 'Thank You Girl', 'PS I Love You', slowing down to Paul's solo 'Till There Was You'. From then on Paul McCartney was my favourite, my teenage passion. The tempo built up again with John Lennon taking the lead after the tantalising build up to 'Twist and Shout'. The fans were going wild by the time their latest release, 'She Loves You', was introduced, I think by Paul, to end a really memorable performance.

It was a real treat for Liverpool fans just before The Beatles were to become a musical legend, far removed from them. From then on The Beatles, The Merseybeat and live music at the Cavern Club were at the centre of my teenage years and helped to make them memorable and magical. I bought the first LP, *Please Please Me*, at NEMS music store in Whitechapel, Liverpool soon after followed by every other LP, EP and single. I joined the fan club and bought the magazines. It was a happy and exciting time.

I WAS THERE: MIKE RIMMER, AGE 13

I was born in June 1950, so too young to see The Beatles in their pre-famous early Cavern Club days. The Beatles only came to my attention through the media, after their recording career was underway. My earliest recollection was chatting with school friends about their first release, 'Love Me Do'. This was late 1962, when I was only twelve years old, but I remember I wasn't all that impressed with the tune!

The first 45 single I ever bought was 'From Me To You'. I bought two copies and gave one to my girlfriend, Linda Sawyer. I can't remember how it was that Linda and I later came buy two tickets to see The Beatles live in Southport. Many of the cinemas at that time had been converted from earlier theatre venues so the cinema could easily be 'morphed back' into a theatre facility for a stage presentation. One such venue was the old Gaumont Theatre in St George's Square on Lord Street. It was then the Odeon Cinema and is now a Sainsbury's supermarket. In keeping with entertainment trends of the time, the Beatles gig was a variety show format. The Beatles were the final act on a variety show which included a comedian and jugglers, plus sets from Sons of the Piltdown Men, The Fourmost and Gerry and the Pacemakers.

Linda and I were sat in the front stalls, towards the right of the stage. I remember there was a compere/comedian and a juggling act, plus several bands. The Fourmost were particularly entertaining, with lots of chat and jokes to the audience. The first half of the show was closed by a set from Gerry and the Pacemakers. My next memory is of The Beatles themselves on stage, with John Lennon directly in front of us. They were dressed in their iconic, collar-less Beatle suits and wore heavy stage make-up. I remember being surprised that they actually looked like the photos and TV images I'd seen of them. The noise from the audience was surprisingly loud, with screaming girls all around us and up in the balcony area. The performance was slick and well presented. The lads tried to talk to the audience between songs but we couldn't hear anything over the shouts and screams. The energy of performances and live music element of the show definitely left a lasting impression on me. Up until then the only live stage entertainment I'd experienced was Christmas pantomime shows as a child.

Circa 1964 there were bands everywhere and a lot of live music being played in those pre disco days. Many of my friends were learning to play guitar. By 1965, I'd joined my first 'proper band' and I've been gigging for most of the following 50 years. Over the years I've played in about 18 different bands from rock 'n' roll to blues to country to folk. I still love playing live music. It can all be traced back to that first Beatles gig and the energy of live music venues in the 1960s. I did have the programme for the evening, but sold it to a collector about 25 years ago.

I WAS THERE: MIKE WINTERS, AGE 12

I went with my sister who was then 20. I don't recall much about the other acts, even Gerry and the Pacemakers who had been top of the charts by then. I recollect all the screaming but you could still just about hear the band. I particularly remember John introducing their new single, 'She Loves You', which had only been released a few days before. My other memory is of leaving the Odeon and standing outside when a car raced from the car park at the rear and sped off down Lord Street carrying the band. It must have been driven by Neil Aspinall. About a week later, I was walking past the Odeon and a guy was taking out the concert poster which I asked him for. I had it up until about 15 years ago when I sold it.

GAUMONT CINEMA
4 SEPTEMBER 1963, WORCESTER, UK

I WAS THERE: ROY TAYLOR, AGE 16

The bill included Gerry and the Pacemakers, The Fourmost and The Dennisons. The Beatles and Gerry alternated between shows as to who would perform 'Twist and Shout'. The show I saw was the first of two that day and Gerry sang it. The MC began to introduce The Beatles and got as far as 'John, Paul...' when the dam burst and the screaming was unleashed! They looked fabulous and sounded wonderful – from what I could hear. I recall 'Till There Was You', 'From Me To You', 'Please Please Me', 'Boys' (sung by Ringo) and 'Love Me Do'. They opened with 'Here's Hoping', a song by Carter Lewis and the Southerners. I'm not sure about the rest – I was too busy looking at the way they stood – George's red Gretsch, Ringo's unique drumming style, Paul's handsomeness and John's whole attitude. What a night!

I WAS THERE: SANDRA LONGMIRE

By now they were very famous but I suppose they still had commitments to keep. On this occasion, we didn't go to the show but waited around the stage door, having run home from school and changed into our black polo neck sweaters. I had embroidered 'PAUL' on the front of mine, as if he would notice! Once again, we handed our books in at the stage door as they didn't come out between shows. We listened at the doors to hear the end of the show and then ran to the front of the theatre – we were quite savvy by then. Our local knowledge paid off and we were able to catch them as they ran to their getaway car via the main entrance. I actually touched Paul McCartney – and he smiled at me!

 # GAUMONT CINEMA
5 SEPTEMBER 1963, TAUNTON, UK

I WAS THERE: CHRISTOPHER BEVAN

In 1963, I was at school in the Lower Sixth and we had lessons on Saturday so I was not able to listen to *Saturday Club* on the radio. It was down to the *Teen and Twenty Disc Club* on Radio Luxembourg and possibly *The Six Five Special* for pop music. Many up-and-coming groups travelled to smaller venues around the country and lots came to Taunton. A school friend who was a regular reader of the *New Musical Express* usually sorted out tickets for us. The Beatles were in top form, but most of their music was drowned out by screaming girls.

 # ODEON CINEMA
6 SEPTEMBER 1963, LUTON, UK

I WAS THERE: TERRY ALLEN

I was a young reporter on the *Tuesday Pictorial*, sister paper at the time to the *Luton News*. The show was one of a series of concerts in a mini-tour granted by Brian Epstein after he cancelled a number of Mersey Beat nights earlier in 1963. The promoter of these shows was John Smith, the compere was Ted King and the supporting acts were Ian Crawford and the Boomerangs, Mike Berry and the Innocents, Freddie Starr and the Midnighters, Rocking Henry and the Hayseeds. The Beatles reputedly earned £250 for the show, equivalent to £4,775 today. A relative bargain, you might think, but those were different times.

I was a general reporter but had a full page to fill every week as the *Tuesday Pictorial*'s film critic which involved reviewing each week's movie offerings at Luton's four cinemas of the time – the Odeon, Ritz, Savoy and Gaumont. In truth, I rarely got to see the films in advance of their release and relied on industry PR and previously published showbiz reviews to give readers some insight into the films' relative merits. One reader told me at the time he found my reviews invaluable in planning his weekly cinema excursion – any film I panned (like the *Carry On* series) he knew he'd enjoy, and any film I praised he avoided like the plague! However, as a result of this work, I was on very good terms with the managers of the four Luton cinemas, and the Odeon's Tom Phillips was my personal favourite amongst this group of uniformly colourful characters, all of whom granted me access to see any film I wanted.

On the night that The Beatles performed at the Odeon, my girlfriend and I were ushered into the auditorium by Tom Phillips and watched the warm-up acts, followed by The Beatles. It was an unforgettable experience, not only seeing such a legendary band perform live but also witnessing the now infamous howling crescendo of screaming girls that virtually drowned out their music.

The Beatles' fame came at a time when sound equipment wasn't what it is today, and the venues were also relatively small compared to today and were typically packed. The Odeon officially housed 1,958 screaming fans, though I suspect a few more sneaked in. The drowning of the music was, in truth, an absolute travesty. But The Beatles were used to it and played on regardless. To my surprise, at the end of the concert, Tom Phillips sought me out in the auditorium and asked me if I'd like to interview The Beatles backstage. Without even thinking, I obviously agreed and he escorted me backstage and showed me into their dressing room, before introducing me to the Fab Four. I had no idea in advance that this was going to happen, which meant I was completely unprepared for it and I must admit the enormity of the situation overwhelmed me.

I recall spluttering a few random questions, which were almost exclusively dealt with, quite warmly in fact, by an ever-smiling Paul McCartney. The others took little interest. In fact, throughout the brief interview, as I remember it, George Harrison sat half smiling – half bored, I suspect – and said nothing, while Ringo Starr was even more detached, just staring at the floor. John Lennon made the odd, slightly caustic interjection, and showed his character when I feebly asked what the group thought of Luton. John fixed me with a withering look and replied in his Merseyside twang 'we arrived in the dark and we'll be leaving in the dark, so you tell me, son.'

The whole episode left me feeling slightly embarrassed and disconsolate at having blown such a unique opportunity, mainly through the lack of opportunity to prepare, mixed with my youth and inexperience. Thoughts of *A Hard Day's Night* and *Help!* crossed my mind, but I consoled myself with the fact that I could not have anticipated getting this opportunity to interview The Beatles. I was thrust into it at a moment's notice, though my two sons subsequently regard this as a highlight of my career and my 15 minutes of fame. I think they've dined out on it with friends far more than I ever have.

Nonetheless, it was a rare experience simply to meet the Fab Four, who were literally a global phenomenon – an accolade the like of which is thrown around too casually with others nowadays – and I'm grateful to my old friend Tom Phillips for giving me the opportunity. There was an interesting postscript to the story.

The following week, when I made my customary call to see Tom and get information on the subsequent week's film screening, he told me that The Beatles had turned up prior to the concert at the front entrance to the cinema, which led to the back of the auditorium, of course. There were no police, no security, no barriers, and the Fab Four just got out of the car and sauntered up the front steps. Fortunately, the audience was oblivious inside the auditorium because had all those hysterical girls realised this, there would have been absolute pandemonium and I doubt whether The Beatles would have ever have made it on stage in Luton that night. The quick-thinking Tom Phillips ushered them back outside and along the facade of the building to a small side door leading to the rear of the stage.

Being a cinema, this door was totally inconspicuous with no signage announcing 'Stage Door' as you would get at a theatre. The design of the Odeon and the fact it had a stage perhaps indicated that it was originally built, in 1938, for vaudeville entertainment as much as for movie screenings, but in all my time there seeing films, I honestly never knew there was a stage door, and it was so innocuous I would actually have guessed it was part of Evelings – the adjacent toy store. Had I learned of this earlier, 'Beatles Almost Mobbed In Odeon Foyer' would have been a great lead story in the paper, but Tom told me about it the following Monday, which was the day the *Tuesday Pictorial* went to press. So we were too late by just a few hours and nobody was ever the wiser – except for Tom and me, my wife and two sons, plus anyone else they've told since.

PUBLIC HALL
13 SEPTEMBER 1963, PRESTON, UK

I WAS THERE: PETE MORRIS

I managed to see The Beatles again at Preston Public Hall the following September. Although it was great to see them again, Beatlemania was in full swing by then and the place was full of screaming girls. They kicked off with 'Roll Over Beethoven' sung by George, and I remember Paul dedicating 'I Saw Her Standing There' to David John Smith (Miffy), who was lead singer with local band David John and the Mood, who was a mate of The Beatles. John called him 'Letters' because he was always writing to the music papers telling them how good The Beatles were.

A group called the Thunderbeats, whose drummer was Keef Hartley, supported The Beatles when they played the Floral Hall in Morecambe in January 1963. The Thunderbeats' van lights stopped working and Paul suggested that they follow close behind him and Ringo on the way back to Preston, which they had to go through to get back to Liverpool. This done, Paul and Ringo stopped off at Miffy's house in Skeffington Road for a fry up. My brother was one of a few lads from Preston who went along to support the Thunderbeats and ended up at Miffy's too. After the meal, Paul got on the old upright piano with Ringo banging rhythms out on an old armchair. They played about for hours, leaving about 7am. My brother remembers Paul playing loads of rock 'n' roll, and 'I Saw Her Standing There', which seemed to be a new song he was still working on. Maybe that's why he dedicated it to Miffy eight months later at the Public Hall.

I WAS THERE: MIKE DRYLAND

They were at a stage where they could mingle with the fans. I went backstage and can remember John Lennon pulling his trousers on – the usual dressing room scene. We had a drink in the Public Hall and Paul McCartney was there. He was very genial, a very pleasant sort of guy. If they had faded into obscurity it wouldn't have meant very much. But you did realise they were unique.

I WAS THERE: MICK GARRY, AGE 13

I'd never been to anything like that before. They'd just released 'She Loves You' and the place was packed. There was condensation running down the walls and we couldn't hear a thing they were singing. I was near the stage and I have this vivid memory of the boots George and the others were wearing. They were scuffed and the heels worn down. George had mentioned in an interview that he liked jelly babies and we were throwing them at him on stage. The following day my brother was in hospital because he'd fallen off the slide on Haslam Park. When he came round, the first thing he did was to ask whether I'd brought any jelly babies back home.

CARLTON THEATRE
6 OCTOBER 1963, KIRKCALDY, UK

I WAS THERE: ALAN FORRESTER, AGE 14

Before The Beatles came along, I had a couple of Elvis Presley singles – 'Teddy Bear' was one I liked. 78s being what they were, I had placed Johnny Duncan's 'Last Train To San Fernando' in the kitchen drawer but opened the drawer too fast and it broke in the middle. On the jukebox in the village I lived in I was punching in The Searchers

– 'Sweets For My Sweet', 'Sugar and Spice' and the *Ain't Gonna Kiss Ya* EP. I loved the harmonies. My friend Chris and I would both sing. We would harmonise. Up until then, we were harmonising on Del Shannon's 'Little Town Flirt', the Everly Brothers and stuff like that whilst walking to the school bus. But they were all lacking any meat and the meat, to me, came in the bass line.

If you've heard Ringo's drumming or McCartney singing 'Long Tall Sally' on the EP, where he gets to the last verse or chorus, he hits it straight away, better than Little Richard did. And this is what The Beatles were doing. They were consistently taking covers and making better versions of them with a cleaner sound. Many of the early rock songs are still fabulous songs but listen to the production. On Chuck Berry – there's a double bass. The electric bass had been invented and by and large the productions are fairly clean but they're not exciting, other than his lead part. The Beatles were taking that and giving that a real kick. You wanted to hear it. You wanted to see it. You wanted to sing it.

I got my tranny in late '63 or early '64 for a fiver. My uncle bought it for me. It was tiny. You were holding it to your ear hoping to try and hear Radio Luxembourg. The musical changes were absolutely driven by The Beatles, because they had taken American music that we hadn't heard yet. They were buying records that were coming into Liverpool on the ships and they were hearing them in Hamburg, records that had also come in on the ships. This is how they got the Motown stuff early. You could hear bass. For the first time you were hearing proper bass. There was a tightness in the production and in the sound quality. Now at the same time as this was happening, you were getting Phil Spector doing this huge Wall of Sound. But you didn't get four guys, a mini-orchestra really, that was so tight, so rehearsed and melodic. It seemed like every time a record came out you could enjoy or love every song that was on the album. You used to get twelve tracks on an album and you would like almost all of them. So what came through was their adaptation and their modification and transformation of American music, distilled so that British society could take it. It was John's driving rhythm and Paul's bass. I think his bass playing was ahead of most people, and that's down to the sheer hard work they put in in Hamburg. They just got ahead of everybody else.

The Beatles were an experience. It was an emotional experience as well as a musical experience. It was huge excitement. You waited. You heard them on the radio. You'd see them on TV. They were funny. So when they were coming to Kirkcaldy, I came into school waving these two tickets saying, 'I've got them! I've got them! Seven and six!' It was fulfilled excitement.

Barbara Dickson, the singer, was in the year above me at Woodmill High in Dunfermline before I moved to Kirkcaldy. She was at the concert too and she paid the same price as me, 7/6. We were right up in the gods, two or three rows from the front of the balcony, and maybe four or five from the back. The support acts were Houston

Wells and the Marksmen, a country act who'd had a hit with 'Only The Heartaches', and The Fortunes who were fantastic.

When the guys came on, I swear I didn't hear any of the first song. I started to hear a little by the third or fourth song in. I found out in the high school playground the next day that they'd opened with 'Roll Over Beethoven', which at that point I'd never heard. I didn't clock the song until the *With The Beatles* album came out. It was just phenomenal. The queues, the atmosphere. I was a 14-year-old boy and the people around me were girls of ten, eleven, twelve right up to late teens. Everyone wanted The Beatles. They were getting calls for The Beatles while the other acts were on. Then it was just everyone standing up, hands in the air from song one to the end. With hindsight you think 'we paid that money and we never heard it'. But we were there.

CAIRD HALL
7 OCTOBER 1963, DUNDEE, UK

I WAS THERE: ANDI LOTHIAN

We got them back to Scotland for three concerts in October '63 and then we had them again in '64 for another three. In Dundee, there was two houses and we sold out both houses. The Caird Hall very, very rarely sold out. Even Frank Sinatra didn't sell it out. But The Beatles? We could have sold them out ten times over.

I WAS THERE: BRIAN MECHAN, AGE 19

Ringo Starr was staying at the Salutation Hotel in Perth, just before the bridge on the right-hand side if you're driving through. I was a hairdresser, working in a salon about 200 yards away. Ringo was my favourite Beatle at that time and I'd read that, at one time, Ringo had wanted to be a hairdresser. On the afternoon before the first Dundee concert, I phoned the Salutation and asked to speak to Mr Richard Starkey, thinking that if I was going to get through, this may work. And it did. The receptionist probably just didn't think. He probably didn't sign in as Ringo Starr. I explained to Ringo who I was, and where I was, that I was going to the concert that night and that if he had a chance to get out, to come across. He said he would if he was able to. Security-wise, I suppose, there wasn't a hope in hell. I went to the concert with a friend. We were only about seven rows from the front, so we heard the first two songs over the screaming, but you just couldn't hear a thing.

I WAS THERE: FRASER ELDER

I drew a cartoon of The Beatles at the Caird Hall. I was the resident cartoonist for the

Dundee Courier. I was also their very first pop editor/reporter. I was sent along to meet The Beatles before they came into Dundee. They were living in Perth at the time at the Salutation Hotel, so that's where I did the drawing. On the afternoon of the show, I took it down to them at the Caird Hall and they stood alongside me in line just like the drawing and I gave them all a drawing each. And the *Dundee Courier* printed ten autographed copies of it and they made it into a competition. That cartoon went all around the world in some shape or form. About thirty years later ,one of the drawings was auctioned and it realised £8,000. I had the original drawing and the drawing is now currently in Liverpool in the Cavern museum. The Beatles also autographed a special one for the kids in the Dundee orphanage.

I actually met them several times. They came back to Dundee the following year. First time around they shared top billing with an American soul singer called Mary Wells, and then the next time they came into the Caird Hall they did a one man show and I went on tour with them in Glasgow, Perth and then Newcastle. I liked George Harrison the best of them all. John, I thought, was a bit of a smart guy – he was always coming away with one-liners. And Ringo was probably the least intelligent of the four of them. McCartney at that time was greatly under the influence of John Lennon. But in later years obviously all that changed. They were good guys. I liked George the best because out of the four of them he was the most accomplished musician, technically, by a mile. And he talked good music. He was a very pleasant guy and that's why I had a lot of time for him.

I WAS THERE: DANIEL FERGUSON

I worked for Dundee District Council. Our office was situated behind the Caird Hall stage with a door access to the stage. When The Beatles came to Dundee, we were able in the office to hear them practising. When all went quiet, we went on stage and picked up broken guitar strings and of course everybody came to believe them as having been used by The Beatles. I still have my guitar strings after all these years. Late in the afternoon came a knock on the common door and who should come into our office but Paul. He asked us if he could use our phone and sat for quite a while chatting away. We could hardly believe it!

I WAS THERE: ANDI LOTHIAN

I had to take the group through the back entrance of this fairly long concert hall, walking over huge coal bins to the least used service door to escape the manic throng awaiting the group outside. My claim is that I invented the word 'Beatlemania'. It happened at one of The Beatles' concerts in October '63, when the fans were rushing the stage and we were about to be overwhelmed. We were all trying to keep them all back, including the

St John's Ambulance men, and we were losing the fight. The BBC reporter stood beside me turned to me and he said 'for God's sake, Andi, what's happening?' I said, 'It's okay, it's only Beatlemania.' Ten days or so later, it appeared in the national papers having been picked up by one of The Beatles' managers at another concert.

I WAS THERE: KATHLEEN MASON, AGE 15

I went to see them on the Caird Hall. We got backstage because a cousin of mine's husband was a reporter at the time. I got their autographs on my arm. I didn't wash it for two days. A couple of years ago, there was a picture in the paper of myself on Ringo's knee.

I WAS THERE: WILMA HART, AGE 17

I remember the excitement, the noise and the thrill of seeing them in person. Mary Wells was also there, singing her hit song 'My Guy'. When we came out at the end, my friend and I had both been temporarily deafened by all the noise. Once we'd had a juice in a local cafe, our hearing gradually returned. I worked in the offices of DC Thomson, the publisher. The morning after the concert, I learned that one of my workmates had been invited by some of the reporters to a party at St Fillans in Perthshire, where The Beatles were staying. Most hurtful to me was the fact that she wasn't even a Beatles fan. Unlike myself, who was in their fan club and had all their records as well as scrap books full of photos of my heroes.

I WAS THERE: MORAG THOMPSON, AGE 15

I was still at school and this was my first concert. My pal had left school and was working next to the box office so offered to get the tickets. Thanks to her we had tickets for the front row, centre right. We could see Ringo's grey streak. We were carried away with it all and joined in the screaming like everyone else. We came out after in a daze and our ears ringing. Next morning, there were photos of the audience in the *Courier* and the girl sitting next to me was there screaming her head off. My parents were horrified so I didn't let on that I was next to her and in a similar state. I was quizzed but assured them that I was sitting quietly! Next day at school, it was all we thought about or talked about.

I WAS THERE: NORMA MCGOVERN (NEE WARD), AGE 12

I was allowed to go with my brother Tommy, who was 14 at the time. I can remember wearing a green mohair coat and stopping in to a sweet shop in Reform Street and buying a packet of toffees. My family were not well off so we were in the cheapest seats at the back of the balcony, The tickets were five shillings – 25p in today's money. It didn't bother us, we were just so glad to be there. You couldn't really hear the boys for all of us young girls screaming. My husband Jim is an even bigger fan of The Beatles than I am and he goes green with envy when I remind him that I actually saw them live. I am now a local councillor and if they were to come back to Dundee at this present time, I might have been able to wangle a back stage pass. Well, a girl can dream!

 ## ODEON THEATRE
11 OCTOBER 1963, BIRMINGHAM, UK

I WAS THERE: NEIL REYNOLDS

By the last time I saw them you couldn't hear anything. Only girls screaming!

 ## PALLADIUM
13 OCTOBER 1963, LONDON, UK

I WAS THERE: ANTHEA CRAIG (NEE GREEN)

The Beatles appeared live on *Sunday Night at the London Palladium*. As it was a TV show, one could arrive and queue and hope to get in. I arrived early afternoon and was almost first in the queue. I think we were allowed in about 7.30pm. The first ten rows were reserved and I got a seat in the eleventh row! They came on at the beginning for a short while, and for the rest of the show compere Bruce Forsyth kept teasing us until they appeared at the end as the top of the bill. I loved every minute of it, albeit we were all screaming for most of their act!

 ## ALPHA TELEVISION STUDIOS
20 OCTOBER 1963, ASTON, BIRMINGHAM, UK

I WAS THERE: SYLVIA ELLIS

I used to go to the studios in Aston where they made the TV programme *Thank Your Lucky Stars* and I was in the crowd when The Beatles were appearing. It was mayhem and when someone as much as opened a window we all screamed! I remember chasing a black cab down the road with my mates as we were sure we saw Paul inside. I was in the studio audience when they announced The Beatles were on the following week. I was so miffed that I missed them by one week. Crazy times – but happy times too!

A PEOPLE'S HISTORY OF THE BEATLES

LEEDS-BRADFORD AIRPORT
NOVEMBER 1963, WEST RIDING OF YORKSHIRE, UK

I WAS THERE: JOHN FIELDS

I worked at Hepworth and Grandage, an engineering firm making Rolls-Royce engines, near Leeds-Bradford Airport. One day a rumour went around at work that The Beatles were due to land at the airport. We were busy working when hundreds of young folk began to pass by. They were mostly girls and on foot and were seemingly getting off the bus. More and more came, all heading for the airport. Some carried homemade banners saying things like 'We love you John', 'Lindsay loves Paul', 'The Beatles Forever', etc. We had to get on with our work but were still very interested in the fact that The Beatles had chosen to come to our small airport. We waited and waited. Nothing happened. No one came, least of all The Beatles, and eventually everyone came back the way they had gone, now trailing their carefully made banners behind them. Dejected and forlorn, some girls were inconsolable, crying brokenheartedly as they passed by. We were quite naughty as we began taking the mickey over these pretty young girls crying over a group that would probably never give them a second look. But that soon changed to dejection when we realised that no one had ever cried like that over us!

ADELPHI THEATRE
5 NOVEMBER 1963, SLOUGH, UK

I WAS THERE: TERRY BAILEY, AGE 11

There was mass hysteria and you couldn't hear their little Vox amps over the screaming. I remember Lennon wearing glasses for some of the show, which isn't always shown in the pictures of the time. I know subsequently people have written about the smell of urine as the girls lost control but I was only eleven and blissfully unaware!

I WAS THERE: ROD WATSON, AGE 17

I went to that concert with a classmate called Andrew Clancy and his sister Charlotte, or Lottie as the family called her. I had just turned 17 in the October and was at Maidenhead College doing a commercial course prior to joining the Berkshire Constabulary as a police cadet and going on to be a police officer for 31 years. We were all from Windsor and caught the bus to Slough bus station and walked to the Adelphi. We were sat about 20 rows from the front of the stage. The Swinging Blue Jeans were the warm up group. It was controlled mayhem but no one attempted to get on the stage. There were lots of hysterical girls though, even Andy's sister. The evening was full of excitement and screaming girls, especially when The Beatles came on singing 'Twist and Shout'. It got to a stage where your hearing started to suffer until they went off at the end. I later became a Beatles fan club member and wore a collarless Beatles jacket and Cuban heel boots. I stopped short of combing my hair forward though!

I WAS THERE: HENRY WRIGHT, AGE 27

I went with my wife Sheila. It was brilliant. The Troggs and Gene Pitney were there too. We had to queue a long way to get in but it was worth it. We didn't get very good seats. And cold an' all, it was.

I WAS THERE: NORMA ZACHARCZUK

I was there with my boyfriend, who I later married. We were about five rows from the front. The screaming was unbelievable. You actually could not hear them playing or singing, the noise was so bad. We also went to the Adelphi disco on Sundays to dance. We went to see everyone who came to the Adelphi. My boyfriend also liked the Stones. They played a few weeks later at the Carlton in Slough High Street, on a Sunday afternoon. We went there regularly to the disco and sometimes to see live bands. We also went on Saturdays to Burtons in Uxbridge as they had live bands too. But not The Beatles. They got too big too quickly.

ABC THEATRE
6 NOVEMBER 1963, NORTHAMPTON, UK

I WAS THERE: JACKIE GOODFELLOW, AGE 16

I queued all night for tickets and the queue was so long I was way back around the corner. They sold the tickets on a Saturday so I did not have to worry about going to work. When the booking office eventually opened, I got two tickets for my friend and myself and I could still only get on Row J, ten rows from the front. What an experience it was just to see them. You could not hear them through all the screaming but it was well worth it. The memories of seeing the fantastic four will be with me forever.

I WAS THERE: JACKIE SHORTTAND, AGE 11

I was there, although I got into rather a lot of trouble from my mother. I was eleven going on 20. An older girl who was a neighbour persuaded me and my best friend to say we were staying at hers for the night. Instead, the three of us spent all night queuing for tickets. It was very exciting and we were about fourth in the queue. When we got inside, there was a plan of the seating and we were able to get front row right in the middle. Unfortunately, the *Chronicle & Echo* printed a photo of the queue on the front page the next day and there we were for all the world to see. I wasn't aware of this until I got home from school the next day. All hell broke loose and my mother said I couldn't go. I begged and cried for hours.

By the morning, my lovely dad had talked her into letting me go. My mum even bought me a new dress with a Peter Pan collar and a big red bow for my hair – I must have looked a sight! On the night I was so excited, but because of all the screaming girl in the audience I didn't really hear the songs at all. I was however lucky enough to get the autographs of all four of them afterwards. My favourite Beatle was Ringo. Most of my friends couldn't understand why. I went on to see the Rolling Stones and several other bands at the ABC. Great times!

I WAS THERE: LINDA GROOM, AGE 14

My mum went and queued for ages to get us some tickets, as we were at school. I went with my cousin Pat and my brother Ronnie. I was 14 and the others were about twelve years old. At one of the shows, we had the fifth row from the front on the right-hand side, because John Lennon was my favourite and he always stood on the right. As soon as they came on and played the first chord, the room just erupted with deafening screams. In my naivety, I thought that if I didn't scream like all the others John would notice me and look at me. But he didn't and so I gave up in the end and joined in with the screaming. At the end of the show, everyone stayed outside to see if they could catch a glimpse of them but as Mum was picking us up to go back home, about ten miles away, we weren't allowed to. I think we had to go to school the next day. I still have the two programmes, but not the tickets. In my diary for 1963, all I put was 'caught bus to see The Beatles, they were Fab, couldn't hear much.' And the next day 'went to school, everyone was talking about The Beatles'.

I WAS THERE: GEORGINA JEYES (NEE TAYLOR), AGE 13

I was there. As school girls aged 13 to 14, we hardly missed a concert. The Beatles, the Stones, Gene Pitney, The Kinks etc. A comedian also had a slot – I think he was Canadian Frank Berry. I can even remember one of his jokes! We were all country girls who came into the Derngate bus station every day for school. Luckily my nan lived in The Drive, so I was nominated to stay overnight with her in order to be first in the queue for the tickets. We would go and hang about outside The Grand or the stage door hoping for a pre-concert glance or scream at our heroes. We would also rush to the stage door in time to see them being whisked away to a place of safety by a posh black car.

I cannot remember much of school learning but I can remember which of my friends fancied which Beatle and I still see these same friends over long chatty lunches. There used to be rugby players at the foot of the stage to stop us running down the aisle and trying to get onto the stage. After one Beatle concert, there appeared a photo of me, arms outstretched and screaming, being held back in the aisle in the office window of the *Chron* at the top of the Market Square, My mother was not pleased and thought I would be expelled! My nan, although thinking that the length of The Beatles' hair was disgusting, was brilliant and loved the tales we told when we returned.

I have always felt that those concerts were not acknowledged as important in the careers of so many legends, and if I ever talk about them, I'm sure today's generation don't believe me as they buy tickets on line to groups who only perform in arenas. We also went to concerts to raise money for the Spastic Society (as it was then called) at Wembley. The Beatles and loads of groups all appeared and by the end of the evening The Beatles had to climb over all the equipment to get to the front to perform. Famous stars of the day from shows like *Coronation Street* would walk about outside signing autographs. Somewhere, I have Albert Tatlock's!

I WAS THERE: WENDY IRONS

My recall of the event is of a long queue outside on the pavement with the police in attendance, but they were talking to us and did not understand the reason for all the excitement. We stood up once inside and were asked to sit but continued to stand. We were unable to hear most of the songs as the screams were so loud and girls were crying. It was over in such a short time, like most good events. My ears were ringing with all the noises from the concert as we made our way home.

I WAS THERE: JULIE CAUSEBROOK, AGE 14

The second time The Beatles came to Northampton, my best friend and I were ready. We had saved up our pocket money (half a crown a week) and the day before the tickets were sold, we wagged school in the afternoon to go and queue outside the cinema where the tickets were being sold. I can remember we were about twentieth in the queue, and we sat on the path outside the cinema intending to stay all night until the ticket office opened the next morning. I didn't tell my parents because I knew they wouldn't let me do this but my friend had told her dad. We didn't think about food or a blanket to keep us warm; we just desperately wanted a ticket (my friend liked John Lennon but it was Paul for me all the way).

Everyone queuing with us was so nice and friendly and we struck up some new instant friendships with like-minded girls. At around 7pm, I decided to go to my nan's to get some provisions i.e. food, etc., as she lived in Edith Street which was not too far away. My best friend Glennis stayed and held our spot. My nan gave me some sandwiches and a blanket and also a flask of tea plus a short sharp telling off for not informing my parents where I was. I went back up to my friend Glennis who was getting on fine with our new friends and we shared the sandwiches around our close group.

Everything was fine until 10.15pm, when my dad turned up and demanded I go home with him immediately. I begged and begged to stay but he was not having any, so I had to go home with him. However, Glennis stayed all night and I went back at around 7.30am taking her and our new friends some breakfast. I was so grateful that they let me in the queue again because, really, they need not have done. Eventually, the ticket office opened at about 10am and we got our precious tickets.

On the day of the performance, we sat on the second row front, on the left hand side of the stage near to Paul McCartney. The show was terrific and everything I thought it would be. After about three songs, there was a surge to the edge of the stage and Glennis and I went too. I was quite tall and my friend much shorter than me so I was the barrage that made us a space. Paul came over to our side of the stage and for a brief moment he touched my hand – being so tall had benefits!

We didn't see The Beatles live again and we didn't see any of the friends we had made in the queue either. Glennis's mum never forgave me for leaving her daughter to queue all night for my ticket and said I had led her daughter astray (her dad was fine with me). My mum was not too pleased with me either but – hey! – my dad understood and I was soon forgiven. My nan had got a bus up to my parent's house that night to tell them where I was (no mobiles or phones in every household then). That is the first and only brave thing I did, and quite dangerous really when you think of today's world. Still, it is a memory that I will always treasure. My love of The Beatles waned when they started to go all hippy, and always in the background was my first love, Elvis Presley, who I've been a fan of since 1959. But I will never forget the short couple of years and Beatlemania. I named my son, born in 1978, Paul in tribute to Paul McCartney. My husband wouldn't let me call him Elvis!

I WAS THERE: KEITH SHURVILLE

When the second visit to the ABC as headliners was publicised, it was obviously a major event in the town and I had to get my mother to drive me and a friend to Northampton early one Saturday morning to join a queue for tickets. The Beatlemania frenzy was in full force and even the lads were dressing up in Beatle tops and had Beatle hair dos, me included. Dressing in similar fashion to The Beatles, I resembled Billy J Kramer and was close to being mobbed when he visited the ABC.

I WAS THERE: JAN DEAN, AGE 14

My friend Lynne and myself were 14 years old. We played the wag from school. We went to what was called Lynn's cafe and climbed through a window in the ladies' toilets to

Clockwise from top left: Valerie Curtis remembers the Northampton show; Malcolm Reynolds recalls The Beatles having to wear policemen's helmets as a disguise to escape Birmingham's Hippodrome; Linda Kitson still has her fan club photo; Karina Billet's dad was in the Adelaide police force and on duty when The Beatles came to town; Christine McDermott's mum accompanied her to the Manchester show and waited outside for her; Tim Tree was in a band called The Thunderbirds when he went to see The Beatles; Jill Phillips (left) got to hold Ringo's hand at Bristol.

Clockwise from top left: Gill Ribis won tickets to see The Beatles in a hairspray competition; Campbell Ford saw The Beatles in Sydney in 1964 before he met and married girlfriend Diana – he also worked on *Yellow Submarine*; Tom Stalnaker turned down the chance of a ticket to see The Beatles in Cincinnati; Sandra Longmire has a fruit gum 'as chewed by Ringo Starr' in her autograph book; Roger Unett clapped so much that he broke his watch; Louise Morris was a very excited 14-year-old; Margaret Vincent saw the Fab Four in Sydney.

access the car park of the ABC. We then got into the back door of the theatre and made our way up the stairs and ended up hiding in a dressing room. After a while, we thought 'we can't stay in here as it would be ages before The Beatles will be in the theatre.' So we then went up more stairs and ended up on the roof of the theatre. After running across the roof trying to find somewhere to hide, we were spotted by some workmen working on an adjoining building and they called the police. The manager of the theatre then came up to the roof and they took us to the upper circle of the theatre and told us we were very lucky not to have fallen through the roof when we were running across it. They took it no further. The story of two girls being up on the roof of the ABC hoping to get up close to The Beatles made the local paper. My friend Lynne did not get to go to see them as her mum would not let her go. But I did. It was all great fun.

I WAS THERE: VALERIE CURTIS, AGE 20

The curtain was about to rise amid the buzz of excitement. But I was filled with dread at the prospect of them not appearing. The Beatles, having performed at the London Palladium and with a recent number one record, would surely not now show up at this unknown venue in a small Midlands town? My boyfriend had purchased the tickets earlier on in the year, having seen The Beatles support Tommy Roe at the same venue. Although we lived in the town, we would travel on our Lambretta scooter to see most of the concerts of the pop stars of the time. This concert felt different, as the popularity of The Beatles was unlike anything we had seen before. As a child, I would get asked in the playground 'are you Labour or Conservative?' Now it was 'who is your favourite Beatle?' by the girls in the office.

We thought The Beatles had been a great support act and looked forward to seeing them in their own show. But they had suddenly become very successful and previous pop concerts sometimes made announcements that certain artists would not be appearing for various reasons. None of my friends had been lucky enough to get tickets, so I looked forward to reporting back to them. I was filled with excitement and also dreading a non-appearance. I found myself saying 'please turn up!' over and over. Suddenly, there was the twang of their familiar chords and we were enveloped in a wall of sound. No words, just pounding beats deadened by screaming shouts to Paul, George and John. Ringo just smiled and nodded his head in time. He was my favourite!

I was so happy and caught up in the excitement too. I quickly realised that the hysterical screaming was not going to stop, even in the gentler songs which I wanted to hear. The younger girls screamed until they were hoarse. I remember feeling concerned and embarrassed that The Beatles would dislike Northampton after this! But seeing the way that they smiled and carried on with their numbers anyway made me realise that they were used to this reaction. My boyfriend was very amused by the whole scene but I longed for someone to intervene and quieten down the screaming. However, we both knew that this was the best concert that we had ever seen and that we were witness to something unforgettable. Next day, my father expressed his opinion strongly. 'Bing Crosby did not need all that amplification and no girls screamed the place down for him,' he said proudly. I understood then The Beatles' place in popular music and how lucky I had been to witness it.

I WAS THERE: MARGARET COLE

I lived with my parents in a village roughly twelve miles away. They thought I was mad to go. I took my brother-in-law along. He drove to Northampton as he was familiar with town driving. It was so loud – everyone screaming and shouting. Getting outside afterwards, goodness – my head was ringing! We both had work next day, my brother-in-law at Wolverton railway works and me at a printing company. Great fun and never to be forgotten.

I WAS THERE: ROGER FRISBY

By the time of the next show, my girlfriend had got tickets near the front of the cinema. Beatlemania had now gripped the country and Northampton was no exception. The support included the Brook Brothers. This was my chance to use the loo and, going around the back seats, a girl grabbed my shoulder and asked if I was Brian Epstein. I said that I was and she asked if I could get their autograph for her youth club in Moulton. I said that of course I would and 'stay where you are'. I now had a problem because I would have to go past her on my way back to my seat so I had to go around the other way all around the cinema and had difficulty finding my seat again and also explaining to the girlfriend what I had been up to. The show was noisy but I had seen the Fab Four twice in eight months!

I WAS THERE: COLIN LITTLE

I went to see The Beatles at the Gayeway dance club in Northampton when they were the Quarrymen and Pete Best was the drummer. I later went to see them at the ABC. My mother was an usherette there and she met The Beatles after the show and they signed their names on a programme for her. The show was incredible, with young girls screaming and dancing in the aisles. I was one of the first to have a Beatles suit made without a collar on the jacket. I don't know what happened to the programme and I no longer have the suit!

I WAS THERE: DI NEWBERRY (NEE BENSON), AGE 13

The second Northampton show, when they were at the height of their fame, was brilliant. I don't remember too much of what they sang as I, along with most of the audience, screamed the whole way through it. I was in a picture on the front of the *Chronicle & Echo*, looking wild!

I WAS THERE: KEITH WHEELER

I managed to get a ticket through Rodex Coats, which turned out to be a complete waste of time as you couldn't hear a thing for girls screaming.

I WAS THERE: PETE SPENCER, AGE 13

Their second performance in Northampton, when they were top of the bill – and after appearing there in March 1963 – was completely drowned out by screaming girls, including my sister. It was continuous and ear splitting. I'm sure I never heard a note, certainly not from their instruments with the rudimentary amplification of the time. Although I took up guitar soon after, and did the rounds of the folk clubs, my appreciation of The Beatles grew and *Abbey Road* is certainly one of my top ten albums – if not top five. Two years later, I went to see Dylan at De Montfort, about two months before he went electric. Now *that* was a concert.

I WAS THERE: GISELA OAKES, AGE 14

Friends and I also went to see The Beatles seven months later at their 6.30pm performance at the ABC on 6 November, but they had become so popular by then it was difficult to hear the music above the screaming.

I WAS THERE: ANN TAYLOR (NEE TODD), AGE 13

I was just a month short of turning 14 years old when I and my twin sister Wendy saw them in concert. We were big fans and had all their records. We lived a few miles out of town in a village and had no chance to get home from school to change to go out. Instead, as soon as school finished, we rushed out of school to get the bus from Moulton into Northampton. I remember feeling embarrassed about wearing my school uniform whilst at the concert. The Beatles sounded just like their records, but there was so much screaming that my sister says she couldn't hear them play at all. When the concert ended, we went straight to the old bus station in Derngate to get our bus home. It was a great treat for us as we never usually had any opportunity to go out anywhere.

I WAS THERE: DAVE YOUDALE

I went to see both Beatle shows in Northampton in 1963. It was the boys in our group who got into The Beatles first, buying the first two singles and getting tickets to the Tommy Roe and Chris Montez tour, where The Beatles started off at the bottom of the bill but had a number one single by the time they had reached Northampton. It was three of us boys who forked out for their first LP on the day it was released – five weeks' paper round money! The girls stayed true to their idols – Cliff, Mark Wynter and co. For a time, anyway...

By November 1963, I was at work and we were in full-fledged Beatlemania. Now the girls were on board. Some would say overboard. I met my mates in a coffee bar called Guys and Dolls in Albert Place, just off Abington Street. As showtime approached, we headed towards the ABC only to meet the first house coming away. A lot has been said about mass hysteria and, true, some were putting it on. But many were not. We passed the girls we knew who were in a daze and had no recollection of seeing us the next day. A lot has also been said about mass urination, but I don't remember any evidence of that. Mind you, we were in the circle so perhaps only people in the stalls wee themselves!

It was a normal package tour with about five other acts, The Beatles only doing the last 20 minutes or so, but the girls screamed from start to finish no matter who was on. I had to ask some girls I knew who were sitting at the front what songs The Beatles had sung as I couldn't hear. During the half time interval, we went to the toilets where we could hear the girls from the first show still outside, chanting 'we want The Beatles'. One of my mates climbed onto the sink and opened a small window. When he stuck his head out, there was a load of screaming from below. It was a dark November evening, the girls were gathered in an alley behind the ABC and the only lights were the toilet windows set high in the wall. We took it in turns to climb on the sink and be screamed at – Beatlemania first hand. I sometimes wonder if there are girls who have spent the last 50 odd years thinking their vigil in that dark alley paid off with a sighting of their heroes. It was a great time to be young. Today's kids can keep their Twitter and their Facebook. I wouldn't have missed that time for anything.

I WAS THERE: CLIVE GEDDES

I had the good fortune to attend The Beatles show in November 1963 with my then girlfriend. I didn't have any tickets so I asked my father, a police sergeant in the old Northampton Borough Police Force, who was in charge of the security operation getting the band in and out of the cinema that evening, if he could have a word with the manager of the Savoy. He duly did so and I was told to ask for the manager at the front kiosk on the night of the concert. Arriving at the kiosk and saying who I was, the manager came and led the two of us in to the cinema and down to the middle of the central aisle. Sitting there were two table chairs from the manager's office. There was no health and safety in those days! We had an uninterrupted view and room to dance.

The atmosphere was electric but when The Beatles came on stage, the noise level was overwhelming. Constant screaming from the ecstatic fans made it rather difficult to hear the band singing. This continued from start to finish but I realised we were privileged to be present at such a momentous occasion. Leaving the concert, it took some time for my ears to get back to normal.

Next day at work, where I was working as an unqualified teacher before going to university, the eleven-year-olds were spellbound as I told them all about the evening. My street credibility was well and truly enhanced. My father wasn't especially enamoured by them. After the concert, a dummy limousine went to the front of the Savoy. My father and others led the group through a back door and across the car park to a 15 foot high brick wall. A ladder was placed against the wall. They went up the ladder and through Tricker's shoe factory, which much later featured in the film *Kinky Boots*. Waiting in St Michael's Road was the getaway vehicle which departed with no problems. My father, a sixteen stone former heavyweight boxer, was not impressed by how lightweight they were when he helped them on to the ladder. 'Could have picked Ringo Starr up with one hand,' he informed me when I got home. Their music did not interest him.

It was amazing to see an early performance of such a worldwide phenomenon. Throughout my teaching career, all my classes heard my story when I regularly took assembly. I used their story as a way to aspire children to be interested in music and to learn to play an instrument. My children grew up listening to 1950s and '60s music while my grandchildren suffer the same fate. Indeed, my granddaughters dance to music from this era in their dance shows.

MY NAN WAS THERE: PAUL WOODROOF

My nan, who was a real character, used to work at the Wedgewood pub in Northampton. One night, after closing, she was clearing up when someone said The Beatles were coming in. They came in and asked for food and Nan, who was only employed as a cleaner, was asked to cook them something. She knew who they were but was busy and wanted to get cleared up and go home. So she scraped old chips from plates of food that had been cleared away from tables earlier in the evening, refried them in the deep fat fryer and then served them to the group. She was a great cook so probably cooked the chips very nicely but perhaps didn't appreciate that the band she was serving secondhand food too was one of the biggest groups in the world!

I WAS THERE: ANNA CIVIL

My mother Ann Edwards saw The Beatles perform in Northampton in 1963. She remembers it well and says that her and her sister Maureen (Tilney) and their friend Rita Keedle were right near the front screaming their heads off. They had also seen the Rolling Stones perform there and remember the audience laughing at the Stones' unusual long hair and scruffy appearance. Mum recalls a photograph that was taken at the time of them in the crowd which was later in the paper.

My other claim to Beatles fame is that my late uncle, Alan Civil, was from

Northampton and played the famous horn solo on the track 'For No One' from the *Revolver* album. He also played in the orchestra on 'A Day In The Life' on the album *Sgt. Pepper's Lonely Hearts Club Band*.

 # GRANADA CINEMA
9 NOVEMBER 1963, EAST HAM, LONDON, UK

I WAS THERE: MICHAEL BAILEY

John at the Granada café, which was then opposite the venue, supplied food for The Beatles when they played. He later tried to auction off the unwashed plates.

 # HIPPODROME
10 NOVEMBER 1963, BIRMINGHAM, UK

I WAS THERE: SUE FLANAGAN

The Hippodrome was manic. Screams, yells, etc. all through the performance. We didn't need drugs. We all just let it all out. There was nothing to compare it to. You had to be there. Do I remember the Sixties? Yes, I do. Because I kept a diary!

I WAS THERE: DAVID LAWRENCE, AGE 12

I saw The Beatles at the Hippodrome and again at the Odeon on 9 December 1965, the day after my 15th birthday. I went with my school friend Paul. He had queued all night for the tickets. In those days the sets only lasted about 25 minutes and my lasting memory is of the noise and the screaming. I'm sure we couldn't hear a great deal of what was being played.

I WAS THERE: MALCOLM REYNOLDS, AGE 16

I'd gone to the show on my own because I wasn't dating a girl at the time. I had a good seat in the circle and remember The Beatles looking very smart. The amplifiers behind them and the PA speakers were small compared with present day gear. Consequently, when they started playing it was difficult to hear them because of the screaming of the girls in the audience. In the back of my old exercise book of reel-to-reel tape recordings from the '60s, I pencilled a list of the numbers that they performed and the order that they played them. I was interested in this because I was learning to play guitar at the time and was a fan. They played: 'I Saw Her Standing There', 'From Me To You', 'All My Loving', 'You Really Got a Hold on Me', 'Roll Over Beethoven', 'Boys', 'Till There

Was You', 'She Loves You', 'Money', and 'Twist and Shout'.

I was really pleased to hear them do 'All My Loving', as it was only released the previous month on the *With The Beatles* LP and I really loved it – and still do! I remember the concert programme being very nice and having a bright orange textured cover. Unfortunately, it was thrown away with my ticket stub and a lot of other concert progammes in the '70s. When the show had finished, I made a quick exit to catch the last Midland Red bus back to Sutton Coldfield, which wasn't part of Birmingham back then. The Birmingham Corporation buses only travelled to the city boundary, so if I missed that bus I would have to walk the last four miles home. The following week the local paper, the *Evening Mail*, showed pictures of the boys after the concert wearing policemen's helmets. Apparently, they had borrowed them to try to disguise themselves to make an easier getaway.

ABC CINEMA
13 NOVEMBER 1963, PLYMOUTH, UK

I WAS THERE: GERALDINE LAWRIE

My father was a Conservative and much to his disgust I joined the Young Liberals as they were doing a coach trip outing from where we lived in Bude to see The Beatles. It was wonderful!

ABC CINEMA
14 NOVEMBER 1963, EXETER, UK

I WAS THERE: CHRIS GALE

When they came to Exeter a second time, they were big. My wife's father was in the police force and so she knew one of the policemen that had escorted them in. He said, 'Do you want to come in and meet the group?' So she met them and said 'hello' and they said 'do you want our autographs?' She said, 'No, not really.'

I WAS THERE: LYN HOPE, AGE 16

I went to the concerts in Exeter on 14 November 1963 and 28 October 1964. I still have the programmes, and stuck the ticket stubs inside the cover. The first concert was 10/6 (53p) and the second 15/- (75p). I was lucky enough to be in the third and fourth rows. From about six rows back, everyone stood up and it must have been very difficult to see or hear a thing, not that we were really bothered. Just to be there was enough!

I remember there was great consternation before one of the concerts as Paul had the flu and there was a possibility that it might be cancelled. A friend of mine was lucky enough to get all The Beatles autographs – I think it must have been at the first concert when they were not top of the bill. She was in the dressing room of one of the other performers getting their autograph when in walked Paul carrying a bottle of milk and he got all the Beatles' autographs for her. I was a pupil at the Maynard School in the 1960s and we went up to the ABC after school one day in full school uniform and asked a policeman standing outside if The Beatles had arrived yet. He looked us up and down and said, 'I should have thought girls like you would know better!' I can't remember what we said in reply, but it is astonishing to think how The Beatles were viewed then as they look so neat and well dressed. Even the newsagent where I ordered *The Beatles Book* every month told my mother he was surprised she bought it for me!

I WAS THERE: TIMOTHY TREE

I lived in a place called Sourton and played in a group called The Thunderbirds. My mum used to run the village youth club – the Twist Club – and my dad would drive us around in an old Austin Sheerline ambulance. We'd use this to take people from our village to see all the acts playing in Exeter. When we saw The Beatles were coming in, Mum block bought tickets for both years so we all got in to see them.

There was a then unknown compere for the show called Jimmy Tarbuck. He was brand new and he was very good. I wasn't terribly impressed with what I could hear of The Beatles' performance, which was not a lot because of the screaming and shouting. Their live performance wasn't up to the standard of their records. They were on with Peter Jay and the Jaywalkers, who used to mimic other groups. The lights went down, the curtains closed and Peter Jay and the Jaywalkers struck up the tune to 'Twist and Shout', which was exactly like the record. The girls went screaming mad because they thought The Beatles were on. Then the lights came up, the curtain went back and the girls saw it was Peter Jay and the Jaywalkers and it all went quiet!

There was screaming at the Rolling Stones shows, like at The Beatles shows, but not quite as loud – you could actually hear what the Stones were playing. But with The Beatles it was very difficult to pick out what they were playing. Being a musician, I could hear them. Whether they weren't putting in the effort because there was so much noise I don't know, but it wasn't what I would call terribly good the first time. But they looked the part. Afterwards, the girls were expecting The Beatles to come out of the main side entrance. They were sneaked out of the back entrance of the ABC instead. The car went past and The Beatles were all in it.

COLSTON HALL
15 NOVEMBER 1963, BRISTOL, UK

I WAS THERE: JILL PHILLIPS, AGE 16

I had been crazy about The Beatles ever since I saw them on *Juke Box Jury*. When I found out they were coming to Bristol as part of their 1963 tour, I was beside myself. I worked opposite the Colston Hall where they would be performing so I spent the entire day hanging out of the window waiting for them to arrive, much to my boss's annoyance. I did not care. My patience was rewarded when suddenly a large black car with blacked out windows appeared and the side gates magically opened and they were in. Gradually, the crowds built up until it was impossible for any traffic to move. Bristol was brought to a standstill, which was a very strange sight and one I had never seen before or since.

I told my parents I was going to see a play as they strongly disapproved of The Beatles because they had taken over my mind! I was very glad my friends and I had already bought our tickets. Because of this, we were able to push past what seemed like thousands of people and take our seats. I was later to become ashamed of my behaviour twice that evening although I did not think so at the time. The first time was that we unfortunately had to sit through several acts before we got to The Beatles, who were top of the bill. I only remember two of the acts, Millicent Martin and Roger Whittaker. Through all of the supporting acts, the audience were shouting 'off, off, off' and I joined in until we had drowned out their singing. That seems so cruel now but we were only there for one reason. The second time was during one of the support acts. I decided to visit the loo, only to find loads of people outside the frosted windows begging to be let in. I opened the window and people immediately piled in. Someone opened all the other windows, causing a stampede. When I got back to my friends, I told them I'd done something terrible!

What seemed like a lifetime later, the MC announced 'now is the moment you have all been waiting for' and I heard nothing after that. My ears were popping because of the high-pitched screaming, most of which was coming from me! I cannot tell you what they sang – I didn't hear one word or one note. John Lennon said later that they could have been singing nursery rhymes and no one would have known. People were dropping like flies and the St John's Ambulance people were very busy ferrying people out on stretchers. I also remember one girl getting on the stage and making a bee line for John, only to faint at his feet. John picked her up and carried her to the wings. He went back a couple of times to check she was all right, which only provoked louder screaming. I was cursing that I hadn't managed to get tickets for the front row.

I thought my ears would never return to normal but on leaving the venue I remembered there was a small side street behind the Colston Hall and we might be able to get sight of them. A few other people had had the same idea. Just in front of the railings was a window with a light on and curtains drawn. I started shouting for John and, to our amazement, the curtains parted and the window opened and there was a smiling Ringo. He stretched out his arm which I grasped, telling him that I wanted to hold his hand.

ARDWICK APOLLO
20 NOVEMBER 1963, MANCHESTER, UK

I WAS THERE: CHRISTINE MCDERMOTT, AGE 12

I'd seen The Beatles for the first time on an early evening Granada news programme. They used to have a music slot. The first time I saw them they'd just released 'Love Me Do' and I was absolutely floored by the record. I'd never heard anything like it and I was really, really keen on them right from that point. I went out and bought the single and then, when I realised they were touring, I just had to go and see them. I finally persuaded my mother to let me go on the condition that she accompanied me. I got front stall seats. I was in XD35 and it cost me 10/6 (53p). My friends would have liked to have gone but none of their parents would let them go.

My mum and dad had an outdoor off licence shop, a 24-hour open all hours-type shop, in Ardwick. She gave in and said 'you can go'. By then I was going to school on my own, crossing over Manchester on two buses, at that age. But it was the night time that she didn't like the idea of. She said she would come over with me and wait outside for me, which was amazing really. It was just an amazing experience. I'd never been in anything like that before. And the noise when they came on was just incredible. I was on the side of the stage near Paul, which was a bit of a disappointment because I was a real John Lennon fan and he was on the other side of the stage. But it was just amazing. You couldn't hear a thing that they were playing, you really couldn't. Because the screaming and the noise was just so intense and I think you were just so amazed by it all you just stood and stared. You couldn't take your eyes off them.

Why did everyone scream? I think it was the reaction of the time. In that period, we were all expected to be little replicas of our parents. And the music was beginning to get quite exciting because you'd had Cliff Richard and Adam Faith and Lonnie Donegan and Tommy Steele and all that. But that was all very parentally approved, in a way. And The Beatles came on and they were just so totally different. For a start, there was four of them and they all of them appealed to different people, especially girls, and I think it just gained momentum.

They had quite a following in the North West anyway, so you were very aware of them if you were old enough to be going to concerts and gigs. There was definitely a sort of following around them and a buzz about them. It was something to do with the fact that there was a type of music, especially an English type of music, that was yours and that was definitely for you and not for your parents. Because your parents didn't necessarily approve of it. And it was all bound up with the fashion, with Mary Quant, and everybody was suddenly conscious that you could dress differently from your parents and you could be somebody different from your parents. I remember my mother still buying me clothes that really were almost like clothes you found in fashion magazines that were meant for older women. You had to wear the miniature version of it. And then, all of a sudden, the whole thing blew up. And it became a thing about fashion and music and everything. That's certainly how I felt – that all of a sudden I could see a freedom to be somebody different and it all became very exciting. And I think that excitement engendered the whole frenzy around the groups, both The Beatles and the Rolling Stones. And, of course, in Manchester we had the Hollies and Wayne Fontana and the Mindbenders.

Eric Stewart used to live in the next street to me. He was in the Mindbenders and he used to let his sister Debbie know when we could go over and get into *Top of the Pops* in Dickenson Road when they were filming it. And it was all that sort of excitement, and the collectivism of a cinema full of girls roughly between the ages of 12 up to 16, 17. The hysteria thing, the excitement, bred the initial scream and then it just got hysterical. But it was an amazing experience. It was a truly wonderful time to be a teenager. It was brilliant being in Manchester and it was probably the same in Liverpool because you had a really vibrant music scene. And the thing was they were all people you vaguely knew anyway. My cousin went to school with both Eric Stewart and Wayne Fontana, so you had a knowledge of all these people. Two of The Hollies worked for my uncle in his furniture shop in Salford, and when they got the recording contract they just came in and said 'Harry, we're leaving.' 'What do you mean, you're leaving?' 'Well, we've got a recording contract.' He thought they were mad.

GLOBE THEATRE
22 NOVEMBER 1963, STOCKTON-ON-TEES, UK

I WAS THERE: GEORGE MORLAND, AGE 15

We went to see them on the day that Kennedy was assassinated. I was still at school. I thought I'd go and queue for a ticket when they went on sale at the Globe. There was no chance of me queuing overnight because my mother and father wouldn't have let me. Stockton was a four-mile bike ride from where I lived in Middlesbrough, so I got up at about six o'clock in the morning and cycled over to Stockton and waited in the queue to try and get a ticket. But by the time I got round the corner from the entrance they had sold out. That was it as far as I was concerned, but luckily for me a lad who lived over the road from me said his brother was a driver for a local coach firm and they were down to take people to the show and he had been given two complimentary tickets. So he gave them to his brother and his brother said to me 'do you fancy going then?' And I said 'of course I do'.

The only trouble with the complimentary tickets was that it was right at the back in the downstairs stalls and the audience was mainly girls. The show wasn't too bad but as soon as The Beatles came on you couldn't hear a thing with the screaming and what have you. You could barely make out what songs they were singing. I do remember one because it was going to be their next number one hit – 'I Want To Hold Your Hand'. They played that one that night and you could just about make out what it was. We were chuffed we'd even got in. To actually see them on stage, you know?

We went to the first performance, at six o'clock, and it was just after eight when we were leaving. We were going across the road and this policeman stopped us and said 'did you enjoy the show?' We said, 'We couldn't hear a bloody thing, mate.' And then we walked down to where we would catch a bus home. We got on the bus and that's when we found out that Kennedy had been shot. My mate kept saying 'what's gonna happen now? What's gonna happen now?' On Monday, I went back to school and people asked if I'd been to see The Beatles but people weren't really interested. All they were really interested in was talking about Kennedy.

MY MAM WAS THERE: LESLEY JOHNSON

My mam saw them three times. On one occasion, in all her excitement she threw her handbag, containing her purse and keys, onto the stage and towards John, her favourite. He looked down mid-song and kicked it back to her.

I WAS THERE: BARRY PARKIN

When The Beatles appeared in Stockton, myself and three pals were driving through the High Street near the Globe Theatre when we were stopped by a policeman. We thought we were in some sort of trouble, but to our surprise a large black limo came out of the alleyway next to the Globe and passed in front of us. The policeman waved us on and, as we followed the limo, we noticed that John Lennon and Paul McCartney were looking out of the rear window laughing and waving to us. As we tried to catch the limo up, the driver suddenly accelerated and Lennon and McCartney stuck two fingers up and then waved us goodbye. That's as near as we got to seeing The Beatles!

ABC CINEMA
24 NOVEMBER 1963, HULL, UK

I WAS THERE: CHRISTINE PINDER

The Beatles played at the ABC Cinema in Hull in November 1963 and October 1964, and I was there on both occasions, my friend's mum having queued all night to get us the tickets. The now demolished ABC cinema was at the corner of the only access road to Hull's central bus station. Despite the police efforts to control the huge crowds of fans, they spilled out right across this road, bringing the bus services more or less to a halt for the rest of the evening. In 1963, the support acts included Peter Jay and the Jaywalkers, the Brook Brothers and the Vernons Girls.

RIALTO THEATRE
27 NOVEMBER 1963, YORK, UK

I WAS THERE: SUSAN YORK, AGE 15

I was attending York College of Commerce doing a course in commerce, shorthand, typing and book keeping when tickets went on sale. As my Mum did not want me to miss lessons, she queued all day to get tickets for me and three of my friends, sitting on a little chair with her flask of tea. I don't remember any of other acts that appeared, but I do remember screaming throughout most of The Beatles' performance! I don't think we listened to the music.

I WAS THERE: DUNCAN CURRY

When I saw them again in November you just couldn't hear them. We were out on the balcony and looking out from the Rialto was just people as far as you could see. People who couldn't get in, who hadn't got tickets. And anybody who went to that window of that balcony – well, the screaming just went mad outside because any face that went to the balcony to look out, they thought you were The Beatles looking out. You could hardly hear them at all. It was just screaming non-stop when they came on. They had gold Beatle suits on.

I WAS THERE: EUNICE HAINSWORTH (NEE WADLEY)

I was a fifth form pupil at Queen Anne Grammar School and in November 1963 I was lucky enough to see The Beatles. I say 'lucky' as getting the tickets was difficult. They went on sale during the morning on a school day so we couldn't all miss school to buy them. Three girls volunteered to go to buy them and pretended to have dental appointments. Of course, girls from most of the classes also skipped school to buy tickets. Unfortunately, teachers weren't fools and soon realised that rather a lot of girls were missing. Some of the younger teachers had heard about the sale of tickets for The Beatles. When the girls returned, they were stopped and asked if they had bought tickets. Some admitted they had and the tickets were confiscated. However, the girls from our class put on sad faces and said that all the tickets had been sold and that they had none. I don't know if the other tickets were returned. The concert was amazing but I don't think I heard a single word of the songs for all the screaming. But I can say – I was there!

I WAS THERE: GILLIAN THOMPSON, AGE 14

The Rialto was usually a cinema but was used monthly for 'pop concerts'. My parents owned the Edinburgh Arms almost directly opposite. It was the nearest hotel to the Rialto and so anyone who was bottom of the bill would stay with us, as a result of which we often got free tickets. In March 1963, The Beatles weren't top of the bill and we got free tickets. In November '63 we didn't, because they were then exceedingly popular. So I truanted from school to get tickets for myself and my younger brother and got into major trouble for doing it. My brother said that if I went, I was not allowed to scream because it would be an embarrassment. I loved them from the time that they did 'Love Me Do'. That was a wonderful record and it was at that point that people started screaming at concerts. People were screaming and tears were rolling down their eyes. It hadn't happened to such a large extent before The Beatles started.

My dad was quite a well-known publican. He was in the York Licensed Victuallers Association, and he and my mother always went over to the concerts after the pub was closed. In those days, pubs closed at half past ten on Tuesday, Wednesday and Friday and at eleven on Monday and Thursday, which were cattle market days when they stayed open later. Mum and Dad met The Beatles after the concert at the Rialto because they knew the manager. I've got The Beatles' autographs in my autograph album.

ABC CINEMA
29 NOVEMBER 1963, HUDDERSFIELD, UK

I WAS THERE: LINDA KITSON, AGE 16

My best friend from school and I worked together as jewellers and we had money of our own to go dancing and buying records. We lived in Halifax and the Sixties were a magical time for us. We were mad on The Beatles and when we heard they were to appear in Huddersfield, we immediately decided we must get tickets to see them. However, all was not as easy as it sounded. We had seen on the television that all the concerts were booked out and that people were queuing all night to get tickets and many were coming away disappointed. We were only young and lived a bit of a sheltered life and although it was supposed to be the 'swinging Sixties' the 'swinging' bit had not yet reached us – if it ever did! There was just no chance my dad or my friend's mother would allow an all-nighter on the streets of Huddersfield.

We came up with a plan and we each told our respective parents we were staying at each other's houses. After smuggling out a blanket and a flask, we headed over to Huddersfield the evening before tickets went on sale to join the end of an already enormous queue of mainly young girls from all over the North. It was thankfully policed by the local bobbies who chatted to us most of the night. We were also moved as more and more people joined the queue and the police started to worry. The first few hours passed fairly quickly, but sitting on the cold flags was really uncomfortable and it was also cold. As time passed, the singing of Beatle songs trailed off as some in the queue managed to get to sleep while others sat there numb, wondering if it had been a good idea to come at all. Similar thoughts were going through mine and my friend's minds. Even the man selling 'Beatle Soup' (it was Oxo) had packed up and gone. We were moved again but as luck would have it they moved a chunk of us and placed us nearer the front on the steps of the cinema, which up to then had been kept clear. This cheered us up no end but trying to sleep on steps was never going to happen.

We overheard a couple of the police talking. They estimated that the amount of people in the queue would mean some would not get tickets and they were contacting the manager to get the staff down early to open up and begin selling tickets. I'm not sure what time they did actually open up but I think it was something like 6am rather than the 9am or 10am it was supposed to be, as the police were concerned for some of the girls in the queue who had not wrapped up warm and who were freezing. Also, more and more people arriving meant the police were finding it difficult to manage us all.

They opened the doors when my friend was asleep and she was trampled on by someone wearing heels and, as they surged forward, she got shoved into the corner while I got pummelled by some around me, who were fighting to get through. It was horrendous and I felt faint. A part of me was so exhausted I just wanted to give up, but events overtook me as I nearly passed out and was swept up by the Red Cross or similar who had been called out to take care of us. They were only letting a few in at a time to the box office, and with everyone shoving it all got a bit hairy. The ambulance lads were helping you through past the ticket box so I took the opportunity to just join the queue. The young lads were saying 'you should have a lie down' and, although the camp beds in the make shift room looked inviting, I replied 'oh no, please. I've waited all night and there's no way I'm going home without tickets.'

I managed to get tickets – you were allowed to buy four each. I then went out to find my friend still in the corner so we headed back home. I fell asleep on the bus going home and arrived home looking like something the cat dragged in. I went straight to bed and slept all day, so pleased I'd got the tickets. My dad never told me off either. He was just glad I'd arrived home and the anticipation leading up to the concert, which was due to take place a few weeks after, was just so exciting we could hardly wait.

The night of the concert arrived and the four of us – my friend and I and my sister and her friend – set off for Huddersfield, all excited to be seeing The Beatles. My favourite was Paul and my friend liked John. We all got settled into our seats and as soon as The Beatles came on the screaming was horrendous and you couldn't hear them at all. We were screaming too! And then everything was over in a flash. I couldn't even tell you what they sang as we couldn't hear them but it didn't matter. We were there and we saw them. When it finished, we called out for more and they played us on for a bit that they were coming back out but I think it was to give the group time to get out of the building. By the time we ran around the back they had gone. We all lost our voices with the screaming. I couldn't speak for days after. My friend had a job interview the next day for a telephonist at the GPO and she had no voice. We still don't know how she got the job, but she did. When I married from home six years later, I took some things with me from my room and my mum was nagging me to take the rest of my stuff. I ignored her and eventually she threw out some of my memorabilia – my Beatle jumper, photos and stuff. All I have left is a few things from being a member of their fan club.

I WAS THERE: JENNY MASKELL

The second time we went to see them in Leeds, it was just Beatlemania and people everywhere, and that continued when they came to Huddersfield. It just blew up really quickly. When they were on in Huddersfield, I queued all night, sleeping on the pavement with my mum, who was a big fan. She was only about 33 or something. My dad thought we were both mad. It was like when I went to see the Rolling Stones. I didn't actually hear The Beatles at all in Huddersfield. We heard them when they went to the Cavern, obviously, but when it got to Huddersfield and beyond we didn't hear anything.

I WAS THERE: LAURIE STEAD

The actor Gordon Kay, who went on to become the star of the TV show *'Allo 'Allo!*, is from Huddersfield and he and I were in hospital radio together. We teamed up to go around doing interviews, and we did an interview with them. On all the occasions I've gone to previous shows, we'd been able to take our photographer with us but on this one only two of us were allowed to go backstage, so we didn't get photographic evidence of it.

With past interviews it had been by arrangement with the management of the venue. On this occasion, with The Beatles being the biggest band around at the time, I decided to write to Brian Epstein to see if we could get permission and I got a letter back from Brian Epstein giving us permission. And if I hadn't have had that, I don't think we'd have got backstage, because security was really, really tight.

It was the height of Beatlemania. They got so fed up with people asking them questions they tended to send the thing up, the usual sort of zany Beatles really. But we managed to get some comment from all four of them. It was rather a daunting, nerve-wracking experience, going to interview the biggest band around at the time, and I never thought we'd actually get permission to do it. The two of us went backstage and I spoke to all of them. I got some of them to introduce record requests, which they did in a silly way.

We did the interview backstage and we stood at the side to watch them in the theatre. It was really all noise. Everybody was screaming so you didn't hear a great deal of it. You could make out what the songs were. But it was this constant barrage of noise and screams. When we ended up editing the programme, we had about a 20-minute programme out if it, because the previous month we'd interviewed some of the crowd when they started selling tickets. The programme was broadcast on hospital radio in Huddersfield. I sold the interview and the Brian Epstein letter and a signed photograph of The Beatles some years ago at Christies.

I WAS THERE: JENIFER TAYLOR, AGE 15

I saw them at The Ritz. It used to be the ABC. Whichever way round it was. I can't remember now. So top of town, Market Street. It was much like you'd expect those concerts to be. It was heaving. We had to get the tickets by having a rota from school. We were at high school at the time, Huddersfield High School for Girls. I was in the fifth year. I was 15 going on 16. The tickets were going on sale the following day but we knew that people would start queuing. They were starting queuing the full day before, so we decided we'd set up a rota. Some of us had free periods during the day, where you were supposed to go in the library and work or do your homework or whatever, and we said, 'Well, if you've got a free period go and stand in the queue and then whoever else gets a free period the next one will come down on the bus to the Ritz and take over from you in the queue and you can go back to your lessons.' And it worked!

The rota meant you were supposed to stay there all night but I bottled out. I think my parents thought it was ridiculous. 'Yeah, but all my friends are doing it.' In the end, I didn't, but my friend Jean did stay all night. And in the morning, when they opened the doors, it was just a free-for-all. You might just as well not have bothered queuing. It was a nice long queue that went all round the back of that building and all round here, there and everywhere. But in the morning Jean just said it were ridiculous. Everybody piled in and it was like the old football matches, when everybody was pushing and shoving to the front. But we did get tickets. We did get our tickets.

When they came, the only thing I can remember is that it was just absolutely packed to the ginnels. And there were stewards standing down the aisles. Of course, we screamed because that's what you did. We got good tickets, we thought, because we weren't very far back. We were in the first ten rows, if not nearer, and I was more than happy because we were to the right of the auditorium so I was in front of John, because he always stood on the right. It used to be Paul on the left, George in the middle and John on the right, so I was chuffed to bits because he was the one for me, was John.

It were bedlam really. You know, you pretend to faint but you're not really doing it. It was just fun. It was all fun. But they were very, very good. Even in those days. It was just the excitement of it all. It was great. I remember the scenes on television, when they went to America and things like that, and when they came back on the planes and everything. It was great really to be part of that. They were national events really. It was good news in those days.

Being a kid, I wouldn't take notice of anything political or anything like that. But there seemed to be a lot of happy, good news. And that's what we concentrated on of course. We got loads of people at the ABC when it were taking off in the '60s. Then the big acts started going to Batley Variety Club. I went to one or two there but it never seemed the same as just popping down to town on the bus, because our bus used to stop on Market Street right outside the Ritz. We used to hang around outside the side door. If you stood on Market Street, there was a little snicket that went up the side and there was a back door to the Ritz and a car park for the cinema. If we went to the cinema, my boyfriend always used to park there.

If you didn't get in to the show to see whoever it was that was on, we just used to go down and hang about there, in the car park. Because the back door was there and sometimes they'd come and everybody screamed and ran over to the back door. And if you didn't get to see your heroes, sometimes the doorman would come and you'd pass your autograph books in and get your own back if you were lucky. And it'd be signed by loads that you didn't know, like backing bands and parts of the groups that you really had no idea who they were. But I got a few decent autographs – they were good days.

John was me favourite. He was sharp. And I don't know whether that appealed to my sense of humour. It probably would even now. I never liked Paul McCartney much. He looked all right, but to me there just wasn't enough substance to him. I thought George was lovely. He was quiet and serious looking, and he had a lovely shyish smile. Ringo used to sit there and shake his head while he played the drums and it were like 'it's Ringo he's just a bit of a lad really – a bit funny, a bit of a joker.' But for me, it were always definitely John. I liked him all the way through his career as well. Apart from when he married Yoko Ono, which I thought was a travesty.

When any of the songs from those groups come on the radio now, I know the lyrics from back to front. I used to buy the weekly magazine *New Musical Express* and we used to go into Woolworths on a Saturday afternoon and buy this thing that gave you all the lyrics to the new songs in this little magazine. We just used to sing along and learn all the songs. And bopping of course – everybody bopped. At school lunch hours we were lucky because being in the fifth year we weren't kicked out to play after lunch. We were allowed to play music, play records in the hall. So we used to just dance all together, bop away to all these songs. They were good days. I think we had a lucky childhood, a happy childhood.

I WAS THERE: JENNIFER BENTLEY

I never saw The Beatles. I used to sit in front of the TV whenever they were on, screaming my head off. I had jigsaws, necklaces, photos, etc. of them but I wasn't allowed to go to see them as my mum said I was too young at 13. I think I'll always regret it. Then the Stones came along, and I'm afraid I switched allegiance to them and then also to The Kinks, who I did see back then.

DE MONTFORT HALL
1 DECEMBER 1963, LEICESTER, UK

I WAS THERE: ANN STEVEN

It was around the time they released 'I Wanna Hold Your Hand'. I was in Row M on my own. I had paid £1/10s for the ticket off a friend at school. I tried to get to the front but security took me back to my seat. Then a lad jumped off the balcony and onto the stage.

I WAS THERE: PAM CHRITCHLOW

My friend Gloria and I chatted to a couple of guys after the show. They were with two limousines. The bloke I chatted to invited us to The Beatles' after show party, which was taking place in a house in Knighton. Unfortunately, I didn't believe him. After he had driven off, Gloria asked what we'd talked about. She went mad when I told her as she knew he was Brian Epstein! I just thought he seemed very different to anyone I had ever met before.

I WAS THERE: STUART LANGFORD

I used to go to school at the Wyggeston Boys, just up University Road from the De Mont, and I walked to school the day after The Beatles had played. I didn't go and see them – I didn't really know how important they were – but next morning the whole pavement outside was completely covered in a gooey, sticky, multi-coloured mess of trodden-in Jelly Babies. In one of those daft interviews they did, one of The Beatles had foolishly said Jelly Babies were his favourite sweet, so fans were flinging boxes and packets and quarter pounds of Jelly Babies at them wherever they played. I remember walking past with my mate that morning and saying, 'What the hell's happened here?'

ODEON THEATRE
7 DECEMBER 1963, LIVERPOOL, UK

I WAS THERE: COLIN HUGHES, AGE 17

I was a member of the TA in Fraser Street, Liverpool. The Beatles were playing at the Odeon Cinema in London Road. The queue for tickets was reputed to be a mile long but later in the day there was no queue and tickets were still on sale. I telephoned a mate and he said that he would like to go so I bought two tickets and we both went to see The Beatles. Unfortunately, we couldn't hear the music because of the screaming girls.

The Beatles fifth single I Want To Hold Your Hand is released on 11 December 1963.

FUTURIST THEATRE
11 DECEMBER 1963, SCARBOROUGH, UK

I WAS THERE: ELAINE WILSON, AGE 17

When I was in the sixth form at Scarborough Girls' High School, I saw The Beatles in concert at the Futurist in Scarborough. They all wore pale grey mohair suits with Chanel style high necks without collars, white shirts and narrow black bootlace ties in contrast to the Rolling Stones, who wore casual clothing. Charlie Watts alone wore a suit. I could not hear anything of The Beatles singing as girls in front of me just stood up and screamed.

GAUMONT THEATRE
13 DECEMBER 1963, SOUTHAMPTON, UK

I WAS THERE: MICHAEL GREENALL, AGE 13

We won tickets to see the Beatles show at Southampton in 1963 from our local club,

Tollies. It was a long ride in on the bus but an absolutely brilliant show. I had a black plastic bomber jacket on with a Micky Mouse drawing on the back. When they were singing, I walked down the aisle to go to the toilet and saw everybody jumping and screaming. When I got to the bottom of the aisle, John Lennon looked at me and smiled. He must have liked my jacket. I've never forgotten it. My ticket was 7/6.

ASTORIA THEATRE
24 DECEMBER 1963 – 11 JANUARY 1964, LONDON, UK

I WAS THERE: CHRIS EVERETT

I went to see The Beatles' *Christmas Show* with a girl I really fancied. A few days later, I went to see the Rolling Stones at Tooting Granada when they appeared with the Ronettes. Although I liked the Stones, I was more interested in the Ronettes because they were very sexy and 'Be My Baby' was a big hit at the time. It was obvious to people of my age that the times they were a-changing! Pop music was changing and so were attitudes and you could just feel it. They were heady days. There was a lot of optimism around. Bands like the Stones and The Beatles were quick to give credit to their heroes, who were all black – Marvin Gaye, Chuck Jackson, Howlin' Wolf, Muddy Waters, Chuck Berry, Bo Diddley, BB King. And those people were able to launch and relaunch their careers by coming to Britain and Europe thanks to The Beatles and the Stones.

I WAS THERE: MALCOLM PAUL

I last saw the group live with a group of friends including my younger sister, who was a George Harrison fan. Supported by Cilla Black, Tommy Quickly, Billy J. Kramer and The Fourmost amongst others, they used their second LP, *With The Beatles*, as a source for most of their songs, although as ever 'Twist and Shout' closed their performance.

I WAS THERE: FRANCIS CROUCHER

Ten or twelve of us had the chance to go to the Astoria Finsbury Park in London. I remember it was very cold. I could not believe the amount of girls queueing to get in. I remember seeing the Fourmost and Cilla Black as support groups. At the end of the night, The Beatles came on and the place erupted. Everyone made a dash for the front of the stage. A lot of us were standing on the seats to see. You could hardly hear them for the girls screaming and fainting. The highlight of the night was a few of the lads I were with had had a bet with one of them that they could walk on stage and shake hands with John Lennon. Our mate Sid managed it! John Lennon was playing the piano and Sid calmly walked over, held his hand out and John Lennon shook it with no problem. The theatre erupted again. Sid then turned round and walked off stage. No one stopped him or even questioned him. Mind you, he was a big bloke. The other thing I remember was that when we came out you could not hear a thing. You couldn't hear the traffic, just a pinging noise in your ears because of the screaming. Oh, what memories. Brilliant times.

After the Christmas shows, The Beatles go to Paris and play 18 nights and then travel to the USA for **The Ed Sullivan Show.**

THE ED SULLIVAN SHOW
9 FEBRUARY 1964, NEW YORK, NEW YORK

I WAS WATCHING: CATHY SANCHEZ

I remember when they first appeared on *The Ed Sullivan Show*. I hadn't heard of them before as I was into the Beach Boys and surfer songs. But the next day at school, all us girls were talking about The Beatles and who was the cutest. George was mine. I and my friends went out to buy their records.

I WAS WATCHING: CHERI BILL, AGE 7

Like most people I watched The Beatles on *Ed Sullivan* in February 1964. Being seven and a half, I mainly wanted to watch because my siblings wanted to and I didn't care to watch the programme Dad was watching on the other set. So we sat on the bed and I had my first taste of The Beatles. I was hooked for life. I loved the music and the way they smiled while performing, each having their own unique style. And Paul McCartney solidified the fact that I am a heterosexual. He was the most handsome man I had ever seen.

In March, The Beatles film their first full length feature film, A Hard Day's Night.

SCALA THEATRE
23-31 MARCH 1964, LONDON, UK

I WAS THERE: CAROL ALLEN

As a teenager, I worked in Charlotte Street next to the Scala theatre where The Beatles filmed their stage scenes for *A Hard Day's Night*. I worked with a friend and, as you can imagine, knowing that our heroes were next door was almost too much to bear. Our supervisor took pity on us one day and let us finish early so we could wait at the stage door. We stood for quite some time but in the end we were rewarded. Out came the Fab Four and we were within touching distance. They all got into a black limo and the icing on the cake was when John Lennon wound the window down and offered me a Polo, which I obviously took! It's my claim to fame.

On 1 April 1964, the sixth UK single, 'Can't Buy Me Love', is released.

ABC CINEMA
29 APRIL 1964, EDINBURGH, UK

I WAS THERE: MOIRA MORRIS, AGE 13

I was 13 and a half when I heard that The Beatles were coming to Edinburgh so naturally I wanted to see them. The only way to be sure of getting a ticket was to camp out but my mother was a bit over protective as I was an only child and she was not keen to let me go. One girl had camped out for three days and had missed school and there was no way that I would have got to do that. However, on the Friday I pleaded again and was told 'no' again. I went to my room and sobbed solidly for about three hours. My father couldn't stand seeing me so sad and pleaded with my mother to let me go, as by that time my friend was getting to go if I was allowed. I can remember him saying to my mum that I didn't ask for much and that they would never hear the end of it if I didn't get to go. By this time, my mum had said she had had enough and didn't care anymore, so the next thing I heard was my dad knocking on my bedroom door, telling me that I was getting to go.

My friend and I headed up to the ABC cinema where they were due to play and we sat on the pavement along with hundreds of other girls. My friend's mum came up later on with fish suppers and they were the best I had ever tasted as it was March and it was cold. My mum said she wasn't giving me any money and that she would come up the next day with money for my ticket. However, because we were near a dance hall and there were drunks about the place, the police decided to get the cinema to sell the tickets twelve hours earlier than they had intended to. That was okay apart from the fact that I had no money for a ticket – so guess what? I burst into tears again.

This policeman saw me and asked what was wrong and I told him. He said not to worry and that I would get a ticket. They would keep it for me for a day as there would be a lot of people in that position. He then pushed me near the front of the queue, although there had been loads of people in front of me. After a wait of ages,

I was at the desk and managed to get a seat eight rows from the front – I remember the seat number, H33 – and they told me they would put it in an envelope for me to collect the next day. I was excited, to say the least. My friend and I walked down Lothian Road and along Princes Street to get home. There were no night buses at that time and we had no money anyway and we got home about 6am. I had to ring my doorbell as kids didn't get keys then and of course my parents were not expecting me back at that time. When my dad answered the door, I screamed 'I've got a ticket!' and my dad said, 'okay, I know you're excited. Just calm down and get to your bed.'

The next day I went to school and was ecstatic. It was a big deal as only three people in my class had a ticket and I had the best seat. I went after school to get the ticket and my mum told me to give it to her for safe keeping. It cost 12/6 (63p). The first two rows were 15/- (75p). I'll never forget the concert. I couldn't see but there was a boy at either side of me and they lifted me on their shoulders so that I could see. I screamed myself hoarse but it was great. I didn't try to get on the stage as the bouncers were throwing girls off, and not bothering too much about how they did it, and some of them got hurt. I was quite light so didn't fancy getting flung about. Seeing The Beatles is something that'll stay in my memory forever. When we were going out of the theatre, quite a lot of the seats were wet but I managed not to pee on my seat.

I also went to see them in October that year but there was no camping out allowed then. You had to send a postal order and it was first come, first served. I still got a seat in the stalls but it wasn't so near and it cost me 7/6 (38p). The concert was just as good. It's hard to believe it was over 50 years ago.

The Beatles commence their first major overseas tour with shows in Denmark, the Netherlands and Hong Kong.

 # K B HALLEN
4 JUNE 1964, COPENHAGEN, DENMARK

I WAS THERE: LIZ MUNK KNIGHT

It was crazy. I didn't want to take the train home. I wanted to meet them. I screamed a lot through the entire show.

On 11 June 1964 The Beatles arrive in Australia.

CENTENNIAL HALL
12 – 13 JUNE 1964, ADELAIDE, AUSTRALIA

I WAS THERE: RAY BARWELL

I could not believe the people outside the town hall. It was gridlock. There were thousands and thousands. You could not fall over if you tried. Everything came to a standstill. You could not think for the screams, the cars, the trams, everything. When they came onto the verandah at the Town Hall, girls were fainting and medics were trying to revive them. I know it was a long time ago, but I'll never forget seeing The Beatles on stage. They were fantastic.

I WAS THERE: BRENTON MONTGOMERY

I went to one of the concerts, but can't recall which one. There were four in all – two on the 12th and two on the 13th. I was a member of the UK-based Beatles Fan Club and through a promo on Channel 7 won a free ticket in the front row!

I WAS THERE: KARINA KAY BILLETT (NEE MORESEY)

My father Desmond Thomas Moresey was a police officer. He was awarded the Australian Police Medal in 1987, just before he passed away, for his outstanding service to the community. I had a look through his duty logs and I found two brief entries that state he was there. He got the job of crowd control at the Town Hall and pulling hysterical and fainting girls from the front of the stage at the Centennial Hall because he was so tall and he could reach them. I can remember him telling me that he was on crowd control and on stage with The Beatles at their Adelaide concerts. I also remember him not being so complimentary about the band, although this may be an age and an era thing. He said 'they were long-haired Poms' and he couldn't hear a word of what they sang because of the girls screaming. 'Why go to a concert and scream?'

I WAS THERE: SANDRA ADAMSON (NEE WYATT), AGE 22

I was excitedly taken by a boyfriend (whose name I have long forgotten) to see and hear The Beatles at the Centennial Hall in the Wayville Showgrounds. My seating was in the centre of the hall, about halfway back from the stage. Everyone in the audience was standing up and jumping around and not being very tall – about five foot four – all I could see was the topmost part of their heads. The entire concert was a yelling and screaming crescendo of noise, so I heard none of their music or singing. It was a huge disappointment for me and the only concert that I have ever attended since because of this. I might as well have been at a football match.

I WAS THERE: LIZZIE ARMSTRONG

I went with my brother and some girlfriends. We camped out on North Terrace overnight to get tickets. We were six rows from the front!

I WAS THERE: SANDI HOGBEN, AGE 17

My father got the ticket from his friend and so I went with his daughter and her friend. The seats were two rows from the stage – dead centre. Lucky me! Being a young lady at the time, I went with the attitude of not getting caught up with the hysterical girls screaming. However, that changed immediately when those gorgeous, handsome, well-dressed, swanky young Englishmen with their accents opened their mouths. Oh yes – I screamed as loud as anyone! I fell in love with George. Paul, John and Ringo did not get a look in. I can still see them before me in their black stovepipe pants, jackets, tie, white shirts and iconic Beatle clean-cut hairstyle. My boyfriend, now my husband, wore the same style at the time. Paul was the front man, with general banter from John and George being more reserved. The stage setting was simple, with speakers, equipment and microphones all in black. I have the official souvenir Australian tour programme, which shows Johnny Devlin, a popular Australian rocker at the time, as supporting artist. I have a signed photo of Johnny which my older brother got for me. I don't remember the support artists apart from one of the bands, who had a saxophone player who blasted the songs out. Needless to say, I went home exhausted, my throat sore and my voice hoarse, reliving every moment. To this day I am excited to think I was there and so very fortunate to have the perfect seat. Thank you, Dad.

I WAS THERE: SUE CURNOW

My husband slept in the street to get the tickets, much to his mother's disgust. We were five rows from the front. I still have the original programme book and some black and white photos I took myself with my Kodak instamatic camera.

I WAS THERE: SAMELA HARRIS

Who could forget? The hall was packed. The audience was predominantly young and female, like me. I had a good seat four or five rows from the front. It was all very happy, excited and generally nice – until The Beatles came on stage. Perfectly normal girls suddenly went completely mad. They started to scream – and they did not stop. They bounced and jumped and screamed ear piercing, deafening screams. The Beatles played, looking amused and bemused, but one could hear only snatches. Amplification was not as huge as it is these days. I was not a screamer and I was really annoyed at the whole phenomenon. I was thrilled to have seen my pin ups in the flesh but I just could not understand then or now why all these fans would rather scream than listen.

I WAS THERE: NICKY CONNOR

I slept overnight outside Allan's Record Shop in Rundle Street to get an even row, eg. Row B, second row from the front. The supporting acts were Johnny Chester and Sounds Unlimited, plus a few more top bands that I don't remember. The Beatles came on for 30 minutes. They sang ten songs of three minutes each – 'Please Please Me', 'Love Me Do', 'I Want To Hold Your Hand', 'She Loves You', 'From Me To You', 'Can't Buy Me Love', 'Rock 'n' roll Music', 'A Hard Day's Night' and two other songs I don't recall. I never remembered too much about it because I was screaming the whole time and never heard anything!

I WAS THERE: HELEN JORASLAFSKY

I wagged school, slept in Grenfell Street to get tickets, and our tickets were in the very last row! As we were in the back row, we had no reservations about standing on the seats in order to see above the waving arms of those in front of us. I can't remember whether it worked! What do I remember? All that screaming! I don't think I actually heard a note or a word during their performance. And Roy Orbison was their support act – who would have thought?

I WAS THERE: JULIE TOLLEY (NEE BENNETT), AGE 14

I went with my very first serious boyfriend, Gary Saunders, who lived next door to my mothers' friends, Uncle Jack and Aunty Lila Dawe on Bundarra Avenue in the northern suburb of Blair Athol. Although unrelated, in those days the terms 'aunty' and 'uncle' were a sign of respect. Gary's mother would drive him to my place at Dover Gardens, in the south and near the coast, and we would sit in the lounge room and listen to 45rpm records whilst my Mum and Gary's mum would sit in the kitchen chatting and drinking tea. Gary gave me a ticket for the concert for my 14th birthday. I do not have any recollection of getting to Centennial Hall, but his or my mum probably drove us there and picked us up after the concert finished.

Our seats were about five or six from the front. Despite what the newspaper and TV reports said, the only screaming was between songs. While The Beatles were singing, everyone was listening. I suspect this was for several reasons. Firstly, we were polite and it was polite to listen. And the tickets were probably expensive, although I never knew the cost. We were also spellbound by the appearance of a fabulous group from overseas, ie. not just local acts such as The Twilights (who later become the Little River Band), The Easybeats or Johnny Farnham. The hall has since been demolished.

I WAS THERE: JENNY LESLIE, AGE 16

It was my first concert. My parents bought the ticket from a neighbour (who couldn't go) for 30 shillings as a birthday gift for me. It was the best gift ever. I was seated seven rows from the front and everybody screamed, which did make them a bit hard to hear at times. The acoustics in Centennial Hall weren't the best, but who cared? Along with them were the group Sounds Incorporated and Johnny Chester, who wore red shoes. I always remembered that. I took my dad's binoculars but didn't need them. I became the 21st member of the SA Beatles fan club. I've always loved them. George was my favourite. I didn't get to see Ringo though. Jimmy Nicol filled in. I've never forgotten that night.

I WAS THERE: JO ROGERS, AGE 20

They weren't actually gonna come here. But radio DJ Bob Francis got a petition up because they were going to miss out Adelaide altogether. My younger sister and her friend went and queued up as soon as they finished work on Friday night. Fans were queuing up outside the market, the big stores that were selling the tickets, all along North Terrace, which is quite a long street, and right round the corner, right down one road and round the other road. There were crowds of them for four days.

They did a procession up King William Street, which is a main street, to the town hall. I was on the median strip and I put my foot out just to see as a copper was coming round on his motorbike. I ended up with it under his footpeg and around his knee, and I ended up with my elbow on his shoulder because he had to stop. So the cars stopped. I think it was an open top Rolls-Royce convertible. We were taking photos of them but none of them came out. It was such a mess, it was just so shaky. It looked like someone's operation actually. Terrible. But this poor policeman – I let him go in the end, but I had stopped the whole parade with my foot!

We got front row tickets both nights. Mum came with us the first night but we were sitting just at the side in the front. We were right in the front the next night, right in front of the microphones. But they needn't have sung really, even when we were sitting right in front, because there was so much screaming you could only just about hear them. The three of us walked home and that was a fair old way because it was a half hour drive. We got offers of rides but we were walking on Cloud Nine singing all The Beatles songs going along the road. That was absolutely great. The only thing was that Ringo wasn't there. I think he had tonsillitis. Jimmy Nicol was there instead.

When they left, my dad and mum took my sister and I to the airport. But we didn't go into the airport. Going down to the beach is a side where there's all this grass and hedges. It's all fenced off and Dad parked there because you could just about see the planes from there. Sis and I got out, jumped the fence and ran across this paddock and down into the ditch before anyone saw us. And then we got up and ran again to get to another ditch. These guards saw us and made us go back, so that's as far as we got and so we didn't see them take off. But there were crowds. There were so many people. And they reckon that even though they weren't going to come here, The Beatles got the best reception in Adeliade of anywhere they played in Australia. They were so natural and down to earth. They weren't putting on any airs and graces. With Australians that doesn't go down too well anyway. I think it was just that everyone found they were just so easy to get on with. And there wasn't all this prima donna stuff that you get with a lot of people. That's why Adelaide liked them.

FESTIVAL HALL
15 – 17 JUNE 1964, MELBOURNE, AUSTRALIA

I WAS THERE: GILL RIBIS, AGE 19

In June 1964 I won tickets to watch The Beatles live on stage by winning an Elnett hairspray competition. We were living in Melbourne and I worked in a pharmacy and got to know about the Elnett competition. You had to answer the question 'why do you use Elnett?'. I can't remember what I wrote, but whatever it was I won it! I took my eldest brother. We couldn't hear. We could hardly see. But I did see it on television afterwards and it was fantastic. The atmosphere was great. Paul was my favourite Beatle.

THE STADIUM
18 – 20 JUNE 1964, SYDNEY, AUSTRALIA

I WAS THERE: JOYCE ALLAN, AGE 13

My friend and I took the day off school when they arrived in Sydney. We spent the day under umbrellas and an awning of the Chevron Hotel, opposite the Sheraton Hotel, waiting for them to appear, which they finally did in the afternoon. The young policemen who were keeping us in check were very friendly and there were no hassles. We were just so excited. Two girls from our school went to the airport and were on the front of the *Sydney Morning Herald* the next day. Despite the fact that their mothers had given them notes saying they were sick, the school was very accommodating, with teachers asking if they had fun! My mother had queued up previously to buy us the tickets for the show. This was an unusual thing for her to do, as she was usually more interested in us getting on with our studies.

Four of us went – my sister and her friend, who was four years older than us but mad about John Lennon, and my school friend and I. We were in the middle section of the stadium, with mesh fences between us and ringside but with a reasonable view. We had such a great time. We were thrilled that Ringo had been able to come in time for the Sydney show after his illness. I had binoculars and remember him wearing lime green socks! When they came on the screams were deafening, but we all swear we could still hear them singing. Mum and Dad came to pick us up and said they saw The Beatles leaving in their car. I think they had a quick getaway quite a while before we were all let out of our seats. Mum always says she wishes she had gone too. It had reminded her of her own teenage years when she was mad about Frank Sinatra. It was such a special time and I'm only sorry now that I didn't keep my scrapbook and ticket for posterity. Years later, when I was coming home from work and heard about John Lennon's death, I immediately thought that my sister would be upset, so had to write to her in London to say how sorry I was. It felt like they were people who were special friends.

I WAS THERE: GEOFFREY OGDEN BROWNE, AGE 13

I went to the Sydney Stadium by some sort of serendipity. My elder sister Mo was married at the time to a colleague at Radio 2SM who was give two ringside seats to The Beatles concert but could not make it so I went with her instead. The tickets we had as a comp cost 37/6 each which was quite a lot of money in those days – you could get a pie for sixpence. Even outside the hysteria had started. I had just turned 13 and could not in my wildest dreams have seen so many nubile teenage girls, especially that night as it was Paul McCartney's birthday. The smells when we got to our seats were amazing. It was a mixture of lust, musk and pheromones.

The Stadium was like a huge barn. The seats were ancient. The air of anticipation was electric, absolutely electric – you could actually feel it. We were seven rows from the front but the noise from what were called 'the bleachers', ie. the cheap seats at the back, was getting louder every minute, a bit like a thunderstorm approaching. Sounds Incorporated, the support act, came on and did a decent set and by and large the audience gave them due respect for their efforts. But no one had come to see Sounds Incorporated!

Then you could practically hear the pounding heartbeats of all the girls as the lads came on. It's so very hard all these years later to describe it... let's just say the room went from 240 volts to about 10,000. It really was a case of 'you had to be there'. The boys looked so natty and clean by today's standards but in those days the haircuts alone raised eyebrows as well as derision from anyone over the age of 30. I remember George having a go at counting in the first number. I heard 'She was just seventeen and you know...' and then the screaming really started! It was deafening, truly on the threshold of pain. From then on, they may as well have been miming. In true stoic Liverpudlian spirit the boys soldiered on. They were battle-hardened by this stage. They make 'em tough in Liverpool.

In just over half an hour it was all over. Or was it? I had witnessed something I have seen to this day only on film and that was mass hysteria. In the stadium that night everyone was standing on those wooden seats. I was in disbelief as if I were observing from another world. The teenage girls were right next to me crying, sighing, screaming and some most probably wetting their pants as well! A medical person would call it rapture. In those days, there were no drugs as we know them today nor even much pre-fuelled alcohol. It was just pure unadulterated fun. Carefree. Part of my life changed that night. For days I ran it through my head trying to figure out what had happened. I remember one thing above all about that night at the Sydney Stadium. Even at the age of 13 I knew I was witnessing history. I shudder to think, though, about what I did when given the album *A Hard Day's Night* one Christmas. I took it back to the shop and exchanged it for Beethoven's *Fifth Symphony*, played by the London Symphony Orchestra.

I WAS THERE: TONY CHAPLIN, AGE 15

I was in the third year of high school when I went to the Saturday show at the Sydney Stadium. I think there were two other acts that night – Johnny Chester and Johnny Devlin and a great English rock band called Sounds Incorporated. I remember The Beatles running on to the rotating stage and them singing about ten songs. You could just make out the words above all the noise. Then they ran off the stage. There were no encores. The place was packed and I loved the show.

I WAS THERE: SANDRA DEE, AGE 16

My friends and I were four rows from the front. Ringo wasn't playing as he had tonsillitis. We didn't take photos – there were no mobiles or videos then. We were 16 years old and my friend's sister was eleven. I felt so very fortunate to be there. The tickets were £12 each and, no, we didn't run to the Sheraton Hotel afterwards!

I WAS THERE: GAIL FAHEY, AGE 15

I came over to Sydney where I stayed with my aunt and grandmother and while I was living with them they took me to nearly every show that came to the Stadium. I can remember the gate man saying to my grandmother that she was the oldest person to go through the gate that night. She would have been 62 years old! We entered though a very small door into the stadium that day. I think it was because I was with the older people and a man took us with him to avoid us being shoved around. I had a wonderful time. We were about 15 rows from the front and could see very well. Everyone was screaming and having a wonderful time. The Beatles looked immaculate in their suits on the stage of the old building. My biggest regret was I didn't keep the tickets. I don't know if I even saw the tickets, as my aunt would have had them and in those days I never thought of keeping tickets.

I WAS THERE: JUNE GRANLAND (NEE CONNELL), AGE 14

I went with a girlfriend to the Saturday matinee show. To this day, I can't believe my mother let me go. I don't remember how we got the tickets. I think my friend had a relative in the entertainment industry. We caught a train in from Parramatta. I can't remember what station we went to but I remember walking a fair way in new high heel T-Bar shoes which were all the rage. On arriving at the stadium there were thousands of people – mainly girls like us. We had to stand behind wooden barriers waiting to go in. Then, all of a sudden, The Beatles' car pulled up and out they got. I could reach out and touch George. He was my favourite! Everyone was screaming but I was just in total amazement that I was so close to them. We were ushered to our seats. Ours were in the bleachers so they were only tiny specks on the stage and the noise of the girls screaming was unbelievable. But I remember them singing 'I Saw Her Standing There'. It was incredible.

I WAS THERE: MARGARET HYDE

My father worked for 2SM at the time. He came home and announced that he had tickets for the concert. My two brothers, my sister and I just about went ballistic and off we went – by public transport, I might add – from Lane Cove. We were in the third row from the front.

I WAS THERE: ROGER UNETT, AGE 20

I had arrived from England on 22 December 1963 and was staying at the migrant hostel at Heathcote. As soon as we found out about the tour, me and some other lads at the hostel including a guy called Jeff arranged for a girl who was also a Beatles fan to go into Sydney very early and queue for tickets. On the day, I drove three mates in my VW Beetle into Sydney and we parked as close to the stadium as we could get, at Rushcutters Bay. We presented our tickets with much excitement and went into the stadium. What I remember most is the revolving stage and the screaming. The noise generated was incredible. I was clapping throughout the concert so enthusiastically that when we got out I realised I had broken my watch.

I WAS THERE: PHIL MARTIN

I was there and I still have my original souvenir programme and my ringside seat ticket.

I WAS THERE: NOELENE JOHNSTON

I was sat in the front row. Honestly, you couldn't hear a thing they sang because of the screaming from the audience. I wasn't one of them because I was with my boyfriend who had said that, if he came, I wasn't allowed to scream. I still have the original programme. I'm not sure why I have saved it all these years as none of my family are interested. They might be when I die, but it will probably just be thrown in a skip.

I WAS THERE: GERRY KEEFE, AGE 24

I went with my friend Bob Muirhead. There were about 15,000 in the crowd and the females outnumbered the males by 14 to one. Because of the continuous female screaming throughout the whole show, I did not hear one word of the songs. Still – what a night!

I WAS THERE: SANDRA MILLHOUSE, AGE 16

I remember it very well. I was standing up in the bleachers with my girlfriend. I kept lighting matches and calling out Paul's name. There were two guys that kept blowing out my match and my friend said I wouldn't do that if I were you because I was crazy and she didn't know what I would do. Well, I put the match out on one of their hands. They didn't do it again!

I WAS THERE: LOUISE MORRIS, AGE 14

I was a very excited 14-year-old in 1964 when my older brother bought me two tickets to see the Fab Four. It was a hard choice as to which girlfriend I would take! We left Drummoyne where we lived at 3pm to head to the stadium, much to the concern of our parents as we had to go up William Street and through Kings Cross. This in itself was an exciting adventure for two very naive teenagers! It was a long wait until The Beatles came on at 9pm to the deafening screaming of the crowd. There were no ear plugs in those days. I remember the advice from DJ Bob Roberts to stick your fingers in your ears and press forward to eliminate some of the screaming noise, which was as loud and ear piercing as a tree full of cicadas. It sort of worked. We were in the second last row of the bleachers, so the stage was very far away but we were able to see Paul – our favourite – shake his Beatlemop while singing 'I Want To Hold Your Hand'. At school the next day, we were the envy of our friends but in trouble with the headmistress as we had wagged school after lunch!

I WAS THERE: SANDRA ORSZACZKY, AGE 17

I still recall the excitement of it all and the incredible wall of noise that endured for the length of the concert! I lived in Sydney in 1964 when the beloved Beatles arrived for concerts. I, along with countless young girls, was completely in love with Paul. I was a working girl and so was able to invest in tickets to the most exciting night out I had ever had. I attended the show with a work girlfriend who shared my love of the band. We arrived at the Sydney Stadium to find the place packed to the rafters. The anticipation was palpable!

The old building shook when the music started and I can honestly say we all heard no singing at all, just the screaming of a stadium full of love-struck girls accompanied by a sprinkling of brave young men. The concert has remained one of my favourite memories of that time in my life and whilst those memories are no longer so sharp, I am so grateful to have seen and experienced the joy of seeing The Beatles. One firm memory I have is of Lesley and I taking the train home and walking down the road singing at the top of our voices all the favourite songs we had seen but not really heard! I can even remember what we wore – tight black pants, sloppy purple jumpers and white boots with a fur trim. So cool!

I WAS THERE: DON BROWN, AGE 17

I'll never forget that period. Parties in those days would play Beatles records only, even though there were only two or three LPs released at that time. It's amazing that we call it such a memorable event – but it was! I was there and so were The Beatles and that was all that mattered. It was June 1964 at the old Sydney Stadium at Rushcutters Bay. I drove there in my MGA. I was working with an advertising agency and the social club organised the tickets, which might have cost 30/- ($3.00). I attended many stadium concerts in the late '50s and the '60s and The Beatles concert was without doubt the pinnacle of all of them. But it shouldn't have been, because I couldn't hear a thing other than the non-stop screaming of the girls for the duration of their stage appearance. It was unbelievable – the worst I had ever heard, and all of this in the giant chook house called Sydney Stadium. The noise was the one thing that made it different to any other concert I had been to, and yet the atmosphere was electric. I think I went to a Saturday show, as we didn't take time off work, and possibly one that started in daylight hours. I remember that The Beatles didn't relate to the audience too much other than singing their five or six songs. And then they were gone.

I WAS THERE: MARGARET VINCENT

I was a lowly student nurse at the time, earning about four pounds a fortnight. I queued for hours to buy the tickets for myself and my sister, by which times the ringside seats were all sold so we had to be satisfied with terrace seats which were just like long benches with numbers painted on them, which cost 17/6 (88p) each. They were elevated in long rows with bare ground underneath, so that if you dropped anything it was lost forever. We waited with great anticipation for weeks and guarded those tickets with our lives.

For several days before The Beatles arrived in Australia, a local radio station had one of their staff travelling with the group, and I listened to the radio every chance I got and hung on every detail. I was heartbroken when we were told that Ringo would not be coming for the first of the shows but would play Sydney. The same radio station then announced a competition for people to attend Paul's 22nd birthday celebrations so I entered the competition, only finding out years later that my mother did not post the entry!

My father drove us to the stadium with strict instructions that we were to behave like young ladies and not talk to any strangers. He would return to pick us up after the show. It was pouring rain and freezing cold, with a very leaking roof and terrible acoustics. The stadium was constructed mainly of corrugated iron and the noise of the pouring rain on the roof often drowned out the singing. And if that didn't do it, the screaming fans did.

Sounds Incorporated were playing first and I think they were greeted with choruses of very loud boos. From what I remember, the songs sung by The Beatles were not terribly good, the acoustics were terrible and they often seemed quite flat and/or out of tune. In hindsight, they seemed to be quite detached from the audience and reacted very little to them. They did their songs and just left the stage, which seemed quite anticlimactic. They almost looked to be reading a script some of the time. The stage was circular and the centre of it revolved, so maybe they were just dizzy. Between the noise of the screams and the very loud rain and howling wind, it was very hard to hear anything much, but – it was The Beatles! Who cared how bad or good they were? After the show, we piled out of the stadium past ambulance officers and fainting girls, into the weather for Dad to collect us, assuring him that we did behave like young ladies. Not!

A group of us went down to Kings Cross on the Saturday morning and stood in the street outside the Sheraton Hotel where they were staying for hours, again in the freezing cold, just waiting for them to make an appearance on the balcony. We were chanting and singing Beatles songs for hours on end until, at about five o'clock, some heads eventually appeared over the balcony railing. We were sure it was them! After a few waves from them and deafening screams from us, it was all over and they were gone. Of course, from a distance of about ten floors up, it could have been anyone up there, and we would never have known.

We lived very close to Sydney Airport, so I went down to the airport to see them leave but the weather was still awful. I think they were driven out onto the tarmac and up the steps undercover. We won tickets to an early screening of *A Hard Day's Night* and the umbrella that Paul used at the airport was used as a lucky door prize. It was filled with confetti which went all over the stage when the winner was announced. I didn't win the prize but I did get a piece of the confetti, which I carried around in my purse for several years.

I WAS THERE: TED ORAM

My mate Max and I had bought our tickets some time before. The big night finally arrived and we trained into Sydney not knowing what to really expect as neither of us had been to anything like this before. Our seats were not bad considering the size of the venue, although quite small by today's standards. The first act was Jonhny Devlin, an Aussie singer. I managed to shout to Max 'what do we do when everyone starts screaming?' 'Dunno,' he said. It did not take long to find out. The next act up was Sounds Incorporated, the volume of the crowd increased and we shouted louder to match it. Sounds Incorporated finished their set and The Beatles were next. The feeling of seeing one's idols suddenly took hold of the crowd. The sense of expectation grew like something alive in that stadium. Words cannot really describe it. The sound and volume of the crowd went up to something I have never heard since. Then four mop tops could be seen trying to get through the crowd to the stage. We had heard of the term mass hysteria. Well, now Max and I were suddenly part of it. Standing on our seats, we screamed along with everyone else until The Beatles were finished. We did not hear much and did not see much – but what an experience, one that is still clear many years later. Hoarse from screaming, we came out not quite believing what we had just been part of. So much so that we took the chance and went back in to Palings Music store in Sydney the next morning, a Saturday, and managed to buy two more tickets. These seats were a bit further back than the night before but we still managed to go through the whole fantastic experience again.

I WAS THERE: CAMPBELL FORD

As a young man in the 1950s and '60s I went to many a concert at the Sydney Stadium – Frank Sinatra, the Beach Boys and Spike Jones – but I didn't go to The Beatles show. Whilst I liked their music, I was unable to buy tickets as their performances were booked out in minutes! However, I did book for the premiere of a sensational new performance of Henry V on the same day, with a young John Bell and his wife Anna Volska as Katherine in an innovative in-the-round presentation in a pavilion tent erected in Rushcutter's Bay Park just across the road from the stadium. All started well until The Beatles' concert began a few minutes later. The music didn't bother us since the deafening screaming and stamping of the audience from across the road drowned out any other sound at all, including the dialogue of the actors onstage in the tent! John Bell and his troupe valiantly continued their performance but it was all in vain – nobody could hear a word! Fortunately, the audience saw the funny side of it all.

I was in my mid-twenties and had been working as a film animator for TV for some time. I was booked to leave Australia to try my luck in England just a couple of weeks after this 'Beatles vs the Bard' event. I was also interested in a pretty Australian girl who was already in London. With several friends and a VW Kombi, we sailed to India and, in true '60s tradition, unloaded it in Bombay and drove overland to London where, by a strange coincidence, I was later hired to work as an animator on The Beatles' *Yellow Submarine* feature cartoon. It was the most memorable year of my life. I met The Beatles briefly during production and found them easy to talk to and totally fascinated by the

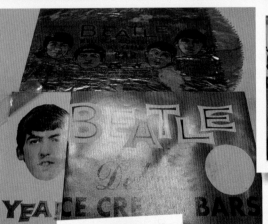

Clockwise from top left: Kelly Wright met The Beatles in 1964; Martha Serafin saw The Beatles at Boston Garden; Daniel Smith will never forget being at the Municipal Stadium in Kansas; items from Bethena Smith's memorabilia collection (four photos).

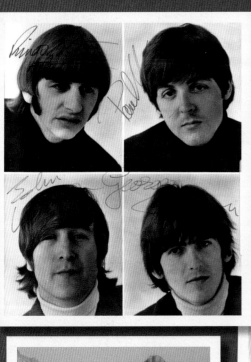

Clockwise from top left: Items from Bethena Smith's memorabilia collection (three photos); Elaine Bender helped run the Fort Worth chapter of The Beatles' fan club; Alistair Fyffe recalls jelly babies being thrown in Dundee; Morag Thompson won tickets in a *Daily Express* competition; Christine Pinder saw The Beatles twice in Hull.

cartoon versions of themselves. The pretty girl also came to work on *Yellow Submarine* and we became engaged during production. We married back in Australia in 1969.

I WAS THERE: BRUCE HAMLIN, AGE 14

In 1964 I was still at school way down in Narrandera and couldn't make it to Sydney even though I had my accommodation booked with a family friend and had a mate willing to share the adventure with me. Being only 14, it was a little difficult to convince my parents to let me come to Sydney, although all of my life I had spent the January school holidays at Manly literally every year since I was born. I now live in the next suburb up from Manly, so I have always been a frustrated Beatles fan.

TOWN HALL
26 JUNE 1964, DUNEDIN, NEW ZEALAND

I WAS THERE: BARRY IDOUR, AGE 23

I attended The Beatles' press conference and reviewed the concert for the *Evening Star*, the now defunct Dunedin evening newspaper of the day. I was one of four Star reporters to attend the press conference and recall being staggered by the massive crowds blocking Princes Street outside the City Hotel where The Beatles were staying. When they arrived, they were literally thrown into the hotel lift by police as they battled against the crowd. I suspect John Lennon may have been mildly injured in this incident as he didn't make it to the press conference, although it was claimed a bit of flu was the reason. Apparently of this incident George Harrison said to a police officer that the police had badly underestimated the crowd control problem, to which the policeman replied along the lines of 'don't worry son, we know what we're doing. We looked after Gracie Fields when she was here.'

The conference itself got off to a grand start once The Beatles got seated when the *Star*'s chief reporter David Exel attempted to get things under way by saying 'right, now before we start can you tell us which of you is which?' The 100 or so people in the room erupted with cries of amazement and George summed it up by replying 'if you don't know by now, what the hell are you doing here?' I felt sorry for Dave because in many interview situations like this it was probably a reasonable suggestion, but it was totally farcical in the context of The Beatles. Quick as a flash, Ringo announced that he was John, Paul said he was Ringo and George said he was Paul. This certainly eased the tension in the room. The rest of the session went pretty much without incident, although John's absence diminished things a bit.

On to the first concert of two in the 2,500 seat Town Hall. I and another reporter, the late Frank Campbell, were lucky enough to be the chosen reviewers although in hindsight there was little to review except the crowd reaction. This was because the volume of the sound system coupled with the screaming crowd made it almost impossible to hear what The Beatles were singing. Frank and I discovered early that if we put our fingers in our ears some of the music did filter through, but not much. Not that it really mattered much as The Beatles were only on stage for 20 to 25 minutes. I don't know what all the audience around us in the dress circle thought about these two dorks sitting there with fingers stuck in our ears. It was an experience that has remained vividly in my memory, being an impressionable 23 -year-old at the time and being part of one of the most exciting performer visits to the city up to that time.

SPEKE AIRPORT
JULY 1964, LIVERPOOL, UK

I WAS THERE: ANDREA CREED

Some of the planes that flew the London route were DC3s which required only one cabin crew. The ground crew pushed the very heavy door from the outside and the hostess was responsible for securing it on the inside. On one occasion, the plane was taxiing down the runway when to my horror the door opened, a bag was thrown in, followed by Paul McCartney. He was very apologetic. I wasn't best pleased because in the split second that all this happened, I had been wondering how I was to deal with what seemed an emergency. At the time, Liverpool was a homely little airport; I doubt the ground staff or airline pilot of what is now John Lennon International Airport would have been so accommodating.

'A Hard Day's Night' is released as a single on 10 July 1964.

On returning from their world tour, The Beatles are given a civic reception at Liverpool Town Hall.

SPEKE AIRPORT
10 JULY 1964, LIVERPOOL, UK

I WAS THERE: ERIC ROBERTS

I remember queuing up. You know the fire station on the corner by the old Speke airport? The Bryant and May matchstick factory was on the other corner, and I was in that road, looking through the mesh. I saw them coming off the aeroplane, and when they came past in the Rolls-Royce, heading to the Town Hall, I saw them there as well. There was thousands of us, all lining the road.

TOWN HALL
10 JULY 1964, LIVERPOOL, UK

I WAS THERE: COLIN HUGHES

I went to see The Beatles at their civic reception at Liverpool's Town Hall. The crowds were phenomenal and the crush unbelievable. I was next to a police horse who continually bit me. The only way to escape it was to tell a first aider who took me to an ambulance. I was taken to the Royal Northern Hospital for treatment but I only sustained bruising and was able to return to the crowds. My cousin, Ritchie Hughes (aka Ritchie Galvin) was a drummer with another band and was asked to become The Beatles drummer when Pete Best was dismissed from the band. My cousin declined as he did not get on well with John Lennon.

ODEON CINEMA
10 JULY 1964, LIVERPOOL, UK

I WAS THERE: EDWINA SWADEN

I went to see The Beatles when they came back for the northern premiere of the film *A Hard Day's Night*. I was standing on a bus shelter roof and I was seen. My mother found out and I was grounded for two weeks.

HIPPODROME
12 JULY 1964, BRIGHTON, UK

I WAS THERE: CHRIS HORLOCK

Singer Ray Charles appeared at the Dome in July, but this month in Brighton 1964 is remembered for Beatlemania taking the town by storm. 'The Beatles Show', as it was quaintly called, came to the Hippodrome with a ticket in the stalls costing 15/- (75p). Most of those present say they couldn't hear what was being sung at all due to the screaming girl fans, and when the sound system packed up for a short period, no one noticed because of the din. In fact, no one interviewed about the concert can recall a specific song at all, such was the row. Getting The Beatles into the Hippodrome without being mobbed caused some managerial head scratching until someone decided to utilise a garage building that stood immediately opposite the theatre. Middle Street was closed off and the van containing the Fab Four drove down West Street, which no one was expecting, then into the garage, which had a West Street entrance. The group dashed through to the Middle Street entrance and ran across the street and through the Hippodrome's front doors, with the crowds getting all but a fleeting glimpse of them as they passed.

I WAS THERE: JEREMY KNIGHT, AGE 13

I had a front row seat along with my 15-year-old sister Belinda. My parents would not normally have let me out at night but even they recognised it was a major event and, as I was being chaperoned by my sister, they let me go. Some of her school friends had slept out in front of the Hippodrome for at least one night to be at the head of the queue for tickets. A couple of her friends spotted The Beatles arriving by car and had chased the car up the road. One of them was thrilled to have been knocked down by it. She wasn't hurt but she felt that she had actually sort of touched them.

I WAS THERE: FRED AVERY, AGE 23

I was working in the London Borough of Fulham as a quantity surveyor. In 1962, a colleague asked me if I had seen The Beatles yet on TV and what long hair they all had. They were a really weird looking group. The Beatles show I saw in July 1964 was the second performance commencing at 8.30pm. I travelled from Burgess Hill to Brighton by train with my 19-year-old brother Philip and our father, whose name was Horace but who was known by everyone as Syd. We arrived at the Hippodrome half an hour before the show started and there were a lot of teenagers in and around Middle Street and outside the Hippodrome. Many of them were waiting to get a glimpse of The Beatles and some of them no doubt saw the first performance and couldn't go home! Our tickets were for the centre circle and cost 15/- (75p) each. My mother had spent a very long time outside of the ticket agents in Burgess Hill a few days before, queuing and not knowing if there would be enough to go round.

The evening opened with The Jynx, who were not mentioned at all in the programme and was compered by comedian Tony Marsh. He introduced boy band Jimmy Nicol and the Shubdubs and then The Fourmost. After the interval, we had The Jynx again and then the McKinleys, who were singing sisters Sheila and Jeanette. Then Tony Marsh came back on and introduced The Beatles. The Beatles were on the stage for about 40 minutes but it seemed like three hours! Most of the audience were teenagers –

80 per cent girls and ten per cent boys, and another ten per cent were parents or other adults. The audience had little interest in the first eight acts but when compere Tony Marsh came on for the last time, the screaming started even before he could begin to announce The Beatles.

By the time The Beatles appeared, the noise level increased to such a pitch that none of the music they were playing could be heard. It was at this point that several of the adults and parents got up and walked out of the auditorium with hands over their ears! Young girls tried to climb on stage and others passed out, and had to be lifted above the agitated mainly female young crowd so that they could be treated by the medical attendants outside of the theatre. Front line girls were throwing jelly babies, which Paul McCartney reputedly loved. The noise level never decreased even though The Beatles tried to announce the songs and, after they had finished, the ringing in my ears went on for half an hour after leaving the theatre. My father stayed throughout the performance but was heard to say 'that's the first and last time that I will ever see The Beatles!' Of course, that was the same for all of us.

I WAS THERE: ROSALIND DAVIDSON (NEE MERRIMAN), AGE 14

The first time I became aware of The Beatles was when two class mates started singing 'Please Please Me' while we were lining up to go into a lesson at school. They were dancing together while singing and I thought it sounded pretty good. It must have been 1963. When The Beatles were due to appear at the Hippodrome the next year, someone in the class organised a rota to take turns overnight in the queue for tickets. I heard about this and was very keen to take part, and even though I was only 14, I was allowed by my parents to cycle from my home in Hove to the Hippodrome in Brighton in the middle of the night so that I could take my place sitting on the pavement. I recall being stopped on the way by a policeman who asked where I was going – the roads were dark and deserted – and when I told him he just smiled and waved me on.

I ended up getting tickets for both performances, first in the right hand box and then in the left. Of course, with all the screaming you couldn't hear much. I didn't scream. I just took it all in, spellbound. They were wearing those dark suits with the mandarin collars. I took some photos but there wasn't enough light and they didn't come out. How thrilling their music sounded to me then. I still get a kind of shiver if I hear it today, 50 years later. I saw the Rolling Stones at the Hippodrome later that year. I was in the stalls and remember getting up to dance in the aisle. They seemed so wild and unkempt compared to The Beatles. Funny how they don't seem that way at all now when you look at photos of that time. I remember my dad sending off to the *Radio Times* for a large black and white print of The Beatles for me, saying knowingly that they'd be finished in six months. How wrong could you be?

I WAS THERE: GRAHAM FRANKS, AGE 16

My recollection of seeing The Beatles at the Brighton Hippodrome is now rather patchy although at the time it was a momentous occasion. I went to see them with a friend, an apprentice carpenter at the time called Chris Harmes. He was 17 and I was 16. I worked for the tailors John Colliers so was able to have suits made with velvet collars on inspired by The Beatles. They influenced a lot of our fashion, shirts, suits, etc., depending on what we could afford. We both lived in Burgess Hill, about eleven miles from Brighton, so travelled down on the train that evening.

I remember sitting in the stalls at the Hippodrome, a small venue for such a huge group by today's standards and watching the support act, The Fourmost. Also on the bill that night was a drummer called Jimmy Nicol. He had replaced Ringo for a short while when Ringo apparently had tonsillitis. The atmosphere in the theatre was electric, with people shouting and screaming. I remember looking at the closed curtains on the stage, again very old-fashioned compared with the O2. The curtains didn't quite touch the stage floor so we could see boots walking about behind the curtains. Was that The Beatles? The curtains opened to an eruption of hysteria and there they were on stage. It was almost surreal, and hard to believe that it was actually them. They had amplifiers and speakers of course but nothing by today's huge sound systems in auditoriums. The screaming and shouting by the audience, including me, was intense but you could hear them and I remember thinking, as they played, that they sounded just like their LPs and singles. It was very tight professional music and you couldn't help but admire them. 'A Hard Day's Night' was high in the charts at the time and I remember it being played. After the show, walking away from the Hippodrome, I noticed all the discarded ticket stubs from the show littering the street. I wish I had known then what I know now and stopped to pick some up!

I WAS THERE: PATRICIA HAWES, AGE 15

I attended The Beatles concert at the Hippodrome. Alas all I can remember is sitting in the stalls, near the front, in the northern part of the theatre and being extremely cross that the girls were all screaming so loudly that I couldn't hear any of the performance! I don't remember how I acquired tickets but I certainly didn't cycle in the dead of night like my friend Rosalind. She says we were dancing in the aisles.

I WAS THERE: MIKE GRAVES

In the weeks before The Beatles performed at the Hippodrome, I and some young school friends thought up a small money-making scheme to profit us all which revolved around six young Roedean School girls who wanted to go to the concert. My suggestion was that queued up for me for several hours to buy two tickets, which was the limit, for a few bob, with me offering them one free ticket for their time. All went well and I finished up with six spare tickets which I raffled at the local coffee bars – the Cottage, the Penny Farthing, etc. – making around £10 profit. When the day arrived, all of us were outside the Hippodrome to see and experience the Beatlemania. The girls who got in said they could hear very little of the band's voices because of the screaming teenagers. Although I was not a fan, as I was into the Stones, it was an amazing experience just to soak up the atmosphere as they stepped out of their limousine!

I WAS THERE: LYNDA PEARCE

I was lucky enough to see The Beatles in Brighton at much the same time as I saw the Rolling Stones, but whilst it was a brilliant concert, they really couldn't match the Stones. I went with friends and the main impression was that it was very difficult to hear because of the screaming. I remember lots of dolly mixtures were thrown on the stage. I assume at some time one of The Beatles had said that they liked them. I enjoyed being there but I was never a great fan and much preferred the Stones' much lower key – but much better – concert in Tunbridge Wells. When the Stones played, everyone just stood and listened and it was a completely different atmosphere.

OPERA HOUSE
26 JULY 1964, BLACKPOOL, UK

I WAS THERE: EILEEN CORNES, AGE 16

I was on holiday with my parents, brother and my cousin Jean at the Claremont Hotel. The show had been sold out weeks ago but the waiters in the hotel had tickets to sell and did not charge any extra for them. Our seats were on the balcony on the front row. The show was in the Winter Gardens complex. Paul, John, George and Ringo wore identical black suits to match their black hair, leading the way in fashion. There were no boys in my circle who dressed like them. The audience was mostly young girls with their mothers. There were a few teenage boys.

I don't feel I was into Beatlemania – I was keen on Elvis, Del Shannon, the Everly Brothers and Motown – but I was keen to see them so I could show off to my friends. From what I remember of the concert, there wasn't a tremendous amount of hysteria. The boys sang about ten songs, mostly about boy and girl relationships, like 'Love Me Do', 'PS I Love You' and 'From Me To You'. The show had other 'boy' bands taking part, and Gerry and the Pacemakers may have been one of them. A few of my class mates at Market Drayton Grammar School elected to attend colleges and university in Liverpool because they were especially attracted to the Merseybeat sound. The

Beatles were good looking and they were not copying or sounding like anyone else. Over the years, I have appreciated them more and my favourite songs are 'Lucy In The Sky With Diamonds' and 'Paperback Writer'.

I WAS THERE: CHRIS SYKES

In my teen years I worked in a textile mill in Huddersfield and went with my mates to Blackpool every year for our holidays in late July or early August and nearly always finished up at the Tower every night. Brilliant days and nights. One year we arrived on the Saturday and on the Sunday morning, one of the lads' dads came over from Huddersfield and told us he had won a lot of money on horses and bought seven tickets for us to see The Beatles. We couldn't believe it, because we hadn't seen any advertising or heard they were coming anywhere.

Really excited, we went along to the Opera House. The accompanying groups which were on before them were the High Numbers – later to become The Who – who were fairly new and who did three numbers, smashing their equipment on the last one, and The Kinks. They were brilliant and then we got a countdown from ten to one for The Beatles. We could hardly hear the countdown for the incessant screaming from all the girls – and some of the lads! They kept this up until the very end of about ten numbers, finishing with 'Twist and Shout'. What a fantastic night to see three top groups like them on one night. It was brilliant, even though we were up in the gods. There were even opera glasses attached to the seat for you to use at a cost of 6d (3p) if I remember right. The other thing I remember was a bank of four Vox speakers on either side of the stage, which I thought was a lot but if they had 40 speakers it still wouldn't have drowned out the girls screaming. My parents didn't know I had been until I got home after the holiday, but they weren't surprised. I used to buy all The Beatles, Rolling Stones and Bob Dylan records at that time.

I WAS THERE: SANDRA LONGMIRE

I have The Beatles autographs from this show. Oh, and Ringo's fruit gum. I'm really not sure if it was Ringo's fruit gum but it was given to me by Mal Evans when they were packing the van. I was easily impressed at 14 years of age!

# GAUMONT THEATRE
2 AUGUST 1964, BOURNEMOUTH, UK

I WAS THERE: DAVID FELSENSTEIN, AGE 12

I was on holiday with my parents in Bournemouth and became friends with a boy of my age from Liverpool who was staying in the same hotel with his family. His family lived on Queens Drive in Liverpool, where Brian Epstein's family also lived. The Beatles were appearing at the Gaumont Theatre that night and we had tickets. I can't remember who else was on the bill but The Beatles closed both the first and second halves of the show. We sat on the front row of the Royal Circle and although the other well-known pop acts on the bill were well received, I remember there was an excited air of expectancy as we waited to see the main act.

At the end of the first half, when The Beatles were announced and they ran on stage, there was an explosion of screams and cheering so loud that even from our good seats, the volume from their Vox amplifiers wasn't enough for us to hear clearly what they were singing. Nevertheless, they were amazing, and as they played all their hits, we were on our feet shouting and clapping along with everyone else. By the time The Beatles closed the second half, my pal and I were buzzing with excitement at how fab they were and that we were actually there! The following morning, we rushed to the local Bournemouth record shop to buy Beatles records, including the *Twist and Shout* EP, which I've still got today. Since that night I've been a lifelong Beatles fan with a treasured collection of all their music, loads of books plus their movies. I've followed them all through their solo years and still get a buzz from anything Beatle related.

Having appeared on **The Ed Sullivan Show** *in February 1964, The Beatles return in August 1964 for their first North American tour.*

EMPIRE STADIUM
22 AUGUST 1964, VANCOUVER, CANADA

I WAS THERE: CHERYL THOMPSON

I worked as a dishwasher all summer in my parents' restaurant to save enough money to go to the PNE to see them. God bless my mother. She took me over to Vancouver on the ferry. Our seats were so high up I could barely see them, even with binoculars. Every time a carful of police drove up to the stage, we all went crazy screaming. I spilt my mom's coffee all over her and I was hoarse before they even arrived.

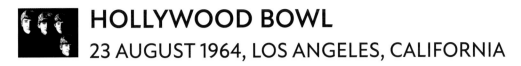

HOLLYWOOD BOWL
23 AUGUST 1964, LOS ANGELES, CALIFORNIA

I WAS THERE: ANNE STASKEWICZ, AGE 13

It was a Sunday evening and it began what would be for me a long relationship with the Hollywood Bowl, my first concert venture into the big city. The Beatles were playing the Hollywood Bowl. Somehow, Dad was always able to procure great concert tickets for me and my friends. I never asked him but in retrospect perhaps it was no coincidence that I made the front page of the Los Angeles *Herald Examiner* the next day, screaming my head off at The Beatles concert. I don't really remember actually hearing them play as the screaming was so loud. But I noted visual details like their dark suits and quirky movements because we were so close to the stage. The Bowl is a smallish venue of 17,000.

THE GARDENS
27 AUGUST 1964, CINCINATTI, OHIO

I WAS THERE: CHERI BILL, AGE 7

Having seen them on *Ed Sullivan*, when The Beatles came to Cincinnati Gardens in August of 1964, I wanted to go. Two of my sisters, my brother, my mom – yes, my mom – and I attended. We were seated upper deck, middle. The stage looked a long way off. Before the concert began, my brother leaned over and said 'when The Beatles come out, don't scream.' 'Why?' I asked. 'Only idiots scream,' he replied. Not wanting to appear like an idiot, I agreed not to scream. And the curtain opened and the light shone on The Beatles and everyone began to scream, including myself. I just couldn't help it. It's what you did to release pent up adrenaline. The girls in the row in front of us had binoculars and were kind enough to share them with us. My sister, having used them first, leaned over my brother and said to me, 'Cheri! I can see Paul's freckles!' She then handed the binoculars to me and, yes, I saw Paul's freckles too.

I WAS THERE: PAULA BROCK, AGE 11

It was sold out. We had to sit in the seats that were assigned to us. At the Stones concert in the same venue just a little over a year later, it must have been more than half empty. I have a photo of The Beatles getting off the plane at Lunken Airport in Cincinnati, Ohio and a photo of them performing on stage. The radio station WSAI brought them to Cincinnati, Ohio and put out a magazine after the concert. There's a close-up photo of girls screaming outside of the glass doors leading into the Cincinnati Gardens before they opened the venue. I know this because I am in the photo – I am the shortest one on the left with dark bangs and mouth open, and my sister is the blonde in striped shirt to the right with her eyes shut.

It had to be 100 degrees outside and 120 degrees inside the arena. I don't think they had air conditioning. Electric fans blowing would have been it. I was pretty far back even though I had bought the more expensive ticket of $5.50. I think the cheap seats were $4.50. It was very noisy.

The Righteous Brothers and Jackie DeShannon were the opening acts. The Beatles were on stage for about 25 to 30 minutes. I couldn't hear a thing but I was screaming so much it didn't matter. Before the show started, we were milling around and every time someone screamed, we would all start screaming having no clue as to what we were screaming about! My future husband, who I didn't know back then but who was there too, told me that he told his youngest sister not to scream like an idiot. She promised she wouldn't but did anyway. He also said there was a guy walking around who looked a little like George Harrison, dressed in full Beatle attire, and he had all the girls screaming at him. He was lucky he didn't get hurt. Someone was selling small squares of bed sheets for a dollar and we were told they were the sheets The Beatles slept on at the hotel. I don't know if they even stayed in Cincinatti that long.

I WASN'T THERE: THOMAS STALNAKER

In late August 1964, a classmate came over to our swimming area at the subdivision my family and I lived. He was all excited because he had gotten four tickets to The Beatles concert. The good news was that he had an extra and would I like to go with him and his friends? Like an idiot, I made an excuse and turned it down. When my friend came back, he told me that after the concert, and as he was exiting the venue, a car passed in front of him and through the window Ringo smiled and waved at him. Yeah – like that happened! After giving him a bad time about that story, he smiled and pulled out a photo of Ringo in a car pulling away.

CONVENTION HALL
2 SEPTEMBER 1964, PHILADELPHIA, PENNSYLVANIA

I WAS THERE: KELLY A WRIGHT

I met The Beatles in September of 1964 when they played at Convention Hall in Philadelphia. Although I was a month away from my tenth birthday, I still remember this surreal experience, and especially a connection with John that I still feel all these years later. My father was a disc jockey on Philly's famous rock 'n' roll station, WIBG-99 (WIBBAGE)

- that hosted the Beatles' appearance. My older brother, our babysitter and I took the train from our home, arriving in time so that I could attend the press conference, held before the show. I clutched my brand-new autograph book, with the giddy anticipation that it was going to have the signatures of a lifetime in it before the night ended.

Some horrible rule about 'no one under the age of 18' suddenly reared its ugly head, and this little girl's heart was on the verge of being broken beyond compare. It was at this point that my dad, the WIBBAGE Good Guy Hy Lit and even Police Commissioner Frank Rizzo devised a plan, that little Miss Kelly Anne Wright was to present to the Fab Four a plaque of appreciation from 'The Girls of Philadelphia'. (The large, engraved brass-on-wood plaque was pulled from an array of gifts and commendations that had arrived at Convention Hall prior to the day of the show.)

When the time came for me to present the plaque, I was to stand on a folding chair with John and Paul to my left and George and Ringo to my right. As I was nervously climbing up on the chair, I lost my footing. As I was about to fall, John reached over and firmly yet gently held my right arm to steady me. It was at this moment in time that his spirit touched mine, reassuring me, telling me not to be afraid, letting this broken little girl know that he would be with me and that I would be okay.

What John did not know, and the reason that the powers-that-be bent over backwards to make certain I not be turned away from this opportunity, was the terrible fact that, only eighteen months earlier, on April 22, 1963, my mother had died. Cancer killed this beautiful, artistic, loving 35-year-old angel. I was an eight-year-old child, thrust into a quagmire of confusion, desertion and abandonment.

The miracle began to trickle in just as the promotional copies of the Beatle 45s my dad brought home from the station did. From 'I Want to Hold Your Hand' to the mesmerising appearance on *The Ed Sullivan Show*, to the breath-taking news that The Beatles were coming to my town, I believe that my mother sent the Beatles to me, to help ease my pain. And they did. But when John took my arm on that magical day, it was as though my mother chose the one whose heart and soul would stay with me, and help me to continue to cherish music, humor, empathy and kindness.

John has stayed with me ever since; he's hanging out with Mommy.

INDIANAPOLIS STATE FAIRGROUNDS
3 SEPTEMBER 1964, INDIANAPOLIS, INDIANA

I WAS THERE: MICK VALENTI

The day I saw The Beatles is a day in my life I will never forget. When I was a child, my parents used to use part of their summer vacations to run their food concessions at different state and county fairs. One of the fairs they always went to was the Indiana State Fair and it just so happened that The Beatles were scheduled to perform. They were booked to do two performances there, one in the early evening at the Coliseum, and a second one later at the Grandstand. As soon as my brother Terry and I heard this, we ran straight to my mom for money to buy tickets. My mom, knowing we were big Beatle fans, readily gave us five dollars each, the cost of a ticket. I remember it was on a Monday that we went to the ticket office. We stood in line forever and, when we got up to the window, the old guy selling tickets looked up with a sombre look and said, 'Sorry boys, the Coliseum is sold out.' My mouth dropped in surprise and disappointment. But, just as quickly, a smile came over the old geezer's face. 'Would you like tickets to see them at the Grandstand, the late show?' he said with a slight chuckle. I'm sure that old man had a great day teasing ticket buyers.

On the day of the concert, the fairground streets were packed by noon even though the first concert wasn't scheduled until early evening. I remember my parents saying they had never seen the fair so full of people. I also remember my dad making the comment that 'in six months' time you won't even hear about The Beatles.' I jokingly reminded him of that statement many times over the years. As packed as the fair was, my parents were busy beyond belief and even though we were only eleven and nine, my brother and I were expected to help out. But around 2pm, more help had arrived and my dad said we could leave for the day.

Even though our tickets were for the late show at the Grandstand, we decided to walk over to the Coliseum and see if we could spot them. Others obviously had the same idea and we soon became sandwiched between hundreds of people, all pressed against the glass doors surrounding the building. I remember suddenly people screaming as someone thought they saw John. But it turned out it wasn't him. Then at some point we could all hear them playing and knew that any chance of seeing them was over. My brother and I decided to go back to the concession and eat before we made our way to the Grandstand. As we broke free from the crowd, we looked at each other in horror. The white t-shirts we had been wearing were covered in blood. We realised then that some of the screaming we had heard earlier came from someone being pushed into the glass doors. Upon returning to the concession, our parents rushed out to make sure we were OK. I remember them then being hesitant about letting us go to the Grandstand.

We washed up, changed shirts, ate some dinner and headed for the Grandstand. It seems we were very lucky that day as we managed to get race track seats just to the right of the stage and a perfect view. I remember a lot of Boy Scouts being there and thinking to myself 'do they need that many ushers?'. The place filled up fast. Never had I seen so many girls in all my life. My brother and I had girls sitting all around us. I remember one girl, who couldn't have been over 15, lighting up a cigarette. It was a Lucky Strike, and the reason I remember that so distinctly is that I jokingly told her that The Beatles all smoked Winston brand. She believed me, put out the Lucky Strike and got a Winston from one of her friends.

The house lights were now dimming as the noise level began to climb. Suddenly, a single spot light turned on as a little man stood centre stage. 'Good evening, everyone, and welcome to the 1964 Indiana State Fair.' The noise level continued to climb as he tried to speak. Then all I heard was a loud shout of 'The Beatles!'

The noise level was unbelievable. The girls were yelling and crying and screaming. Never in my life had I seen anything like that. The stage lights suddenly seemed to all turn on at once. No colour. Nothing fancy. Just super bright light. And there they were! Standing there, guitars in hand – John, Paul and George broke into 'Twist and Shout' while Ringo paced the music with a hard-driving beat of the drums. It was unbelievable. The crowd went wild. Girls were yelling out the name of their favourite Beatle. And every time one of the group shook their head, it seemed like there was even more screaming. About halfway through the concert, I realised why so many Boy Scouts were there. They were running up and down the aisles, putting the girls that had fainted on cots and taking them to first aid. Girls were crying, fainting, screaming. The music was straining to be heard above the noise of the crowd. It wasn't the best quality sound by any stretch of the imagination, but it was the most complete music experience anyone could ever hope for. Then, as suddenly as it started, it was over. It seemed like they were only on stage minutes when in fact it was a half hour, or so I was told later. They took their final bow in unison and left the stage. The Beatles have impacted so many lives and continue to do so even today. My nine-year-old grandson Julian recently learned 'Let It Be' on the piano. Their music and fame will live for ever. They are the greatest group of all time.

MIDWAY AIRPORT
5 SEPTEMBER 1964, CHICAGO, ILLINOIS

I WAS THERE: PAUL DUBIEL, AGE 11

In 1964 I was eleven, my sister was 13 and we were playing their new album, *Meet The Beatles*, before they came to the US. My sister found out from her girlfriends that they would land at Midway Airport in Chicago and not O'Hare, which was more appropriate, and so we got on a bus and went to meet them there. As they got off the plane, fans started jumping the fence, screaming and crying. I didn't know what to make of all this. My sister and her friends made the headlines as there was a photograph of them clinging to the fence and crying. One girl managed to grab a clump of the grass they had walked on and held it close to her face!

OLYMPIA STADIUM
6 SEPTEMBER 1964, DETROIT, MICHIGAN

I WAS THERE: ALBERT ANDRUS, AGE 17

I was a 17-year-old eleventh grader living in Hamtramck, Michigan, five or six miles from the Olympia Stadium. I went with a friend who lived two doors away. It was the two o'clock show. We didn't call them concerts back then. We started out with balcony standing room tickets, but the place got so crazy with screaming I ended up right at the stage front and took some really nice black and white photos. At the time, I was into film developing and made lots of copies that I gave to friends. But I have nothing now, not even a negative, and neither does anyone I remember giving a set to. We saw them again in Detroit in 1966.

MAPLE LEAF GARDENS
7 SEPTEMBER 1964, TORONTO, CANADA

I WAS THERE: WAYNE PARSONS, AGE 16

Like most 16-year-olds in 1964, I was consumed by the music and aura of The Beatles. There had been an NBC news report the previous November about The Beatles' phenomenon in the UK and later a clip of the group performing 'She Loves You' on *The Jack Paar Show*, an American talk show. Then in February 1964, The Beatles performed on *The Ed Sullivan Show* to a then-record 70 million viewers. By the summer of 1964, and after the release of the movie and album *A Hard Day's Night*, I was filled with anticipation of their impending visit to Toronto's Maple Leaf Gardens. I desperately wanted tickets to the show and since my dad had worked at The Gardens since 1949, I thought for sure I would have the inside track to scoring a pair. Alas, he informed me that the tickets had sold out in a matter of minutes and not a single ducat was available, not even to him. I was crestfallen.

I had a friend called Linda White who – to my great surprise – had a crush on me. She came to my rescue. When she asked me to go to the concert with her, I couldn't have cared less how she got that pair of tickets and, of course, I said yes. I had little interest in Linda as a girlfriend but even less shame in attending the show with her. Linda's tickets were in the second row of Greens, not the best seats in the house but certainly not the worst. I was on top of the world as 7th September approached.

One week before the concert my dad had a surprise for me. He had somehow managed to get a single ticket. The seat was AA-1, the first seat in the first row, about ten feet from where Paul McCartney would soon be stomping his Spanish-heeled boots. What a dilemma. Take the best seat in the Gardens and take Linda's heart and break it (which I would later do anyway)? Or give the ticket to my best friend Dave and let Linda have her night with The Beatles and me that she had been hoping for? I did the right thing. And I have regretted it ever since.

Dave knew exactly where we were sitting, and every two minutes during the show he would look up in our direction with his best shit-eating grin while the Fab Four shouted, sang and pranced a few steps from his seat. Linda soon had a different crush in her bomb sights. Her broken heart mended in about an hour. The show and the experience were unforgettable just the same.

While I sat in the Greens with Linda White, somewhere else in that crowd of 17,000 was a girl who would turn 14 a week later named Janice Cowan. Janice's parents were not happy about their young daughter going to her first concert with her friend Bev Ballantyne and no adult supervision. But, ultimately, they relented and gave their permission on condition that under no circumstances was she to go downtown to join the raucous crowd that was amassing at the King Edward Hotel, where it was rumoured that The Beatles would be staying. As her parents waited for Janice to come home for dinner before the big show, they settled down to watch the five o'clock news on TV only to see – in living black and white – their darling, sensible and well-behaved daughter at the King Edward Hotel. 'You are not going to the show' was the announcement that greeted Janice's arrival home.

Her brother Rick was almost apoplectic with joy. Janice pleaded, wept, moaned and spoke in tongues and finally her parents showed some mercy and allowed her, at the very last minute, to go. Janice ended up having the best night of her life in the same building where I was and where we both would be, 14 years later, when we had our wedding reception at Maple Leaf Gardens. The reception was to be the second-best night of her life – and the best of mine.

I WAS THERE: KITTY BOTBYL, AGE 13

I loved The Beatles, and George in particular, but I only saw them once, in Toronto. Of course, no one really heard the music because of the obviously happy screaming young ladies, myself included. I was thrilled at being able to be in the same room with them!

THE FORUM
8 SEPTEMBER 1964, MONTREAL, CANADA

I WAS THERE: TED BRENNAN, AGE 15

I was 15 when they played their only Montreal concerts. I remember a feeling of electricity up and down my spine while watching them. I kept thinking that I was in the same place and breathing the same air as them. Their set consisted of eleven songs, which meant they were only stage for about 30 minutes, not much by current standards. My other memory is of the constant sound of screaming fans during the show, which resembled jet engines. It only subsided long enough between songs for me to hear Paul's voice introduce the next song, whereupon the sound of screaming would instantly rise again. It was almost impossible to hear them singing.

In hindsight, a Beatles show was not so much a musical concert as a social and cultural experience. I was also lucky to see them twice more, in Toronto in 1965 and 1966. The experience of these two shows was very similar to the 1964 Montreal show. My belief is that they decided to stop touring in 1966 mainly because most of the fans, especially in North America, only wanted them to remain as 'mop tops' frozen in time. They realised it didn't really matter what songs were played, there was no seeming end in sight to the screaming and hysteria. *Revolver* had just been released before the 1966 North American tour yet they chose not to perform any of its new songs on this tour. This decision to exclude their latest product went against every rule of marketing and promotion.

GATOR BOWL STADIUM
11 SEPTEMBER 1964, JACKSONVILLE, FLORIDA

I WAS THERE: RICK DOESCHLER, AGE 14

I grew up listening to the British Invasion bands. I was very lucky to talk my parents into taking me and my brother to see The Beatles in Jacksonville. That changed everything for me. I was hooked on music and the guitar.

I WAS THERE: STEVE JONES

The Beatles were coming to town, town being Jacksonville, Florida. We lived just a few blocks from the Gator Bowl in a very poor neighbourhood but money was sparse for a 12-year-old boy. Hurricane Dora made a direct hit but there was a silver lining to that black cloud. After the storm, yards needed to be cleaned and I was their man. Here was my opportunity to earn enough money to buy a ticket to see The Beatles, and I did. The price of tickets ranged from $3.50 to $5.00 and I bought the cheapest one. It was enough for me. The stage was at the north end of the stadium, and I was in the second tier, along the 30-yard line at the east side. It was a good spot with a good view.

The vibe was inexplicable. No words could really describe the magic of the evening. I believe there was over 20,000 people who showed up, not bad just a week after that devastating hurricane. When The Beatles were introduced, the crowd went wild. I had goosebumps and the hairs on my arms and the back of my neck were on ends from the screaming and sheer excitement of the moment. I could only make out a few songs they sung because of the noise but that was part of the magic.

I wanted to get as close to seeing The Beatles as I could, so right after the show I scampered down to the exit for the north end of the stadium, figuring they would leave from that spot since it was close to the expressway. (I had a paper route in that neighbourhood and knew the area well.) By the time I got to the exit, a crowd had gathered, everyone thinking the same thing as me, that The Beatles had to be leaving from here in their limousine. A cop came out of the door, looked around and told the crowd that The Beatles would be leaving across the way. They all started to rush to the other exit. That didn't make sense to me and a few others so we hung back.

About a minute later, the gate opened and out came the limo. It was going to speed up but a few people rushed the car and grabbed the door handles. They slowed down to a crawl. I saw John grab his door from the inside, looking out with a smile on his face. Ringo was next to him. That was the closest I ever got to them, but what a memory. I only knew it was a segregated show a few years after the fact, but I can tell you there was no problem from anyone in the audience, before or after the show. I remember seeing black girls with buttons pinned to their dress that read 'I love Paul' or 'I love Ringo', etc. What we had that night was music from what is the greatest band to have ever existed… bar none.

BOSTON GARDEN
12 SEPTEMBER 1964, BOSTON, MASSACHUSETTS

I WAS THERE: GAIL NASON, AGE 16
On 27 August I wrote in my diary:

I got in the mail today – I am almost too excited to write; when I opened the envelope I did a cartwheel and my mom thought I had gone mad – I got in the mail a letter. And in that letter there were words and the words read: Congratulations, etc! I won a contest and the prize was two tickets to see The Beatles in person at Boston Garden. I was going to see The Beatles in person – The Beatles, the most popular singing group in the world. Thousands of fans gather wherever they go. It is something you dream about. I can't believe it!

On the day, my friend Marie Ceramicoli and I stood outside the hotel for five hours hoping to get a look at them. As the kids got over excited outside the hotel, some boys actually started rocking a parked car which brought the mounted police who proceeded to rush at everyone with their horses. I actually had to climb over a car to avoid being hit by the horse. It must have been scary for the police too as such screaming crowds were new to all of us.

We got in with ten thousand screaming girls. When we were finally inside the long halls of the Garden, a few girls actually fainted and could not fall to the ground because we were packed in like sardines. That was scary. I didn't scream and neither did Marie. We wanted to hear them. We could only hear a few notes because of the girls screaming but they were beautiful. I will never forget the screaming kids who must have been jumping up and down, because the floor was shaking. The Garden actually vibrated from the sound of the screaming, jumping girls.

Seeing The Beatles live was such an exciting thing. Of course, we were all mad about them. You could see The Beatles but could not hear them. I could not understand them screaming like that so that you missed them singing. That summer was wonderful. My friends and I saw The Beatles, the Rolling Stones, Dave Clark Five, The Animals, and The Kingsmen. What an exciting time for music. So lively and upbeat – just what we all needed. Except, of course, our parents who hated the look and the sound! I will never forget those years. I have often thought about the 'madness' of it all, the screaming crowds. I think after the Kennedy assassination we were like balloons ready to explode. The Beatles' joyfulness allowed us to explode.

I WAS THERE: SHAMO JANIE BISHOP, AGE 16

I did not have a ticket and some friends did. I tried all summer and bought a ticket at the last minute from a kid who could not go. Of course, I dressed mod like the British girls with tweed skirt and vest and bangs. I didn't ever go to my seat.

I WAS THERE: JODY ELIZABETH TUBERT, AGE 13

I was almost 14 when I got to see The Beatles in concert. That was a magical age, a magical time. Little did I know that I would leave the Boston Garden that night with my very own autographed Beatles programme. The Beatles meant everything to me. Not only did I have their autographs, but I also had their drinking glasses, ash trays and cigarette butts. Wow! Back in early 1964 I was attending junior high school and starting to get boy crazy. Months earlier, the world had been grief stricken and in total shock when President Kennedy was assassinated. I was pretty naïve and had not seen much in the way of tragedy. President Kennedy's death was devastating to me. The world would never be the same. Innocence was lost. The holidays were sad. Winter was upon us.

Then something magical happened. The radio stations everywhere started to play some new happy sounding songs by a new group from Liverpool, England. 'She Loves You' and 'I Saw Her Standing There' were about a young teenage girl just like me. The tide started to turn. The British had invaded. There were more songs and albums. Then the best thing happened. This new group The Beatles were going to be on *The Ed Sullivan Show* in February. They had taken the world by storm. The veil of grief started to lift. History was being made. A whole new era was about to begin. Music and life would never be the same.

Yeah, yeah, yeah! Beatlemania had taken over. You could buy everything from Beatles bubble gum cards to lunch boxes and pins. Everything was The Beatles. The radio stations held contests such as how many words you could make out of the word 'Beatles'. One of my friends nicknamed herself Beatlette and would call into the radio station for requests. One of my younger brothers had his hair styled into the first Beatle haircut in the city. It was a crazy time! It was electrifying and exciting.

Late in the summer of 1964, while The Beatles were on their first US tour, my father – a reporter for the Worcester *Telegram & Gazette* newspaper in Massachusetts – received a dreaded assignment: 'Jack, go to Boston and interview these four moptop boys at the Boston Garden and find out what is causing all this hysteria!' Lucky for me, he was able to take four of his seven kids with him. Of course, we each had to buy our own $5.50 ticket, which at that time was an outrageous amount! The four of us did everything we could do earn our $5.50 from mowing lawns, to babysitting – eleven hours at 50 cents an hour – to caddying at the local golf course. We were all huge fans and had been buying and listening to all The Beatles albums and records since earlier that year. Of course, our record player had to be shared with Mom and Dad and the likes of Frank Sinatra, Tony Bennett and Anthony Newley. The older folks just couldn't understand what the fascination was with these 'long-haired hippies' who sang such silly songs! Weren't they surprised when their crooners started singing some of the Fab Four songs themselves?

Finally, the day arrived. We didn't own a car so my father had to borrow one. We drove into Boston and stood outside the Garden for what seemed like eternity. I remember a hotel close by and rumours that The Beatles were staying there, so we joined the crowd and just stood there looking up. Everyone screaming, pointing, believing we just saw 'them' peeking out the window. It was like the feeling you had as a seven-year-old when you know you just saw Santa Claus on Christmas Eve and heard the sleigh bells. At some point in the afternoon, my father had to go to 'work' to interview The Beatles. Oh, how I wished I could go with him!

After the interview, he came to our balcony seats and surprised each of us with our very own autographed programme. There I was, sitting inside the Boston Garden holding my newly autographed Beatles programme, waving at the cameraman along with my siblings. We were in ecstasy and waiting anxiously for The Beatles to come on stage. What a night! Finally, the wait was over. There they were, singing and shaking their heads and laughing and jumping around and waving. The pandemonium was indescribable. This is what they sang that night – 'She Loves You', 'A Hard Day's Night', 'If I Fell', 'Long Tall Sally', 'All My Loving', 'Roll Over Beethoven', 'Boys', 'Can't Buy Me Love', 'Things We Said Today', 'You Can't Do That' and 'Twist and Shout'. My father's article appeared in the Feature Parade Section of the Worcester *Sunday Telegram* on November 15, 1964… the day after I officially turned 14. I was the luckiest girl in the world. It was the opportunity of a lifetime and one that I will cherish forever. As the commercial says – priceless.

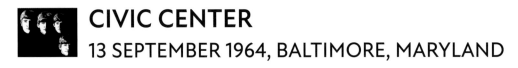

CIVIC CENTER
13 SEPTEMBER 1964, BALTIMORE, MARYLAND

I WAS THERE: DONNA CERNOHORSKY-CASENOVE, AGE 13

Imagine being 13 years old, never having been to a concert and being absolutely crazy about The Beatles. My mother took me, my sister and brother and a few friends to see them. The Civic Center was packed. We were so excited. When John, Paul, George and Ringo walked out onto the stage there was a deafening roar of screaming girls and thousands of flashing cameras. All I could think of is 'they they are, in the same building as me, breathing the same air.' Everyone was standing on their seats. The ushers couldn't get anyone to get down. I was so overwhelmed I thought I was going to explode. All I could do was cry. The Beatles were fantastic. The concert ended. We all went home with the memory that will remain in our hearts forever. Even today, when I see pictures of The Beatles or play their music, that wonderful youthful feeling comes flooding back to me. I will love John, Paul, George and Ringo forever!

I WAS THERE: NANCY MCFADDEN KERFOOT

Picture this: a twelve-year-old girl, dressed in a Beatles sweatshirt and Beatle boots. My fourteen-year-old sister, dressed the same, leads the way. The cheap boots pinch our toes and we are awkward and unsteady on the Cuban heels, but we don't care. We are going to see The Beatles! We know nothing, as we have never been to a concert, or anything like it. We've never been on our own in a big city before either, but Daddy dropped us off in front of the Civic Center and told us where to meet him afterwards.

It's a dreary, rainy Sunday afternoon. A school night, but our tickets ($2.50 each) and paid for with our allowances, are for the first show at 4pm. We merge into a noisy mob of people, mostly teenage girls, and follow the crowd inside, where our precious tickets are brutally torn, leaving us with just the stubs. Somehow, we manage to find our seats, in the 'Upper Concourse', which we now understand means balcony. But we are looking down on the left side of the stage, not way in the back, so it could be worse. We chat a bit with the girls sitting in front of us. They are just as clueless as we are. We wonder whether we will scream like the girls in the newsreels. We certainly won't cry. Crying is stupid.

Finally, the lights dim and the show begins. The tension is extreme. But we have to endure five or six other acts before our idols take the stage. We clap politely at the end of each song for each of these unwanted performers, then groan audibly as another song begins. Please get off the stage! Please let us see The Beatles!

At long last the magic moment arrives. John, Paul, George and Ringo are in our presence, right below us, breathing our air, breaking our hearts. They smile at us and goof around a bit between the beloved songs. We cup our hands over our ears to muffle the crowd noises so we can hear their voices. Ecstasy. I want to join in with the screaming, but I'm so self-conscious! How to do it? I let out a few tentative squeaks when the surrounding noise is at peak volume, until I work my way up to a full-throated shriek. The girls in front grin and nod at me over their shoulders. Got it!

Now that I know how, I scream and scream. What a way to release the tension! But not while the lads are singing, no. Wouldn't want to drown out their voices!

But then they leave the stage. The magic is over and nothing will bring it back. Reluctantly, we follow the subdued crowd down the stairs. Outside it is early evening. Kids are lined up for the second show. Some of them we even recognise from school. Yeah, I think, it was fab. Yeah, you're gonna love it. And, oh yeah, you might even learn to scream.

 MUNICIPAL STADIUM
17 SEPTEMBER 1964, KANSAS CITY, MISSOURI

I WAS THERE: DANIEL SMITH

Nothing was bigger in American pop culture than The Beatles in 1964. Kansas City was no exception. A medium-sized metropolitan area in the centre of the country, with sprawling suburbs in every direction crossing state and county lines, Kansas City, Missouri had big city amenities, including major league football and baseball. Segregation was not the law, like in the American South, but it was the custom. Municipal Stadium, located in the Jazz District, in the heart of the African American community, was the home of the Kansas City Athletics baseball team, later to become the Oakland Athletics. Charley Finley, owner of the baseball team, was known for his crazy promotions and spats with the other league owners. In the summer of 1964, he made headlines by saying that he was going to bring The Beatles to Kansas City. Updates on his negotiations would periodically appear in *The Kansas City Star* newspaper. In his final attempt to buy a concert from Brian Epstein, it was reported that Charlie offered $150,000, which was more money than anyone had ever been paid for a live show at that time. Epstein accepted and a September date was secured.

My older brother, Mark, was a record collector and ahead of most of his peers on the importance of The Beatles. Having read an article in *Time* magazine in November of 1963 and before their records were even on the radio here, he declared that The Beatles would be bigger than Elvis. He started wearing bangs and bought every Beatles recording that he could find at local music stores. By spring, I was just as enthusiastic about The Beatles and begged to get a drum set. My parents eventually bought a snare drum and paid for drum lessons. I wanted to be Ringo Starr. When *A Hard Day's Night* opened in theatres in Kansas City on August 19, 1964 (my twelfth birthday), my mother drove me and my older sister, Kathleen, to see it.

When The Beatles concert was announced, Mark petitioned our paternal grandmother to convince our parents that seeing The Beatles was a must for her favourite grandson. Mark bought two tickets. I was devastated to learn that he planned to take a date. Knowing I was going to miss a piece of history, I pouted for days. Coming home from school the day of the concert, I walked in on a conversation Mark was having with my mother. I overheard her say, 'Ask Dan. Maybe he'll go.' I asked 'go where?'. Mark said, 'Sherry (his date) can't go. Her father won't let her.' It was my lucky day. I had to give him all the money I had ($2) and my mother covered the rest.

Mark was only 16 and had been driving just since March. It's hard to believe now, but my 16-year-old brother was allowed to take his twelve-year-old brother from the suburb of Overland Park, Kansas to a rock and roll concert in the 'hood' of Kansas City, Missouri on a school night in the family car, unsupervised. It was common in the surrounding neighbourhood of Municipal Stadium for people to rent parking space in their yards for ballgames. We got a kick out of a middle-aged woman waving her flashlight and telling us to hurry or we might miss the game.

Standing on the mezzanine level of the stadium, I saw Ringo's drum kit with the Beatles logo on the bass drum. It was then that it hit me. We were really going to see The Beatles in the flesh and playing their music. Our seats were box seats near the field. The top-priced tickets were on the field, from home plate to the stage at second base. The opening act was trying to keep the crowd's attention, but as soon as a limo arrived backstage, the screaming started. After the MC announced 'The Beatles!', the screaming of teenaged girls hit a fever pitch and we decided to move back under a stadium loudspeaker where we could hear enough of the music.

It was fantastic. They played all their biggest hits, including 'A Hard Day's Night', which was at the top of the charts by then. George Harrison commanded the audience to clap their hands and stomp their feet at one point. The crowd gladly did. The concert was not a sell-out. Half the stadium seating was still available at showtime. Charley Finley lost a lot of money on the concert, but he kept his promise. $150,000 for a thirty-minute concert. That's $5,000 a minute in 1964 money. As long as my brain works, I will never forget being there. My life as a professional musician is rooted in that experience.

MEMORIAL AUDITORIUM
18 SEPTEMBER 1964, DALLAS, TEXAS

I WAS THERE: RODGER BROWNLEE

By the time The Beatles made their first concert appearance in Dallas, I was a full-blown raving Beatlemaniac. It began on a cold December day in 1963 while riding in a friend's car, when suddenly 'one, two, three, bah!' exploded from the radio speakers and the interior was flooded with the thumping beat and rhythm of 'well she was just seventeen, you know what I mean.' That was how it started. I was hooked. I wanted to be a Beatle. Then came 6 February 1964 and *The Ed Sullivan Show*. America got to see and hear what The Beatles looked and sounded like and was given a live glimpse of the reaction of ecstatic Beatles fans. My enthusiasm knew no bounds. I was extremely excited about this new sound and new look and wanted to be part of it in every way. When I learned that The Beatles were coming to Dallas, I knew I had to be there and be a part of the scene. In the intervening months I engaged in a flurry of activity, working on a construction crew by day and hanging out at the local hops on weekends. I learned where to shop for the right duds and soon had myself decked out in a Beatle outfit so I could at least play the part. When the concert tickets finally came on sale, I was first in line and bought two – one for myself and one for the lucky girl I would ask to go with me to the show. Then the day finally arrived.

I donned my Beatle outfit; slim fitting, black stovepipe slacks, white shirt with broad collar, skinny black tie and the crowning touches – my Beatle boots and collarless jacket. Completing the look, I combed my hair down all around just so. Striking a pose in the mirror, I fancied myself 'fab'. I was ready. The lucky girl I had asked to the concert got cold feet and backed out so, as a last-minute substitute, I gave in and told my fourteen-year-old sister Shela to come along. When I could get her to stop yelling and bouncing off the walls, I fired up my 1957 Volkswagen Beetle convertible and off we headed for Dallas and Beatlemania. I couldn't help but notice that girls outnumbered the boys by at least three to one. Not a big surprise there, but I was a little surprised that I didn't see any of the guys decked out as I was in full Beatle regalia, and I was a little more than disappointed that no one seemed to notice that I was!

We located our seats out on the floor, about 20 rows back from the raised stage, slightly right of centre. I had a perfect view of the bandstand for filming with my Brownie 8mm movie camera. A row of wooden barricades encircled the front of the stage and the blue uniforms of the Dallas Police Department were everywhere, including the cordon they formed in front of the bandstand. The steady hum of conversation and clatter of chairs bounced from the walls and increased in volume as the excited fans filed the auditorium to capacity and as the much-anticipated hour of show time fast approached. My heart was thumping wildly with anticipation as the MC made his introductions and the show began but subsided as the audience settled down and rewarded the show openers with ripples of polite applause, punctuated with shouts of 'we want The Beatles, we want The Beatles.' I don't remember much about the show that preceded The Beatles, except that there were two well-known artists, Jackie DeShannon and Clarence 'Frog Man' Henry, and an unknown girl trio known as The Exciters who were three black women in the mould of The Supremes and who wore orange shifts loaded with concentric rows of fringe that really shimmied when they shook. They lived up to their name, doing up tempo numbers that really rocked the house, adding to the overall excitement that filled the air.

The opening acts were done and the lights went down as the last round of applause faded into a low level hum of excited conversation that rattled around the auditorium. Then. stepping out into the spotlight, KLIF disc jockey Irving Harrigan introduced The Beatles and Ringo, followed by Paul, George and John, took the stage. From that point on, pandemonium reigned with a rising level of screams and shrieks coming from the throats of the 10,000 strong audience of mostly teenage girls. Being able to hear The Beatles play and sing was impossible so I concentrated on filming with my 8mm Brownie.

Then suddenly as if on cue, with arms flailing in the air, heads bobbing and shaking from side to side, pulling at their own hair, with tears streaming down their faces and spittle flying from their mouths, ten thousand fans rose from their seats to stand and cheer and jump and shout so that I was also forced up out of my seat in order to be able to see and continue filming. I didn't think that the decibel level of the noise could go any higher but it did.

As The Beatles finished their first song and did their famous Beatle bow, bending over deeply at the waist, the shrieks increased in volume to a crescendo that can only be produced by the frantic, fanatic fervour of fans who are half out of their minds. Then, as they began their next song, everyone began climbing and leaping up to stand in their chairs. My little sister leapt onto her chair and with tears streaming down her contorted face screamed 'Ringo! Ringo!' over and over, pounding me on the head with her right hand, totally unaware of what she was doing and totally out of her mind. In self-defence, and in order to continue filming, I climbed up on to my folding chair, balanced myself as best I could and watched most of the rest of the concert through the half-inch viewfinder of my camera, doing so even after running out of film. I just kept winding and shooting, ending up with only about a minute and a half of decent footage out of a five minute reel of film. My ears were ringing and my head was spinning as I tried to scream along with the rest. I was a little out of control myself.

At the time, I wasn't sure what songs The Beatles performed. I think their big hits 'She Loves You' and 'I Saw Her Standing There' were included and that I caught snatches of 'Twist and Shout', but I could not with any certainty have named all the songs performed if my life had depended on it. From the opening note, the noise level was deafening, something I could never have imagined, even after watching the shots of the screaming fans on *The Ed Sullivan Show*. Except for the random word or phrase, it was simply not possible to hear The Beatles. It was so loud I could not get my sister to quit pounding on me.

Then it was over; a final tidal wave of shrieks and screams burst from ten thousand sets of lungs concussing the eardrums as The Beatles made their final bow and exited the stage. The noise level held for a few remaining minutes, then just as suddenly dropped off to near silence punctuated by the sounds of hundreds of girls sobbing, plaintive last cries of 'Ringo' or 'Paul' and the clatter of ten thousand fans climbing down and untangling themselves from their chairs and heading for the exits. Out of the blue, I was accosted by a number of girls thrusting their programmes at me, asking in rapid fire: 'Are you in a band? Do you play the guitar? What's your band's name? Can I have your autograph?' I was a little taken aback, but pleased that my Beatle outfit had attracted this attention.

I WAS THERE: ELAINE BENDER

Three friends and myself ran a chapter of The Beatles Fan Club out of Fort Worth, Texas. We were interviewed on local KFJZ Radio and I read *The Beatles News* to keep fans updated. To everyone's great delight, The Beatles would include Dallas on their 1964 US tour. I was 14 years old and paid a 17-year-old neighbourhood boy to take me to Dallas and stay with me all night in line at the box office, so I could be first in line to buy tickets when they went on sale the next morning. Well, I wasn't first, but there were only about a dozen ahead of me once I got in line around midnight. Mission accomplished: four tickets at $5.50 each!

Thursday evening, September 17, 1964 and my friends and I were waiting at Redbird Airport (now Dallas Executive Airport), six miles southwest of downtown Dallas. I had received information from the official fan club source as to the time of arrival for our favourite Fab Four. The crowd was not nearly as large as I expected. We got as close as we could and watched as they came down the steps from the airplane and walked toward the waiting limo. They returned our waves before climbing inside.

Next stop was the Cabana Hotel on busy Stemmons Freeway in Dallas. Word had gotten out that The Beatles would be staying here. A crowd of mostly teen girls was pushing, shoving and shouting, trying to get into the lobby. The sound of breaking glass, police sirens, and then ambulance sirens followed as the police moved the crowd back. Those who would not leave were hauled off in police vans. A girl was seriously injured, having been pushed through a huge plate glass window, and others were cut as well. We moved to the large, grassy median of the freeway, where we sat as the entire hotel and parking lot were now off limits. A news team from the local ten o'clock news appeared with a camera in my face. 'Who's your favourite Beatle?' 'Did you witness the accident this evening?' The Beatles spent part of the next day visiting the girl in hospital who had been pushed through the window and phoning others who had been injured in that crush of fans.

As an aside, the hotel later removed the carpet from the suite that had been occupied by John, Paul, George and Ringo for two nights. Some enterprising individual purchased it and sold off small squares mounted on an official-looking certificate which stated 'The Beatles Walked Here'.

The next day, September 18, my friends and I split up and waited around the back of the hotel by exits marked 'Private', hoping at least one of us would catch a glimpse of our beloved Beatles leaving for the concert. Eventually, a limo pulled up to one of the exits and then another limo parked near the other private exit. I reached inside my bag for a hairbrush and lip gloss. Just as I was brushing my long hair, the door behind me burst open. Ringo took the hairbrush from my hand, 'Mind if I borrow this, luv?' and pretended to brush his hair before handing it back and getting into the limo with Paul. I managed to say 'hello' to which Paul replied, 'You coming with us?' as he patted the seat next to him. A man in the front passenger seat shook his head at Paul and I answered 'see you there!' John and George had apparently exited the other private door and were in that limo.

On to Dallas Memorial Auditorium for my first concert. We had floor, centre section, fifth row seats. Showtime was 8.30pm. There may have been several opening acts, but I only remember the very talented singer-songwriter, Jackie DeShannon. People often ask if I could hear The Beatles at all. The answer is 'yes', but only because we were so near the front. I doubt those fans seated further back and or up in the balcony could hear over the roar of screams. The PA systems back then were inadequate for this type of show. The amps were small and there were no microphones on them. John, Paul, George and Ringo were already so skilled at what they did together that it's no surprise they managed to do it at all, and sounded good!

The setlist they played (in order) was: 'Twist and Shout', 'You Can't Do That', 'All My Loving', 'She Loves You', 'Things We Said Today', 'Roll Over Beethoven', 'Can't Buy Me Love', 'If I Fell', 'I Want to Hold Your Hand', 'Boys', 'A Hard Day's Night' and 'Long Tall Sally'.

There was no talking in between each number, other than introducing the next song. It was a very short show, especially by today's standards, with The Beatles being on stage only about 30 minutes.

I WAS THERE: BETHENA BATEMAN SMITH

In Garland, Texas, we had a wonderful music store called Arnold & Morgan Music that carried pianos, guitars, amplifiers, sheet music, you name it. It also had a huge vinyl record section where, as a young teen music fan, I would go hang out and buy all my original 1960s albums. (In the 1970s, my husband worked for Arnold & Morgan, where many big-name bands would come for equipment, or they'd have equipment supplied by Arnold & Morgan. In May 1976, my husband got the absolutely wonderful assignment of delivering some equipment to the stage crew in Fort Worth before the opening night of the *Wings Over America* tour, Paul's first American concert after The Beatles, and of course my husband brought me along! We were able to visit with Denny Laine backstage for a bit and were extremely lucky enough to still be backstage long after the concert ended, as Paul and Linda were walking toward the front of the Fort Worth venue to a waiting limo. We introduced ourselves to both of them, and they were very kind and gracious and shook both of our hands as they were leaving. It was the thrill of a lifetime for me. But I digress…)

On February 9, 1964, my mother and I were having our dinner on TV trays when The Beatles appeared on *Ed Sullivan* for the first time. My mother thought they were very cute, and I fell head over heels in love with the band. I already loved the music from hearing it on KLIF AM in Dallas. As a 13-year-old fan, I became obsessed from that day forward. I wanted to read and listen to everything, anything to do with The Beatles…

As soon as I learned that The Beatles were touring and making a stop in Dallas, Texas, I asked my mother if we could go. Of course, she said yes! We had tickets on the lower balcony. On the morning of September 18, 1964, my mother and I drove off Stemmons Freeway to the Cabana Hotel, where the boys were staying, and I joined the crowd of fans that was watching the windows constantly and endlessly singing 'we love you Beatles, oh yes we do'. A young girl pressed up against the glass doors to the lobby by the crush of the crowd was injured, but I wasn't in that part of the crowd at that time.

My mother was a consistent advertiser in the *Garland Daily News*, and was able to arrange a press pass for me to attend their pre-show press conference. (Earlier that week, I had written 'a letter to the editor' to the newspapers that was published on the day of the press conference, asking my fellow fans to enjoy the music and not scream so much or throw any jelly babies during the show. I'm not sure it made any difference…) Armed with my press pass, I went alone into the press conference and stood along the wall, a nervous observer. I was a teenage emotional mess seeing the boys in person at the front of that room and talking and joking with the press but I managed to hold myself together.

After the press conference, my mother handed me an autographed photo of the boys that she had received from one of the employees at the Cabana Hotel. Then we left to drive past the airport runway just to see their plane on the tarmac, grabbed a late lunch and were off to Memorial Auditorium before the concert was to start that evening.

After the show in Dallas, we drove out to the airport to watch them fly off to another city, another show. They were playing 'A Taste of Honey' on KILF as I watched their plane fly away and I heard the lyrics 'I will return, yes I will return, I'll come back…' and I knew I would see them again. I just knew it.

PARAMOUNT THEATER
20 SEPTEMBER 1964, NEW YORK, NEW YORK

I WAS THERE: TOM LUKAS

The Beatles came to America and I watched them arrive on the TV news. As soon as that segment was finished, I switched to another station and watched them arrive again. I got to watch them arrive about six times! I decided I was going to go and be a part of those screaming girls. I took the subway and went to Penn Station. I thought I was going to find them. I never did.

But a few months later I found Gerry & the Pacemakers. I went to *The Ed Sullivan Theatre* and managed to sneak into their dress rehearsal. Little Stevie Wonder was on the bill. I followed them and after they performed and I went to the toilet because I knew that I had to get to the stage door before they split and I got out of the theatre, the hotel is only a block away and I went back the next day some girls told me what room they were in and said try and get an autograph and we will pay you so I knocked on the door. Brian Epstein answered, I said, 'Hi Mr Epstein, I just wanted to say hello and shake your hand,' and I got invited to the show.

The Beatles played a charity concert at the Paramount Theater in September 1964. I was part of the crowd behind police barricades, directly opposite the stage door, just a few yards away. It was still light out when one long black stretch limousine pulled up in front of us. John and Paul got out on our side of their car, paused and waved to us. They were both so tan and healthy-looking, with huge grins. Then the girls near me pushed over the barricades and tried to rush them before the stage door closed. At the same time, about ten or 20 mounted police galloped into the mass of frenzied girls.

I stayed back on the relative safety of the sidewalk. My hormones were completely different than the girls'. They didn't seem to realise the danger that they were putting themselves into.

The Beatles return to England from the USA in late September 1964. By early October, they are out on the road again.

ODEON THEATRE
11 OCTOBER 1964, BIRMINGHAM, UK

I WAS THERE: SUE MILNER (NEE LANAWAYTHET), AGE 13

One of my mates' mums had queued half the night to get us three girls' tickets for the Fab Four. We were huge fans and had a daily running commentary on our imagined relationship with each of The Beatles. We spent our breaks and the walk home fantasising about them as though we were their girlfriends. Imagine! When we went to the show, we promised each other we would not scream. Well, that didn't last long. Call it mass hysteria or whatever but we screamed our heads off. I am happy to tell you, though, that we didn't wet our knickers! At one point I was convinced Ringo was looking directly at me. That made me scream even louder and he wasn't even my favourite. For years my mum would tell anyone who would listen that 'when Sue saw The Beatles she didn't walk in the door, she floated in and no one could get any sense out of her for a week.' It was a bit like that.

I WAS THERE: JOHN BATES, AGE 12

I was lucky enough to see them twice in Birmingham. I remember them appearing at the Ritz Ballroom in Kings Heath in 1963, which was not far from where I lived at the time, but my father would not let me go as I was considered too young at the age of eleven. However, when they announced they were coming to the Odeon in 1964, my father not only queued up with me overnight when the tickets went on sale but accompanied me to the show, as did my mother. They did two shows that night. I went to the early show. They were the last act on of many acts, as they were touring with Sounds Incorporated, Mary Wells and the Remo Four. The atmosphere was terrific, but you couldn't hear much of them above the screaming. I was upstairs and many were standing up and leaning over the balcony, giving the Odeon staff on duty cause for concern. It did not detract from a memorable occasion.

I WAS THERE: SYLVIA ELLIS

I feel privileged to have seen The Beatles live twice at the Birmingham Odeon, once following the release of their *A Hard Day's Night* album, and then in 1965. I went with my friend Pat Banneville to queue at the box office early in the morning, about 7am, and got Row M. It was all very exciting.

I WAS THERE: LIZ WOLSEY, AGE 12

My friend Julia and I were twelve and queued from 5am to get tickets. There were hundreds of us, mostly females. The queue snaked round the streets and the back of the Odeon. At one point, there was a big surge which was frightening as we were all squashed together. Julia remembers an ambulance had to come when we were queuing for tickets as people fainted in the crush. But eventually we got our tickets. Julia knitted a black polo neck jumper to wear to the concert, just like The Beatles wore sometimes. The atmosphere was electric. Girls were screaming so much you couldn't hear very much. Everyone at the concert had to stand up as you couldn't see anything because those at the front stood up first. I can't remember what they played – but it was a wonderful night!

ABC CINEMA
13 OCTOBER 1964, WIGAN, UK

I WAS THERE: DEAN WALL

My mum Elizabeth saw them at the ABC, which had been known as the Ritz until 1962 and became the Ritz again in 1985. She said they were crap! My dad, Alan, remembers them playing Leigh Casino on Lord Street the previous year. Dad said Mrs Brierley who owned the Casino had booked The Beatles for two shows but when they made it big, they cancelled their second show. She tried to sue them but was unsuccessful. It's a furniture shop now.

ABC CINEMA
16 OCTOBER 1964, HULL, UK

I WAS THERE: CHRISTINE PINDER

In 1964, the support acts included Sounds Incorporated, Tommy Quickly and Mary Wells. I can't remember any of these at all – only The Beatles. Once they came on stage, we couldn't hear anything at all except screaming, including our own! After the second concert of the evening, The Beatles were taken in a police van to the local

Gordon Street police station, until the fuss died down. They changed out of their stage clothes and went to the nearby chippy in Redbourne Street. My friend lived down Redbourne Street, and was very upset to learn that The Beatles had been within yards of her house whilst she was still on the bus coming home from their concert!

LANGLAW ROAD, DALKEITH
19 OCTOBER 1964, EDINBURGH, UK

I WASN'T THERE: JOHN STOBBART, AGE 12

I grew up on Langlaw Road, Dalkeith, just outside Edinburgh, and attended Dalkeith High School. My best friend was Charlie Harrison, and his cousin was George Harrison. After two girls started a petition signed by 8,000 fans to bring them here, The Beatles came to perform at the ABC on Lothian Road in Edinburgh. George decided he wanted to visit his relatives who lived in Dalkeith and arranged everything with Charlie's mum. The visit was kept secret because it was the Swinging Sixties and the time of Beatlemania, so this was going to be something really special on our road. Charlie's mum decided that only friends aged 16 or over could come to the house for the visit after the performance in Edinburgh, because she didn't want the place overrun with kids. Charlie begged his mum for me to join in but she stood firm and would not give in. George and Ringo made their visit to Dalkeith, but I had to stay at home and didn't get to meet them.

CAIRD HALL
20 OCTOBER 1964, DUNDEE, UK

I WAS THERE: SANDY MCGREGOR

As a young reporter with the Dundee *Courier* newspaper, I attended the concert with the then Countess of Strathmore, the late Queen Mother's family, who had called our office asking if we could arrange for her to meet the group. The original idea had been for them to go to Glamis Castle, about 15 miles from Dundee, where she lived. This proved unviable and I then worked on getting them all together for afternoon tea in the home of my then fiancée, my thoughts being that it would make a great yarn for the paper along the lines of 'Countess Dines with Beatles in Council House'. That plan failed because of time difficulties, which didn't go down well with my fiancee's mother, who had used most of that week's family allowance on boiled ham for the sandwiches!

The final proposal, which worked, was for me to take the Countess to the Caird Hall

Clockwise from top left: Sandy McGregor arranged for a minor royal to meet pop royalty in Dundee in 1964; Paul Walters (pictured here with Lulu) was sent to the chippy to get tea for The Beatles; three items from Dena Hubbard's memorabilia collection; Peter Vickery still has his programme from the Exeter show; Gloria Roode's friend disappeared in the melee at the front of the stage at Ipswich.

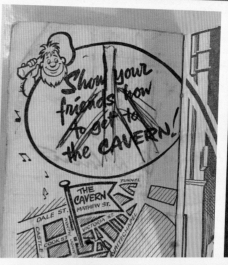

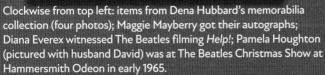

Clockwise from top left: items from Dena Hubbard's memorabilia collection (four photos); Maggie Mayberry got their autographs; Diana Everex witnessed The Beatles filming *Help!*; Pamela Houghton (pictured with husband David) was at The Beatles Christmas Show at Hammersmith Odeon in early 1965.

– the concert venue – where they could all meet for tea in a private room. Things went well and the Countess, in pearl necklace and expensive fur coat, stayed on to watch the concert from a special seat organised for her in the wings. All very strange!

I WAS THERE: DONALD STUART

My group Tommy Dene and the Tremors supported The Beatles at Dundee's Caird Hall in 1964. After playing, we had to act as stewards at the foot of the stage. I was in front of John Lennon and had a good view of them and heard their playing despite the screaming! I saw them again at the Ernst Mercke Halle in Hamburg in 1966, and again they were as good live as on record.

I WAS THERE: ALISTAIR FYFFE, AGE 17

I went with a few friends, one of whom – Bill Russell – organised the tickets. I had only started working some eight weeks beforehand. We lived in Cupar and travelled to Dundee by train. My parents had nothing to say about attending such events. Myself and a group of friends had been attending the Raith Ballroom in Kirkcaldy regularly, something I did most Friday and Saturday evenings until around 1969, and these events were much more likely to expose attendees to fights and assaults. My parents were more concerned for my safety on those nights out.

We were at the 6.30pm session and my seat was Back Stalls A15. The seat cost ten shillings (50p). Somehow, I managed to retain both parts of my ticket unseparated and while no longer in mint condition it is still presentable. Two things stand out in my memory. The noise from the audience came close to completely drowning out The Beatles, although where we were sitting may have exaggerated this, and people were throwing items onto the stage. I have a vague memory that these were sweets. My wife believes they would have been jelly babies as it was known that Ringo liked them. I have no memory at all of the supporting acts. My wife was a Beatles fan but she never saw them. It has always been a bit of an amusement in our house that I have, as I was never a great Beatles fan and was more a fan of the Rolling Stones, who I also saw at the Caird Hall.

I WAS THERE: BRIAN MECHAN

Four of us went and were on the balcony, looking down. I got a Beatles jacket made-to-measure in brown corduroy. It cost £68, which in those days was a lot of money. It was a week before they were coming to Dundee. I'd gone to the JM ballroom, one of the biggest ballrooms in Dundee, and they refused me entry because my hair was longer than most people's, and because I didn't have a collar on my jacket. I was so incensed by this that I wrote a letter to the *Dundee Courier* saying 'I wonder what would have happened if The Beatles had turned up at the door?' They published my letter.

I WAS THERE: MORAG THOMPSON

I was at the Caird Hall when The Beatles returned to Dundee, but not in the front row as I had been the previous year. I had already bought tickets but then won two tickets in a *Daily Express* caption competition. The first I knew was when someone at school spotted my name as a winner in the paper. This was a cause for great excitement as my new friend from school and I were able to give the tickets to our younger sisters – after checking which were the better seats for us! After the show, our wee sisters went running after a decoy van, thinking The Beatles were aboard and in spite of our trying to stop them.

I WAS THERE: MOIRA WALLACE, AGE 13

I was there in the front row. What a night! I was nearly 14 at the time, as was my pal Barbara Davidson. Barbara's father, Wullie Davidson, owned the famous Fort Bar in Broughty Ferry, Dundee. There were many famous regulars at the pub at that time including the Dundee FC team. Wullie Davidson knew Andy Lothian, another regular, who was a famous dance band leader and who brought The Beatles to Dundee through his agency, hence Barbara acquiring the front row tickets. I can't remember the songs sung but everyone was screaming. Some people passed out and were carried out and then had to be brought back into the hall; all girls, of course. After my husband and I got married in 1980, we used to frequent the Brax Hotel in Carnoustie. One of the guys my husband had a drink and a right good craic with was Ian McMillan, who took the famous Abbey Road photograph. One night in the early '80s, Ian never appeared. My husband asked where he was, to be told that Ian had gone to London to photograph Paul McCartney walking over the zebra crossing with his dog for the cover of a new album.

ODEON THEATRE
22 OCTOBER 1964, LEEDS, UK

I WAS THERE: SUSAN BROWN

We managed to get tickets for The Beatles and Mary Wells concert. You could only apply by post, as opposed to hours of queuing. The tickets we got were seven rows from the front in the stalls – brilliant, except that the compere, comedian Bob Bain, wound up the audience to such a pitch that when The Beatles arrived on stage, all the people at the back surged to the front of the auditorium. We had to stand for the whole of the rest of the concert. I remember one of the girls who was trying to get up onto the stage fell down into the orchestra pit. Someone else threw a cigarette lighter onto the stage and hit Paul on the head. The look on his face showed he wasn't amused. The price for the tickets for this concert was 10/6d (53p) each. I have the programmes for both the June 1963 and this concert. I can't remember how much they cost.

I WAS THERE: CAROLINE FIELDS, AGE 17

I remember going to see them at the Odeon on their very last visit to Leeds. I went with a friend from work and had good seats in the centre of stalls. I was appalled that, not only could we hear nothing because of all the screaming, but suddenly everyone began standing on their seats so we couldn't see the stage either. As a professional singer (I am a variety artiste and between the summer season and panto would 'temp' in an office) I remember thinking how awful it was that the seats would be spoilt – I had sung on that very same stage myself with Leeds Girls' Choir for their annual 'Tunes For Toys' concerts supported by the *Yorkshire Evening Post* and hated to see the Odeon being spoilt. The audience of mainly girls waved frantic arms about, stamped their feet, screamed the name of their favourite Beatle, bounced up and down on the seats, threw sweet wrappers everywhere and even stubbed their cigarettes out on the back of the seats. I had worked with the girl I was with for over three years on and off and never knew she smoked. That night she went through a packet of ten!

But I will be eternally grateful that I got to see The Beatles play live. Their music was new, alive, vibrant and easy to learn and sing along to, and all I wanted to do was dance whenever I heard one of their songs. My hero was Paul and I thought he was the best thing since sliced bread – I still admire him today! That night was great and, despite being deaf for the next few hours (due to all the screaming and the volume of the band) I count myself lucky that I was there. I wouldn't have missed it for the world. At work the following day, my friend and I had a smugness about us as we knew we had witnessed something special. The biggest band in the world had played for us!

I WAS THERE: BARBARA MARSDEN

I was unable to go to the concert although I had a ticket. My auntie arrived one day at my home and announced that she had managed to get two tickets for my cousin and myself to go to the concert. However, my dad, who was a special constable at the time and had been on duty for the previous concert and seen all the pushing crowds of screaming fans, made the decision that I couldn't go and no amount of pleading from his sister made any difference. He was adamant that I couldn't go. I can still remember feeling angry at his decision and even now, all these years later, whenever I mention it to my cousin, he just laughs and I get the feeling he doesn't even remember going to the event – which, of course, I would have done as I can very clearly remember going to another concert not long afterwards to see Cliff Richard and the Shadows and Lulu.

HIPPODROME
25 OCTOBER 1964, BRIGHTON, UK

I WAS THERE: RITA HEWETT, AGE 17

The Hippodrome was full of screaming girls, making it impossible to hear the boys singing. I went with my boyfriend at the time who kept questioning me as to which one I most fancied. I told him it was Paul, which led to him going into a mega strop which caused a break down in the relationship. I didn't fancy him much anyway as he was a Rocker and I was a Mod. My parents did not really understand what all the fuss was about when you had such good music like the Black and White Minstrels and Billy Cotton. They really had a great taste in music!

I WAS THERE: BRENDA HILL, AGE 14

My best friend Jackie asked me to queue up for tickets as I was off school ill at the time. I queued for a very long time only to be told the only tickets available were in a box. Fortunately, the lady behind me solved the problem by offering to share a box with us. The gig was on a Sunday and as my parents were very strict (and didn't know about the concert), Jackie and I went to church and tried to creep out during the service only to be stopped by one of the church wardens. I bravely explained what we were doing but I'm not sure he believed me.

   Having never been to a concert before and not knowing what to expect, I had the time of my life. Mary Wells was one of the support acts and I remember that when The Beatles came on stage, the whole theatre erupted. Teddy bears and all sorts of items were thrown on stage and it was hard to hear their music for all the screaming. I didn't tell my parents until a few years later where I went that day.

ABC CINEMA
28 OCTOBER 1964, EXETER, UK

I WAS THERE: MARY JONES, AGE 13

I will never ever forget that night. I had to beg my parents to let me go. My friend and I came out of the venue soaking wet with sweat and hardly able to move or speak, utterly drained. My parents were waiting for us. When we got in the car neither of us could say a word. During the drive home, my mum got angry with us as she thought we were being awkward, but we were both simply dumbstruck and in total shock. What a night!

I WAS THERE: PETER VICKERY

They were promoting *A Hard Day's Night*. The Rustiks opened the show followed by a solo artist named Michael Haslam. Next was Sounds Incorporated, who stayed on stage to back Tamla Motown's Mary Wells. The Remo Four opened the second half, followed by Tommy Quickly and finally The Beatles'. The show was compered by Bob Bain. All I can remember about The Beatles performance is that you could hardly hear a thing for the screaming but at least I was there, and I still have the official programme.

I WAS THERE: PAUL WALTERS, AGE 14

My father owned the gents' hairdressers in Princesshay for years. He was a referee and a cricketer and did loads and loads of sports things, so he knew thousands of people in Exeter. The owner of the ABC, Bob Parker, came across to him and said, 'We had The Beatles here the year before and it cost us a fortune in policing. You know so many people. Would you like to get maybe 40 people together to act as a human barrier and stand across the front of the stage, just to stop people getting onto the stage?' My father said, 'I'll do it as long as my son can come and possibly get to meet The Beatles. Or at least be there and stood by the stage where he gets a good view.'

The Beatles were staying at the Rougemount Hotel in Exeter. When they turned up they came in the side door of the ABC. I held the door open for them. Somebody was filming us, I think it was (TV presenter) Keith Fordyce and his crew, and I got on TV. They did two shows and in between I managed to wander into their dressing room. I said to Lennon, 'I'm playing guitar. Are there any tips you could give me?' He picked up his guitar and said 'here's a good chord'. I sat down between Lennon and McCartney and he gave me the guitar and said, 'This is the end chord for 'Can't Buy Me Love'.' I think it was C diminished 7th. And I said, 'Oh right, that's very useful that.' And Lennon took the guitar away and he said, 'Well, it's not how you start, it's how you finish is the most important thing.'

Ringo came across as he was washing his hair and he said, 'No, you don't want to play guitar. You want to play drums.' And he gave me a pair of his drum sticks, which I've still got. They actually had Ringo Starr imprinted on them. Neil Aspinall, their tour manager, then said, 'Can anybody get some fish and chips for the lads, because we've been watching Liverpool (football team) and we haven't actually eaten? They were so carried away.' So myself and Charlie, an ambulance driver who was actually helping my father, said 'yes, we'll go'. We went down to Cables and they did the fish and chips. Being 14 years old and meeting your idols, and knowing you were getting food to take back to them, I said to the woman behind the counter, 'You won't believe it but these are for The Beatles.' She said 'I don't care who they're for, love. You're not getting any more!'

GAUMONT THEATRE
31 OCTOBER 1964, IPSWICH, UK

I WAS THERE: GLORIA ROODE (NEE WILSON), AGE 16

My friend Carol and I were chambermaids at the Crown and Anchor Hotel in Ipswich. We made sure we booked our tickets for all the shows at the Gaumont Theatre. The first one was in October 1964 to see the Rolling Stones, where we were caught up in the crowd rushing the stage. They called it 'mayhem' in the local paper. When The Beatles came not long after, they had the orchestra pit filled with policeman so that events didn't repeat themselves. Halfway through the show, I noticed Carol was missing. Then I saw the policemen making a move and then some flailing arms and legs. It was her being carried out. I had a split second of thinking 'should I go to her?' but didn't. Afterwards, we all filed out and there she was, with the St. John's Ambulance Brigade. She was soaking wet. She sobbed, 'They chucked a bucket of water over my head!' We laugh about it now, but it was a crazy time. What a great time to be a teenager. I remember smoking cigarettes round my friends' houses at school lunchtimes and listening to the latest Beatles records. Paul was my favourite.

On 9 December 1964, 'I Feel Fine' is released. The Beatles end the year and begin 1965 with another series of Christmas shows, this time at the Hammersmith Odeon in London.

HAMMERSMITH ODEON
24 DECEMBER 1964 – 16 JANUARY 1965, LONDON, UK

I WAS THERE: SUE CORNELL, AGE 16

I went to see them with a friend from college whose parents worked for Marconi in Chelmsford. Their social club arranged a coach trip to Hammersmith Odeon. The line-up was The Beatles, Freddie and The Dreamers and The Yardbirds. I was rather a fan of the Rolling Stones, but my friend persuaded me to go with her as she liked The Beatles and her parents paid for my ticket. I remember The Yardbirds and how good they were – I felt they were far more talented than The Beatles. Freddie and The Dreamers were okay, with a taste of comedy as well. However, when The Beatles came on the stage, I could only hear screams from the fans in the audience which continued throughout their performance, making it difficult to hear a word they sang. I was not impressed and even if there had been no screaming and The Beatles could have been heard it would have not made any difference in my opinion. There was an interval in the performance and my friend and I, along with her parents, went to a pub next to the Hammersmith Odeon. Freddie and The Dreamers were in there and they spoke to us and gave us their autographs. They were extremely friendly. The whole experience of the evening is something I shall never forget and I can still remember seeing The Beatles with their pudding basin haircuts and wearing round-necked jackets and matching trousers. But I still prefer the Rolling Stones and their music any day.

I WAS THERE: PAMELA HOUGHTON (NEE BLENCO), AGE 26

I went with my sister Pauline and my niece Karen to see The Beatles' *Christmas Show*. It was introduced by Jimmy Savile and it was very noisy. You could hardly hear the singing because of the teenagers screaming and shouting. Everybody was shouting, but mainly girls. We were downstairs in the first row of the back stalls. My husband drove us down in his Wolseley 6/90 but he didn't come in to see the show. He went for a pint instead. Either Karen or Pauline got the tickets. In those days, you wrote to a box office and sent the cheque, even an open cheque, if you wanted to get tickets. If the show was on and was going to be a sell out, you put your self-addressed envelope in and wrote to the box office in the hope you'd get tickets. They did 'She Loves You'. They were wearing collarless suits. Karen was a great Ringo Starr fan.

I WAS THERE: KAREN SMITH, AGE 13

It was The Beatles' *Christmas Show*. It had either Rolf Harris or Jimmy Savile in. The Yardbirds were the co-stars. It was very noisy. A girl fainted near us. We were in the stalls, on the end of the row. We weren't that far back. All I can remember is the hysteria really. I couldn't say what they played or anything. They did some sketches and I think George wore a red-and-white spotted headscarf. They did a little panto.

I WAS THERE: DENA HUBBARD

I first saw The Beatles at the ABC Cinema in Northampton. The next time I saw them was on 28 December 1964 at the Odeon in Hammersmith. We sat in the circle and paid £1. I remember Jimmy Savile was compere and the Mike Cotton Sound, The Yardbirds, Elkie Brooks, Freddie and The Dreamers and Sounds Incorporated were on the bill. I saw them a couple of times after that. The four times I saw them, I didn't hear a note because of the screaming, but I can remember that they always looked smart. Three years ago, we were flying back from New Zealand to Los Angeles. We stood at passport control and we heard a voice say 'come on, girls, keep up.' I thought, 'I know that voice.' I turned around and – it was Ringo, stood right next to me!

I WAS THERE: PAUL BAKEWELL, AGE 10

I'm proud to say my very first concert was The Beatles at Hammersmith Odeon in January 1965 at the tender age of ten, which I attended with my older cousin, Maureen. All I can recall is incessant screaming and the crowd going crazy at the front when John dropped his harmonica during 'I'm a Loser'. Maureen was a keen artist and had drawn four portraits of the respective Beatles. These were given to the manager and returned signed. Happy days!

EMPIRE POOL
11 APRIL 1965, WEMBLEY, LONDON, UK

I WAS THERE: KAREN SMITH

I also saw them at an *NME* Pollwinners' Concert. You booked your tickets before the results came out so you didn't know who would be appearing but they weren't a surprise. They had topped pretty much every poll going apart from female vocalist! They used to be fantastic, those concerts. It used to be a Sunday afternoon. There weren't so many things happening or places open.

'Ticket To Ride' is released on 21 April 1965.

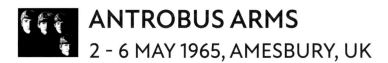

ANTROBUS ARMS
2 – 6 MAY 1965, AMESBURY, UK

I WAS THERE: JEAN DEVINE, AGE 16

When they were filming *Help!* on Salisbury Plain, we heard that they were staying in the hotel in Amesbury, 'we' being a bunch of schoolgirls. We decided to go down into the village and hang around the hotel hoping to get a glimpse of them. There we were in the foyer, five of us, probably surprised that we hadn't been chucked out, and there was no security and nobody around. In the foyer is a staircase that goes up to the rooms, and as we were standing there, in they walked in a straight line, one behind the other like they were walking across Abbey Road. They had the suits on as well. Paul gave me a cigarette – a Peter Styuvesant. At the age of 16, I declined the offer! 'Hello girls,' they all said. They were all chirpy and then they walked up the staircase. Paul was the last one up and when they got to the landing, he turned round and he beckoned to me to go up. I was much too scared to do that – so I didn't!

I WAS THERE: MAGGIE MAYBERRY (NEE DIMMER), AGE 18

I met the group whilst they were staying at the Antrobus Hotel and was able to get their autographs. Amesbury was only a village at that time and although we had the usual cafes with jukeboxes, pubs and dances, where live groups played, Salisbury and Andover were the next biggest towns to us. My friend, Sue Dimer (similar name to mine but one 'm' less!) and I were going out and thought we would have a walk down to the hotel where The Beatles were staying, just to see whether we might see them. It was a spur of the moment thing and certainly not planned, as we never ever really thought that we would see The Beatles.

When we reached the hotel, it was quite quiet and I cannot really recall much, if any, activity outside the hotel – if anyone else was there, it would only have been one or two girls but certainly not a crowd. It was early evening and we discussed whether to go into the hotel bar and have a drink. My friend was a bit unsure, but we finally went in a bit sheepishly, bought a drink and sat down. There was no one else in the bar. We sat and waited, never really thinking that we would see The Beatles.

But after a while they all came into the bar – seemingly to get a drink and take it into the dining room to eat. I scratched around in my bag, found a scrap of paper – I was not prepared in any way to get autographs – and went up to the bar where they were standing. What I remember, quite vividly, is the dandruff on their reefer jackets – not something I expected to see but it was so noticeable against the dark colour!

They did not appear to be hanging around, ie. they were getting their drink and going, so I had to hurry or they would have been gone. I managed to get John, Ringo and Paul and then asked George for his. He wrote Walter Shenson (who was the producer of their film), so I challenged him and asked him for his own name. He then wrote George 'so and so' Harrison. John, Ringo and George left the bar and Paul began to chat briefly with me. He asked me if I was resident there. I said 'no' and so he asked if my father owned the hotel. I laughed, said 'no' and that I just lived locally.

It all seemed a bit surreal and I can't recall anything else Paul said beyond that, but it must have only been brief as he then probably realised that he needed to catch the others up and just said goodbye and left the bar. My friend just sat there and watched us.

I WAS THERE: DIANA EVEREX (NEE WORT)

I remember The Beatles filming a section of *Help!* on Salisbury Plain. I was living with my family at Shrewton Lodge, a lovely house and large farm off the Shrewton-Larkhill road, bordering the road to a remote pub, the Bustard. Remember the scene in the film where The Beatles drove a tank through a straw stack? The stack was specially built by our farm workers and constructed with a hollow centre, strong walls and a single bale full height wall at each end. Of course, we went up to watch the scene being shot, luckily done in one take. I've kicked myself so many times for not getting their autographs.

PALAIS DES SPORTS
20 JUNE 1965, PARIS, FRANCE

I WAS THERE: BETH KAPLAN

I woke up early, set my hair and put on my best dress, the baby blue shift with the teardrop cutout at the front that would have shown off my cleavage – if I'd had any! The rest of the family were driving to the country for the entire day, and there was much nagging; 'be careful, don't be late…'. Blah, blah, blah…

The matinee was at 3pm so I got to the Palais des Sports at 2pm. Maybe we'd see them arrive, I thought, but no such luck. At 2.30pm, they let us in. I bought the big souvenir programme and turned it to the picture of Paul; I was ready. The Palais was round and gigantic – 4500 seats! – and at 2.30pm it was almost empty. But half an hour later it was entirely full. For some reason, the audience all around me was mostly boys, a wall of boys. We all clapped our hands, '1, 2… 1, 2, 3… 1, 2, 3, 4, let's go!'

I wasn't as close to the stage as I'd have liked but, still, the eighth row centre was not bad. A loudspeaker warned us not to use the flashes on our cameras or they would be taken away and to stay in our seats, that any troublemakers would be removed. Welcome to friendly France, Beatles. Finally, it started. The first hour and a half were some lousy groups, lots of noise and some booing. The best known were The Yardbirds. I'd heard of them but they were awful – just not The Beatles.

The Beatles' blue amplifiers were on stage and at one point they brought on Ringo's drums. There was lots of clapping but there was a piece of paper stuck over The 'BeaTles' part. When they all filed in, we applauded, so I didn't expect that there would be any screaming. French kids were so obedient. An intermission was announced but I was trembling so much I didn't budge.

Finally, everybody was in their seats, stamping and howling. The paper had been removed from the drums and I was holding the picture of Paul and I had my Brownie camera with the flash switched off. The announcer came out and got us ready, then counted down 'Dix, neuf, huit, sept, six, cinq, quatre, trois, deux, un, zero – Les Beatles!' He stepped back, a hand pushed aside the curtain and the screams went up to the roof. Scream, yell, sob, cry, adore – there they were, tall and handsome in sober dark grey suits. They smiled at us all screaming and calmly put on their guitars. Paul came to the microphone and said something, but the screams were so loud that no one heard it.

I was waving my picture of Paul – shaking, screaming, stamping my feet, clapping my hands, trying to take a photo and getting ready to pass out, all at the same time. They left the house lights on quite brightly so I was sure they could see us. They opened their gorgeous mouths and sang 'Words of Love'. We calmed down and were quiet during the song, but when it was over and the four heads went down, up went the yells again. Paul, even more handsome and cheerful than I'd ever imagined, spoke French with a Liverpool accent. 'Saloo. Mane-tenn-ante notre prochane chawnsown… chawnsin… chinsown… ' He stopped and scratched his head as he tried to figure out how to say 'now our next song'. The audience all shouted 'oui, oui' so he went on 's'appaile 'She's a Woman'. He leaned forward the way he does, to begin to sing; his teeth gleamed, his eyes twinkled.

It was at this point that, as I waved his photo, I was absolutely sure that he looked down and saw the girl in the eighth row centre in the baby blue shift with a teardrop cutout. He saw me, waving that big picture of his face in a sea of boys, and he grinned at me – right at me – inclining his head a bit. If I had died at that moment, it would have been at the pinnacle of my fine, short life.

Meanwhile, George was standing lost in the middle, looking at the floor, while John was planted firmly, his feet wide apart, surveying the audience. They sang 'I'm a Loser', 'Can't Buy Me Love' and 'Baby's in Black', during which we all swayed back and forth, stamping, clapping, singing and screaming. Then Paul announced Ringo, who sang 'I Wanna Be Your Man', which was the only time in the whole evening I glanced at him. He just sat there at the back, bashing away. His hair was too long anyway.

John's sideburns were a mess, George's was curly at the neck and Paul's was perfect, gleaming, shining. I'd always thought his hair was really dark but it wasn't that much darker than the others. Then they played 'A Hard Day's Night', introduced by John who only said 'merci' and then spoke in English. George sang 'Everybody's Trying To Be My Baby', which was just about the only time I ever looked at him. Then 'Rock 'n' Roll Music', 'I Feel Fine', 'Ticket to Ride' and then Paul said 'main-ten-ant our last song.' I screamed 'no, no' but they heartlessly sang 'Long Tall Sally', bowed, did a little dance, took off their instruments and left.

We howled, screamed, cried. They came back, bowed once more and dashed off. I didn't want to leave, but even more, I didn't want my father to be mad so I rushed out and there he was. I got into the car, croaking, sweaty, nearly blind, I was dreading his usual sarcastic commentary; he hated The Beatles. But Dad was silent. He just sat, looking at the ecstatic kids pouring past the car. 'Daddy,' I said, 'it was just the best, the best. I'll never have an experience like that as long as I live. They played all the best songs and they're so beautiful, so handsome and fun and they tried to speak French.' On the ride home, as I babbled, he didn't make fun or yodel 'yeah yeah yeah'. I kept expecting him to, but he didn't. Not once.

ABC THEATRE
1 AUGUST 1965, BLACKPOOL, UK

I WAS THERE: DERRY JACKSON, AGE 14

I believe it was the first time they sang 'Yesterday', after which John walked on stage with a bunch of flowers. As John turned to walk away, he kept the tops of the flowers and Paul was left just holding the stems! What made the day very special was that I was in the theatre all day watching them rehearse. For some reason, comedian Bob Monkhouse was there. I saw them during rehearsal do a very funny and slightly cruel send up of the Rolling Stones. I watched them laugh and joke together which proved they were very close, not just musically, but also as friends.

The single 'Help!' is released on 4 August 1965.

The Beatles return to North America for their second Stateside tour.

SHEA STADIUM
15 AUGUST 1965, NEW YORK, NEW YORK

I WAS THERE: MAUREEN GROGAN, AGE 15

I was when The Beatles came on *Ed Sullivan* and, along with my 12-year-old sister Kathy, became an obsessed Beatles fan. We were obsessed with the entire British Invasion, which brought us to the Rolling Stones show and Herman's Hermits and others who came to town. But we pretty much lived and died for The Beatles. I used to get a teen magazine every week called *16*. One week in the spring of 1965, I saw an ad for Sid Bernstein Enterprises with a PO box, ticket prices, etc. for The Beatles' Shea Stadium show to be held on August 15, 1965. I immediately freaked out and, naturally, then started asking my mother if I could go, if I could go, if I could go!

My job was babysitting but I got a lot of it so I was able to tell her that I would have the money. The tickets cost $5.65. We lived in central Massachusetts which was close to a four-hour drive to New York City at that time, but she said, 'If you get the tickets your father and I will drive you down.' The key there is she never thought in one million years I would get the tickets. Well ha-ha for her!

Myself, my sister, my two best friends Darlene and Lynn all got our money together and I went and got a money order at the bank and mailed it off to Sid Bernstein. A few weeks passed and one day I went to the mailbox outside our front door on the porch and pulled out the envelope with the tickets. The screaming, the crying, the jumping up and down and the hysteria was heard all over the neighbourhood. Some of the neighbours even joined in – the younger ones!

My dad agreed to drive so he, my mother and my grandmother all got into a three-seat station wagon with four semi-hysterical girls ranging from 13 to 15 years old. That was very brave of them. We made it to New York City on a record-breaking hot day in a non-air-conditioned car. That must've been fun but it wasn't really important to us.

My parents dropped us off outside of Shea Stadium, set up a place where we would meet after the show and four little girls from a very small city went off into the bowels of this huge stadium in the largest city on earth without a thought in our heads but Beatles, Beatles, Beatles!

The outfits were all important and we had shopped to find the most Mod outfits that we could possibly come up with in Worcester. Not quite as good as Carnaby Street but we tried. And the whole stadium looked the same. There were boys there, by the way; a young boy and his father were sitting right in front of us. We were on the very top level, sort of in the corner, and even there we recognised every single song they sang. The myth that no one could hear them has been out there for so long and it's always frustrated me. We wrote down a list of the songs they played in order and it's absolutely correct. All that we have lost is the handwritten list.

According to the note I wrote inside my programme cover, The Beatles came on stage at 9.15pm and I know it was about a 35 minute show. We jumped up and down, we screamed, we sweated, we cried, we threw confetti, we almost fell on top of the people in the row in front of us. We jumped up and down. We screamed and we screamed some more. We had binoculars that we had borrowed from a relative and I tried to put the binoculars up to the little box camera to see if I could get pictures but all we got was black film. I'm sure my hands were none too steady. I was then, as always, madly in love with John and went crazy when he was playing the keyboard with his elbow. It just seemed like typical John Lennon smart ass kind of stuff to me. I didn't know until later on that he was doing it partly because they couldn't hear themselves play and they thought no one could hear what they were doing either. We could hear!

It was 35 minutes of the most manic hysteria that teenage girls could ever withstand. Why none of us passed out considering that heat is a miracle. All of us being girl scouts or former girl scouts, we were prepared with smelling salts. The good thing about being on the top level turned out to be that when The Beatles came into the stadium they came by helicopter. The helicopter was flying around, more or less buzzing the stadium, although I did hear years later that The Beatles were taking a look at the size of the crowd and were just overwhelmed. But we could see them flying back and forth over our heads and we could see them in the doorways waving and peering out the windows. So long before the show started, we were all standing up on our seats stretching, screaming and reaching up to the sky trying to figure out which Beatle was looking out which door. Again, how we didn't fall off the chairs and split our heads open is beyond me. (I am now thinking as the mother not the not the 15-year-old hysteric.)

With the show ending came the most severe mood crash probably ever seen outside a medical setting, from the highest high to the depths of despair in seconds. By the time we got outside to meet up with our folks we were all crying hysterically. We had passed by the driveway where the Wells Fargo truck had driven The Beatles out of the stadium. It was now locked but we and many other girls were down on the ground touching the pavement, kissing it, crying and moaning 'they're gone, they're gone' over and over. This is what my mother came upon. She was not too happy that we were crying when she thought we would be so happy and grateful that they had brought us all the way to New York to see our idols. She had no concept of the emotional roller coaster that goes into something like this. She was a bit angry at first because she thought we would be happy. But in order to make us more happy she, Dad and Gram said they would drive us over to the marina and show us something that would cheer us up. It was just across the road.

We go over, get out of the car, stand along the railing on Flushing Bay and there's a big yacht. They informed us 'the Rolling Stones are on that yacht'. Well guess who started crying and screaming all over again? It turned out that while we were at the concert the yacht with the Stones and The Beatles girlfriends and wives had pulled in. They had all gotten into a limo and driven over to the stadium, passing right in front of my family standing on the sidewalk. My family had seen Cynthia Lennon and Patti Boyd, etc. sitting in the car.

One of the guys working on the boat ran into my grandmother and told her that The Beatles were coming back over there after the show to party with the Stones. My grandmother, who was terrified of water her whole life, asked this gentleman if there was any way she could get an autograph for her granddaughters who were over at the show. He walked her out on a fairly rickety pier to wait while he went into find Mick who, he said, was a really nice guy. He came out with Mick Jagger's ballpoint pen autograph on a little piece of paper from my grandmother's purse. Now if we promised to stop crying and acting crazy, my grandmother was going to give me a surprise. We did, she gave me the surprise and explained it and we all went hysterical all over again. So for a couple of years, I had an authentic partial Mick Jagger autograph with unassailable provenance. However, I eventually cut it in half with my most best friend who had been there. And one year later, I traded most of the first name to a girl who had a double Beatles album that I wanted and had no money for.

I retain a portion of the M in blue ballpoint ink and I know it's Mick's but no one else would. Of course, we did not know then that it would become the most famous concert probably ever held in the world. We just went because we adored The Beatles; they were miraculously within an area that my parents were willing to drive to, and I saw an address where I could mail away for the tickets. Thank you, Sid Bernstein Enterprises and *16* magazine.

I WAS THERE: NANCY RICHY

My first and oldest memory of The Beatles is hearing 'I Want To Hold Your Hand' in

1964. I was a faithful listener to 'The Good Guys' on WMCA in New York, and one night that song came on and I went crazy. The sound, the beat, the harmonies, the way they sang 'oooh'… it was the greatest thing I ever heard. The next day in school, all the girls were talking about this new group from England. Some of us had even brought our portable radios to school hoping to hear them during recess or lunch. I became a Beatlemaniac before the term even existed. I was obsessed with them, collecting anything and everything I could get my hands on, creating scrapbooks, etc. I remember writing to Dandy Dan Daniel, one of the Good Guys, asking how I could get tickets to their concert at Shea.

My mother surprised me and my sister with tickets for the August 15, 1965 concert at Shea Stadium. Imagine a concert having to be held in a stadium because there were just too many people who wanted to go! That's the first time anything like that ever happened. We were beyond excited to see and hear our beloved Beatles, and I remember thinking how all the people in the entire state of New York were probably in the stadium that night. To call it a mob scene is a total understatement. Never did I ever see so many policemen in one place at one time.

The audience was comprised of mainly teenage girls accompanied by their parents. Almost all of us wore dresses or skirts and blouses… that's just the way it was back then. I remember my dress was a home-made yellow and brown plaid sleeve-less A-line; little things like what I wore to the Beatles concert will never be forgotten! From the moment we arrived, there was constant chatter throughout the stadium, which increased exponentially whenever any sign of life showed on stage. Cousin Bruce Morrow was there, and, of course, Ed Sullivan. I remember grabbing the binoculars my mom brought and running down to the lowest level of our tier for a better look.

When they were finally announced, the uproar from the crowd was off the charts. I'm sure the screams could be heard up in the Bronx and down in Manhattan, and I screamed right along with everyone else. There were our idols, our dreams come true, right there in the flesh, singing for us. Who the hell knows what they were singing – the crowd was so loud we could barely hear a note – but it didn't matter because we were in the same place as The Beatles, seeing them in person, breathing the same air as John, Paul, George and Ringo. Girls screamed, cried, hyper-ventilated and fainted. A few even tried to reach the stage. It was a night I will never, ever forget. Even now after all these years, after going to countless concerts by the biggest groups of the day, even after getting married, having kids, seeing my kids get married and have babies or their own, that night in August of 1965 will always be the single most exciting and exhilarating experience of my life.

I WAS THERE: KAREN WALZ

The whole night is somewhat of a blur for me; I was not yet in my teens. My mom had surprised me (to say the least!) with tickets for her, myself and two friends to see the Fab Four at Shea Stadium. I remember dressing up a bit – as though they would see me — for the special occasion. Weather history says it was only in the 80s, but maybe because of the crowd, it seemed like such a hot night. We pretty much sat in the nosebleed section, but luckily facing the stage. I don't remember the opening acts, but do remember The Beatles being introduced and the ensuing joyful pandemonium. No sophisticated sound system, no Jumbotron. I have a vague recollection of briefly borrowing binoculars, but otherwise, from where we sat, they looked more like (as the old joke goes) The Ants. It was all but impossible to hear them, but my most distinct aural memory is discerning 'Can't Buy Me Love'. It was such a thrill to know that I was hearing their voices live! I really didn't want to be a screamer, as I was more intent on being a listener, knowing that this was probably a once-in-a-lifetime event for me – it was. My mom took some photos, and I can picture the one of me looking near hysterical, but I haven't been able to find them for a while. On the way home, Mom goodnaturedly said she couldn't hear a thing but the screaming. I was happy to tell her that I could hear some vocals, as did my friends. It was, of course, a super night to remember; probably the coolest thing my mom had ever done. My friends were so appreciative, as I've always been ever after. Mom's gone now, but I know in her own way she dug it as much as we did.

Simply unforgettable.

I WAS THERE: JO ANN GRUBBS, AGE 14

I saw The Beatles at Shea Stadium in 1965. I was in the press box seats so didn't experience as much of the craziness and I actually heard them. I was almost 15 years old and it is etched in my memory forever. I remember the excitement of the helicopters circling overhead. I had binoculars and my cousin almost ripped them off my throat when they ran on the field. I remember asking my cousins at one point during the concert 'what did Paul just say?' 'I couldn't hear it.' In watching films of that day, I noted that Paul and John were speaking gibberish at points because no one could hear what they said anyway. No matter what they said, I was in awe of just breathing the same air as The Beatles. I could never have imagined what an impact they would have on musical history. I just knew that I loved their music, their beautiful vocal harmonies and their haircuts and suits and I adored Paul the most. He just oozed joy and enthusiasm and was so darn cute. I was smitten. I have seen Paul and Ringo since and love them as much as I did as a teenager. They are incredible!

I WAS THERE: ELIZABETH COLEMAN, AGE 13

Being a small-town girl in the 1960s, seeing The Beatles in concert was just a dream. But it was every 13-year-old girl's dream. And that dream came true for me thanks to a local radio station. They sponsored a contest to see The Beatles at Shea Stadium and I was a winner. The bus ride to the stadium seemed never ending. Singing our favourite

Beatles songs helped some. Finally, we arrived and my eyes lit up with amazement. Never had I experienced anything like this.

Inside, we had our seats and nothing could be heard except our shrill screams. And the show hadn't even started yet! There was an older lady trying to give us candy to stop screaming. Forget about it! When Ed Sullivan appeared on stage, we knew it was time and time stood still. When introduced, The Beatles appeared running out to the stage. This was really happening. The screams didn't stop and I can still see John running his elbow across that keyboard. We screamed every word to whatever song was being sung. I never cried during the concert but as soon as we were on the bus after the show the tears came. I didn't want this to end. And it didn't – these moments live on in my heart forever. Thank you, John, Paul, George and Ringo for making this young girl's dream a reality.

I WAS THERE: JILL LEWIS

I saw The Beatles in '65 at Shea Stadium with my older brother and friends. It was the first time I heard girls screaming. The Fab Four were dots from where I sat and I could not distinguish one song from another. I turned around to see more of those screaming girls, and a girl who was much older than me, maybe 17, was crying and moaning 'George, George'. I thank The Beatles for introducing me to the Sixties!

I WAS THERE: JANIS PRATT

My sister Donna and I were fortunate to attend two Beatle concerts. The first was in our hometown of Baltimore in September 1964 and the second, and most memorable, was at Shea Stadium in New York. We travelled to New York on a charter bus sponsored by a Baltimore radio station with a trip that included a day at the 1965 World's Fair. We very proudly wore our BBII (Beatle Bobbies International Incorporated) uniforms consisting of a long sleeve white shirt, black tie, black skirt, and black arm band with white BBII lettering. I remember that the sun was shining, the sky was blue and there was a sense of anticipation building in the air.

Upon entering Shea Stadium, the sheer size of the stadium and the sea of people pouring in was mind blowing and increased our anticipation and giddiness. We were then filled with anxiety upon arriving at our seats in the nosebleed section and behind the net, realising that our view of the Fab Four was not going to be very good. We immediately scoped the lower bowl to find seats with a better view. Suddenly, everyone was standing and screaming – the roar was deafening! Every now and then we could catch a glimpse of The Beatles and heard a few notes and lyrics, but mostly it was a sea of jumping, crying, screaming teenage girls. We couldn't help but get caught up in the frenzy. Many girls tried to climb the barriers and one girl finally got out onto the field and began running towards the stage. This caught John Lennon's attention and he waved, encouraging her to 'come on'. Unfortunately, she was intercepted by one of New York's finest who promptly escorted her away. As the concert came to a close and The Beatles were whisked away, euphoria and exhaustion swallowed me, but the deafening roar followed me all the way back home to Baltimore. I left Shea loving George.

I WAS THERE: SHAMO JANIE BISHOP

In 1965 they did not have a concert in Boston, so all year two friends and I schemed on going to the concert at Shea Stadium in NYC. Us three high school girls found out the dates and reserved hotel rooms at over 220 NYC hotels. Of course, we lucked out with the Warwick, where The Beatles stayed. We were in the lobby but weren't allowed to check in. We even asked an elderly lady to help but we were turned away so we stayed on the street corner, looking up at the rooms and waiting for them to exit. We met a lot of fans and there was even a fight, with bubble gum, of Beatles versus Stones fans. (The Stones were at the Plaza Hotel at the time.) We only went to our room at another hotel when we needed to get ready for Shea. It was an awesome concert, with The Beatles on a stage at second base. I left before the end and was at the exit when they came out in a Wells Fargo truck. I put my hand on the window and Paul put his hand up and winked. That was over the top for this 17-year-old fan.

ATLANTA STADIUM
18 AUGUST 1965, ATLANTA, GEORGIA

I WAS THERE: DAVID BRYANT

My mother worked at the Bell record shop in High Point, North Carolina and introduced me to Beatle music. I still have in its sleeve the first record she brought home to me, the 45 of 'I Want To Hold Your Hand'. I was smitten at first listen. This was the best thing I had ever heard and from that moment on I was as big of a fan of The Beatles as she was. My mother continued to bring home all The Beatles records to me the day they arrived at her store. I'm sure I had the best collection in town.

Shortly after becoming a Beatle fan, some of my buddies and I decided to learn how to play guitar – rhythm guitar for me – and drums and start a band. It was called The Morlocks. We covered a lot of different bands including The Beatles and enjoyed a few years of local success playing the County Fair, State Fair, local dance clubs, parties, and even a local TV dance show. Music became my life and it was largely inspired by The Beatles! The store where my mother worked also sold tickets to all the rock concerts that came through Greensboro and I did not miss a show. I saw the Rolling Stones, Dave Clark Five, Beach Boys, Herman's Hermits, the Monkees, Jimi Hendrix and just about all the rest at Greensboro Coliseum, but The Beatles never came.

I listened to our local High Point radio station faithfully because they played Beatle music and one morning heard my favourite DJ, John Ferree, announce that he and his wife had put together a bus trip to see The Beatles in Atlanta, Georgia. Wow oh wow! When my mother heard about this she immediately said, 'Well, David, you have to go and I'll pay for you to go!' She did, and I think the whole trip including the ticket cost $50.

I will never forget the excitement I felt as I boarded the bus early that morning and headed to Atlanta to see The Beatles. We got there that afternoon, stopped at a YMCA, freshened up and changed clothes and then grabbed a bite to eat before heading to the baseball stadium. It was filling up quickly with mostly teenage boys and girls, beyond excited at knowing that shortly they would be seeing and hearing the greatest band in the world!

It was amazing. It was hard to believe and surreal. Everyone was scanning the stadium, some standing, to see if The Beatles were to be seen anywhere, perhaps in a dugout or 'look over there!' Sometimes screams would go up in certain sections as they thought they had got a glimpse of them. The atmosphere in that stadium was electric. I had never experienced anything like that before. I can't remember who the opening act was but my feeling was most did not care – 'let's just get on to The Beatles.' Then they were announced and I heard the loudest roar I had ever heard. They walked out to the stage and began to plug in their guitars and get things adjusted. Then they began to play 'Twist and Shout' and the screaming was so loud you really could not hear much music. The PA system was bad, but to be honest nobody cared. The incredible experience of being in that stadium at that moment, being a part of something historical that you would never forget. Seeing The Beatles live and in person!

HOUSTON INTERCONTINENTAL AIRPORT
18 AUGUST 1965, HOUSTON, TEXAS

I WAS THERE: ELAINE BENDER

My three friends and myself made the drive to Houston on August 18th. Running a Beatles Fan Club chapter in Fort Worth, we were fortunate to secure tickets for both shows in Houston through that fan club connection. We had already seen The Beatles in Dallas in 1964 and were eager to see them again. KFJZ Radio in Fort Worth sponsored our fan club chapter and Houston sister station, KILT Radio, was bringing The Beatles to Houston. First stop was KILT Radio, where we had been invited to come in for an interview and stir up excitement about the concert.

We made our way to Houston Intercontinental Airport where we would hand each Beatle a real cowboy shirt upon their arrival. We had obtained their shirt sizes from The Beatles Fan Club headquarters. Each shirt was different. Ringo was very into all things Western, so his shirt was the most colourful – red with the western braid and pearl snaps. The others were more sedate, but authentic. Blue for Paul, yellow for George and navy for John. Excitement was building as we watched their airplane land. What happened next was scary.

Fans broke through the police barricades and rushed toward the airplane. They locked the doors from inside as fans went up the steps, even climbing on the wings. The police did manage to get the girls off the airplane, but could not safely clear the tarmac. I had been knocked over once and my focus was getting out of the way of the mob and over to the side next to the terminal building. I was lucky, in that some of the crowd had been trampled and needed to be taken by ambulance to the hospital. Before long, an elevated catering truck made its way over to the airplane and the four Beatles stepped onto the top platform, protected on three sides, and sat down. I will never forget Paul's lovely face looking down at me, smiling as the truck moved past me, taking them to safety. He waved at me and I waved back. The other three looked terrified. We did eventually get those shirts to the guys. As an aside, I recall John being asked at a press conference how he liked Texas. He stated that they had only been to Texas twice and were nearly killed both times. (In Dallas the previous year, an unruly mob of fans pushed through the plate glass windows to get inside their hotel.)

 SAM HOUSTON COLISEUM
19 AUGUST 1965, HOUSTON, TEXAS

I WAS THERE: ELAINE BENDER

Sam Houston Coliseum was packed. We arrived about 1pm for the 3.30 pm show. Tickets were $5 each. We were centre floor, third row, with my seat being more toward the end of the row, right in front of Paul. I felt like he was staring right at me a few times! Opening for The Beatles were Cannibal and the Headhunters, Brenda Holloway, Sounds Incorporated, and King Curtis and his band with the Discotheque Dancers. Those of us up front could mostly hear the music. I am told by friends further back or up in the balconies that they heard screams and little else. I was focused on trying to hear every bit of the music. Not a screamer myself, I did ask the girl behind me to stop screaming in my ear. The Beatles were on stage little more than 30 minutes.

The setlist was 'Twist and Shout', 'She's a Woman', 'I Feel Fine', 'Dizzy Miss Lizzy', 'Ticket to Ride', 'Everybody's Trying to Be My Baby', 'Can't Buy Me Love', 'Baby's in Black', 'I Wanna Be Your Man', 'A Hard Day's Night', 'Help!' and 'I'm Down'.

After the show, we had dinner and came right back for the 8pm performance. They played the same set. This time, we were sat on the centre floor, fourth row. The audience stood up on their chairs once The Beatles took the stage. I was surprised at the energy level of John, Paul, George and Ringo since it was their second performance that day.

I honestly thought I would get to see them again, but they never came close enough to my hometown in 1966. Then they ceased touring (who can blame them?) and the band broke up. Beatles fans can take comfort in that each one continued to make music individually. I've lost count of just how many times I have seen Paul. A high school friend has been a member of Ringo's All Starr Band since 2014, and I have caught some of his shows too.

I WAS THERE: BETH BATEMAN SMITH

One of my aunts lived in Houston, working for the Texaco Oil company. When I asked if she could arrange for tickets to the two concerts there in August, she surprised me with a pair for each. My friend, neighbour and fellow Beatles fan, Cynthia Burton, and I travelled to Houston with our mothers on August 17th. We talked them into staying downtown in a Sheraton Hotel where the boys were staying and Cynthia and I rode up and down the elevators, along with other fans lucky to be in the hotel that day, hoping that the elevator doors would open and there they'd be! We weren't that lucky that day, but we had a ball meeting other fans and just living in the moment.

Our mothers dropped us off for the afternoon concert at the Sam Houston Coliseum and came back to pick us up that night, after the second, evening concert. It was a different world back then; we felt completely safe wandering around outside the Coliseum between shows. We walked around in a happy daze until we could go back inside to the evening concert, but other fans who were waiting said a limo was expected before the evening concert, so we joined the crowd and ran after the limo as it drove by. I *think* I saw George's face inside the car…

The evening concert was even more amazing. Our seats were in the middle section, on the left side of the floor of the Coliseum, and once The Beatles took the stage, all the fans got up and stood in the chairs to see them over the heads of the crowd in front of them. I remember a wonderful time although it was truly a challenge to hear over the screams. We had a good view of the boys on stage, so we just stood, some listening and some crying, dodging jelly beans, but thoroughly enjoying the sight we were witnessing. We never left our seats during that concert. We did not want to miss a second.

After the show, we went to the backstage area where lots of fans were waiting. We only got to see the stage door opening and closing before our ride arrived. Back at the hotel, Cynthia and I rode the elevator for a bit, not knowing if the boys had been brought back there or not. Then, exhausted, we went to our room and drove back to Dallas the next day.

I WAS THERE: RODGER BROWNLEE

In the year since I had seen them in Dallas, The Beatles had grown in popularity beyond anyone's wildest expectations, their music becoming more popular, more sophisticated and more influential. The British Invasion and The Beatles were not fading away into obscurity and practically everyone in the music and entertainment business wanted to be a part of the scene and was carried along on that wave. I was a member of The Elite, one of the most popular and successful bands in the north Texas area. Our British sound and style led KFJZ radio disc jockey Mark Stevens, to introduce us as 'the band that looks and sounds like they just stepped off the boat from Liverpool.' We revelled in the popularity and attention and became the house band at Teen A Go Go, the largest live music venue for teens in Fort Worth, sponsored by KFJZ. Little did we know that how we looked was going to lead us into trouble.

Eddie Deaton, Bob Barnes, Bruce Lair and myself loaded into Eddie's '62 Chevy Impala and headed to Houston for The Beatles show. KFJZ had provided us with great tickets for the show but hadn't booked us a motel room, so we had to make the 50 mile drive to Galveston to get a hotel room. In the morning, we drove to Houston to do a reconnaissance; we wanted to see the layout, parking and entrances at the Sam Houston Coliseum. It was only mid-morning and there were were already lines forming for the early afternoon show. Having been to The Beatles concert in Dallas the year before, I knew a little of what to expect, but hadn't witnessed anything like this.

As we slowed to a crawl, with the windows down, someone spotted us and let out a yell. Suddenly fans broke from the lines and came running towards our car, screaming and yelling all the way. Just as quickly, cops at the scene ran to intercept the runaways, while one of their number took to a bull horn to announce, 'It's not The Beatles; I repeat, it is NOT The Beatles.' Returning to the Sam Houston Coliseum in the afternoon, we were again spotted by the crowd who again mistook us for The Beatles. A cry went up, the crowd broke ranks and it was a like chase scene right out of the movies.

Thankfully, the alert Houston PD cops noticed our plight and began yelling and frantically waving us towards them. We made it just as the mob was closing on our heels. The cops shoved us through a side door and slammed it shut behind us. We blinked and looked around. The area was cavernous and empty except for a couple of janitor-looking types. It took a minute and then it hit us – we were backstage at The Beatles concert. We began exploring, sticking our noses through every door and checking every alcove. We failed to locate any of the dressing rooms; our best find was a restroom, which we desperately needed by this time. Finished with our business, we finally came to a set of stairs that led up. Looking at each other and shrugging our shoulders, we started climbing.

At the first landing, we could hear the noise and rumble coming from the gathering storm of fans. At the top of the next flight, we stepped out on to a balcony bathed in the brilliance of spot and flood lights. As soon as our eyes adjusted, we could see that we were in the balcony row right above and behind the stage. It only took seconds for the crowed below to spot us, and in one body they rose to their feet with a cheer that rattled the ceiling; at the distance we were from them, they had no idea who we were. Then all the cops located around the front of the stage turned, and looking up, began pointing in our direction and shouting orders.

In a matter of a few seconds, cops were closing in on us from all directions. One angry cop, thinking we were part of the show, demanded to know why we not backstage where we belonged, and instead up here causing all this disruption. Surrounded and intimidated by a ring of angry, scowling faces with badges, we meekly showed them our tickets and told them we were lost. With barked orders and a flurry of activity, we were hastily escorted to our seats, and told to stay put. The seats were great; only a few rows above and on the left side of the stage. The lights were down, and we remained cloaked in darkness and unobserved for a time.

Then the master of ceremonies came out, introduced the opening act and the lights came up. Before we knew it, hundreds of girls were surrounding us. The opening act, Sounds Incorporated, was largely ignored by the fans around us as they jostled to hand us things to autograph, most of which were Beatles album covers. They didn't care at all that we weren't The Beatles or that we weren't even in the show; they thought we were a band, any band, and that's all that seemed to matter. It was too chaotic for questions and answers, so they kept jostling, handing us anything that came to hand and we kept signing.

I don't recall much of the concert up to the time that The Beatles came on. It was impossible to see through the wall of young female bodies and flailing arms. The crush of autograph seekers abated somewhat only when the imminent presence of The Beatles caused them to scurry back to their own seats. Then The Beatles were introduced and pandemonium erupted.

The noise, as in 1964, was deafening, unbelievably loud. Only this time it came from two or three times more sets of lungs than the 10,000 I had witnessed the year before. Even with their new special made Vox Super Beatle amplifiers, each with 100 watts of power, the music hardly made a dent in the impenetrable wall of noise – the shrieks, screams, sobs and yells of the crowd. It was a little better for us. With the location and close proximity of our seats to the stage, we were able to catch snatches and sometimes entire phrases of 'Twist and Shout', 'Dizzy Miss Lizzy', 'Ticket to Ride', 'A Hard Day's Night' and 'Help!' amongst others, and of course McCartney's show stopper, 'I'm Down'.

Our seats also gave us a decent view of the stage, despite the obstructions, and as always, I had along my trusty Kodak Brownie 8mm movie camera and started filming as soon as The Beatles came on stage and kept it up until the film ran out. The goosebumps were crawling and the adrenaline was rushing as George, John, Paul and Ringo played the hits that we had come to hear. And then, after ten or twelve songs, it was over.

The girls continued to scream and shriek and sob and call out the names of their favourite Beatle, even after they had left the stage and the lights came up. But the show was over and fans began making their way to the exits. As we tried to rise up out of our seats, we were once again beset by die-hard autograph seekers who pulled and tugged at us relentlessly until once again we were saved by the Houston PD. They took us to a side door and turned us loose. We made it to our car a few blocks away without further incident and took stock. Other than a few bumps and a few missing tufts of hair, we were intact.

I WAS THERE: DOROTHY GIBSON, AGE 13

My parents allowed me to fly Braniff Air with my good friend to Houston for The Beatles concert. At that moment, I could imagine myself dressed as a classy hostess serving my beloved Beatles on a flight to where all my dreams came true. We were picked up by other parents at the Houston airport and taken to an all-night slumber party in preparation for the next day's event. We filled ourselves with tuna sandwiches and chocolate chip cookies. In 1965, kids were pretty much safe everywhere. About six of us well-dressed young ladies – in very mod navy top and mod dress, that I kept for years and never wore again – were dropped off at 4am for the Back to School Beatles concert to be given at 3pm that afternoon. Believe me, we were at the head of the line to get in. It was, after all, a 'run for your seat' event. Nothing could drag me away from my front-line position.

At least, not until I got sick. Remember those tuna sandwiches? They don't mix with a young girl's emotions. A very nice officer escorted me from line and I remained in his cruiser until 15 minutes before the doors opened. Yes, he made sure my place was secured and I was back in front. I can't remember if I held onto my friend's hand when we charged forward or if we were equally matched for speed. We made it though, eighth row centre.

Oh, it was so hard to get through those opening acts. We, the entire crowd, were on edge and many times thought we spied our favourite peeking through the side curtains. It must have been worse for those performers who were not The Beatles. They never had the crowd and they never had a chance. Then there they were – John, Paul, George and Ringo. I still remember that first chord. It may have been the only one I truly heard, as most everything else was drowned out by our cries of utter abandonment.

We stood not on the seats of our chairs but somehow were balanced up on the backs of the metal folding chairs. And before it even registered it was over. Of course, I can tell you how I bragged when I knew George looked directly at me and we connected. He was truly magical, as I later found out he was able to do that with other girls. Still, I knew then his look at me was personal. A friend, much braver than I, was able to sneak into the Sheridan Hilton and got a picture of George walking the hallway. I still love my copy of that photo. I told a few lies over the next two years or so about who took the picture. I had it and it was proof enough. My children celebrated August 19th with me for many years. My middle son found a video recording of the Houston 3pm concert and gave it to me one Christmas maybe ten years ago.

Then, when we attended his college graduation in Iowa, we returned to Texas via Memphis. In a little souvenir shop across from Graceland, my husband found a memory book with photos from the same concert. There are pictures looking out at the crowd. You really can't identify who's who but I still think I see me right there in that eighth row with a shout on my lips and tears in my eyes. Wow, I surely was blessed. What an experience. When we returned to San Antonio, we started a club of girls – the FLMC. This stood for Father Lennon Many Children. We disbanded when other boys became real…

COMISKEY PARK
20 AUGUST 1965, CHICAGO, ILLINOIS

I WAS THERE: ALBERT HERNANDEZ DE LEON, AGE 16

When my mom and I arrived in Florida from Cuba on one of PanAm's last flights just a week before the October missile crisis in 1962, all we had was the clothes on our back, two small suitcases and an enormous relief to have at last gotten out of that proletarian hell. And I had a list of all the vinyl LPs I was going to buy on arrival. The manager of the building where we lived gave me a small record player that Christmas, which I kept for the next three years. The number one song in the *Billboard* charts was The Four Seasons' 'Big Girls Don't Cry'. I proved to be a hardcore pop fan the moment I got off the plane on that fateful September day in Miami, and in high school in Chicago I nearly spent all my lunch money and allowance on 45s. First it was The Four Seasons – the first group I ever saw on stage in 1963 – and then Leslie Gore, The Beach Boys, Gene Pitney, Connie Francis and more.

It was during my world history class in February 1964 that someone had a copy of a newspaper with the Fab Four on the front page. My first impression was not favourable. I thought they all looked like Moe of the Three Stooges. All that changed a week later when I heard 'I Want To Hold Your Hand'. In my music class we listened to light fare like *Breakfast at Tiffany's*, *The Sound of Music* and *West Side Story*, and my teacher was not crazy about The Beatles. As an assignment, we had to do an essay explaining whether we thought the Fabs were a social phenomenon or just a passing fad. I got an A on mine, and she told me it was by far the best and most convincing one she had graded.

There were roughly 3,000 students at Waller High in Chicago in the spring of 1964, and I was one of only three guys had their hair 'long', which Beatle styles were! At one point, the principal threatened to suspend us unless we cut our hair. Then my French teacher Mme Ivoire intervened. She started a petition and we gathered over 1000 signatures, so the old fart gave up and left us alone. That summer, The Beatles came to town and tickets were gone within an hour. I was shattered. But I did not totally despair. Between my oodles of mags and singles and outings to the local radio station lobby with mod friends with fake Liverpool accents on Saturday afternoon, life went on.

The following year I saw The Hollies, Yardbirds, Herman's Hermits, the Stones, The Animals, The Dave Clark Five and another two dozen other bands. Me and my friends combed every hotel in town until we finally would find the band. Then the pics, autographs and parties would follow. But we were just biding our time for the return of the Fab Four. Finally, the big day was announced. By then, people in school were calling me the fifth Beatle. We were the envy of those unlucky ones who did not get tickets.

On the morning of 20th August, a friend whose aunt worked at the Sahara Inn by the airport called to tell me they were staying there. I was sworn to secrecy, but by the time we got there at noon, there must have been 500 frenzied teenagers in the parking lot screaming at the top of their lungs. A hundred police and security guards firmly stood between the crowd and the entrance. It was absolute pandemonium. I started scheming with my friend Christopher on how we could get in through the back and we sneaked away from the crowd and forced our way through a side door service entrance. We moved stealthily but cautiously, not knowing where the hell we were going.

We heard women's voices and hid in a laundry closet until they had gone. A few feet ahead there was a staircase, so we decided to take it all the way up to the top, while carefully scrutinizing for any movement – or British accents – on every floor. When we reached the top floor, two security guards saw us and gave chase. We scrambled up to the roof and started running. The crowd down below saw the chaos and started cheering for us. They were hysterical as we outran the guards. We went to the far side of the hotel and proceeded down the opposite staircase when suddenly – British accents!

We hid in a broom closet as the two guards continued speeding down the stairs, passing us. We then emerged, thrust the hallway door open and saw a dozen men in suits. And George, walking from one room into another! Obviously, some of these men were roadies and guards protecting them. Like idiots, we screamed 'George!' He turned around and said 'hello' but by then we were already in the arms of two gorillas handing us over to the two security guards. We were unceremoniously marched downstairs and thrown out into the cheering crowd. We were almost crushed by the inquisitive multitude.

In the next issue of *Fabulous 208*, the Chicago correspondent who happened to be present went on to describe this madness in her weekly column 'and suddenly, two blokes wearing matching lavender shirts with black ruffles down the middle were being chased by security guards on the roof, and the crowd went wild with cheers and yells of encouragement, as they soon disappeared into the hotel below.' I was famous! Britain would read about me and Chris!

We arrived at Comiskey Park Stadium shortly after noon. Ticket purchase had been mail order only, with no lines at the box office. Luckily myself and my two best friends, Linda and Rhonda, got tickets to both afternoon and evening shows. We were within the first five rows, but what difference did it make? The stage was almost an entire city block in the distance. We had binoculars and cheap Instamatic cameras, but these could not even begin to capture the four figures which soon broke into song. I did not hear a note. It was just screams and more screams. Looking back on it, I would have loved to hear them as well as seeing them. But, hey, who was complaining? The scenes of total madness and pandemonium were repeated that evening at 8pm. It was more exhilarating at night than in the afternoon! My diary could not hold all the emotions I experienced that day. The next day, I was hoarse and exhausted, as if I had run a marathon. I think half of the 35,000 fans that saw the performances either slept all day Saturday or spoke on the phone. Mom was just beside herself as that's all I talked about for the next month.

I WAS THERE: RICH PINE, AGE 11

I saw them for the first time on *The Ed Sullivan Show*, three days prior to my tenth birthday, so by the time I saw them live, I had been a rabid fan for a year and a half. Besides my wedding and the birth of my children, this was one of the most unforgettable days of my life. How many people can say their first ever concert was The Beatles? They played at old Comiskey Park, a baseball stadium and home to the Chicago White Sox baseball team. A raised platform had been constructed in the vicinity of second base and The Beatles and their opening acts – Brenda Holloway and the King Curtis Band, Cannibal and the Headhunters, Sounds Incorporated – performed from there. There was no audience seating on the field itself, only in the stands where one would normally be during a ball game.

There were two shows that day – one at 3pm and another at 8pm. I was at the three o'clock show with my nine-year-old sister and my aunt's roommate, the person who took us. She was in her early to mid-30s at the time, but was head of the steno pool at the Wrigley Gum Co and had a number of late teen and 20-something women who worked under her. Their enthusiasm for The Beatles had rubbed off on her and, knowing my sister and I were crazy about them, asked my parents if she could take us. Thankfully they agreed, otherwise it never would have happened.

It was a beautiful sunny day and August can be very hot in Chicago. My recollection is that it was warm but not overly so. It seemed to take forever until The Beatles came out – I knew Cannibal and the Headhunters, not so much the other bands. But all I cared about was seeing the Fab Four. When they finally did come out, they had to run across the field from one of the dugouts to the platform and the audience went bananas. The screaming began full force and everyone was on their feet. When they began playing, it was difficult to hear, but you could tell what songs they were playing. I clearly remember John doing runs on the keyboard with his elbow during 'I'm Down' and George at one point turning from his position on the stage and running toward the edge of the platform, facing one part of the audience with his arms open. You could physically see that part of the crowd react as though they'd all been hit by lightning at the same time. They played 'Help!', 'She's a Woman', 'Ticket To Ride' and 'Dizzy Miss Lizzy'. When it was over and they were gone, I remember looking back over my shoulder up into the stands. Here and there were scattered groups of girls – most of them older than me – sitting in their seats and crying.

The Beatles had a huge impact on my life. I started playing drums because of Ringo and just two years ago realised my dream of owning a new black oyster Pearl Ludwig kit, built to the same specifications as one of the kits he used while a Beatle. In high school, I made an animated film with another student using 'You Know My Name, Look Up The Number' that got us an honourable mention in the Kodak Student Film Awards Contest in 1973. I will die a Beatles fan...

MEMORIAL COLISEUM
22 AUGUST 1965, PORTLAND, OREGON

I WAS THERE: PAMELA J LORD

I was 14 and had just started high school. My best friend's father bought her two tickets to see The Beatles at the Memorial Coliseum and she asked me to go with her. This was the first music concert I had ever been to. The air and vibe were electric! It was one of those experiences you will never forget. When we had the chance, we moved from our seats to the sideline with several other screaming girls, waving and shouting as The Beatles played.

HOLLYWOOD BOWL
29 & 30 AUGUST 1965, LOS ANGELES, CALIFORNIA

I WAS THERE: CATHY SANCHEZ

Two of my good friends and I went to the Hollywood Bowl. We had pinstriped pants made especially for the concert, and our black turtle neck tops and boots. I remember all the screaming and crying all around us. One friend, Nancy, was crying and saying how much she loved John. The very next day we went to the movie theatre and watched *Help!*

We even took binoculars to get a real up-close shot. I have a sweatshirt now that I wear out sometimes that says, 'Yes I am old, but I saw The Beatles on stage.' People will come up to me when I'm wearing the sweatshirt and ask me, 'Did you really see The Beatles?'

I WAS THERE: ANNE STASKEWICZ

I attended back-to-back Beatle shows at the Bowl and remember hearing them play. I even wrote down the playlist. They were much less formal than on their first visit to the Bowl the previous year, joking with the audience and skipping around on stage. In those days, there was a water-filled moat in front of the stage and John spat into it several times and nearly fell in at one point. Opening for The Beatles on the first night, which was a Sunday, were The Discotheque Dancers, Sounds Incorporated and others. Our seats were stage right again and even better than the previous year – in the boxes! I recall the celebs who were around and in front of us; Sonny and Cher, Dino Martin, Joey Paige, a Beach Boy or two, Joan Baez, a few Byrds and Shindogs, even Debbie Reynolds. Were we old enough to drive, we'd probably have driven up after the concert to Benedict Canyon, where they were staying.

It was after show number two at the Hollywood Bowl, on the Monday night, that I came closest to The Beatles. When Paul announced that 'I'm Down' would be the last song, the whole audience surged toward the stage. John pointed for someone to jump into the moat and several girls did. By 1965, my friends and I were already veteran groupies and, as all knowledgeable groupies do, we staked out the stage exit and were caught up in the surge of fans surrounding the armoured truck that ferried them out of the Bowl. I somehow got wedged between a policeman and the rear window of the truck and suddenly was face to face with George. That was the closest I ever came to a Beatle!

COW PALACE
31 AUGUST 1965, SAN FRANSICO, CALIFORNIA

I WAS THERE: MICHAEL SCOTT, AGE 16

I went to see The Beatles on their second tour of the US with three buddies from high school. I remember very little about anything that preceded The Beatles taking the stage. When the band began, pandemonium broke out. We left our seats and inched our way towards the stage through a sea of hysterical young girls, winding up three back from the barricade on Paul's side of the stage with security lined up between it and the stage. There was no air and very few boys up front, just batshit crazy young females! One actually bit my ear lobe and said 'boys shouldn't be up front'. 'OK,' I said, 'but I ain't moving.'

The Beatles were dressed in camel tan military-style jackets and black slacks. Paul and John looked amused by it all. George looked freaked out, maybe even scared. There was a cymbal in front of Ringo's face so I don't know how he looked. The screaming was as loud as their playing. It never stopped!

The lack of breathable air started causing girls to pass out. There was no way to get them out of the fracas so the security behind the barricades started passing the girls up to the roadies who were crawling around The Beatles and they would pull them to the back of the stage. Some girls got the idea of faking passing out and, once they were pulled on stage, they would come to life and go after a Beatle. Just frigging crazy. Paul, who was about ten feet from me, was doing his thing whilst keeping an eye on the zombie girls being dragged across the stage. He looked a bit bewildered and amused.

In front of me was a very petite girl with a bigger one in front of her and then the barricade. Then the security cops, then the stage and Paul. I noticed that the little girl seemed to be getting smaller. She was supported by the girl in front and by me from behind. I tried to bring her to with no success. Alerting the security, I passed the little zombie to him. The whole while, Paul was watching what was happening. The security passed her up to a roadie crawling around Paul's feet. This little zombie was out and didn't return to the living. Looking at the floor, I saw a coat where the girl had been. I grabbed it and held it aloft, yelling to get anyone's attention. The roadie was right behind Paul dragging the little zombie. Paul was taking it all in, seemingly concerned. I threw the coat at the stage. Paul caught it with the neck end of his Hofner and pitched it back to the roadie. When he turned back to us, Paul smiled and gave me a wink. It was kind of like 'we got it done!'

I WAS THERE: PAM MAZZUCHELLI

My friend and I had twelfth row seats. I easily got up near the stage when they sang 'Ticket to Ride'. I was on the left side of the stage and got to look up at Paul, who was almost directly above me, and then John joined him to sing. The screaming was deafening, so I only heard muffled voices and odd notes. The show was stopped after a few songs and The Beatles left the stage. Luckily, they returned and continued. The show wasn't long, and my friend got up near the stage only to be pushed back by security. Unfortunately, we missed our ride home to Campbell, 50 miles away, and we ended up at the police station with about thirty other underage girls. I was in big trouble for a long time.

Around 1994, many Beatle fan clubs were cropping up here in the States. One of my cousins, also a Beatle fan, had been flying around the country attending many of these conventions. She told me that at a convention in Chicago she met Alf Bicknell, one of the Beatle chauffeurs. I listened politely thinking, 'Yeah, yeah, yeah, anyone with an English accent could claim that.' A few weeks later, she urged me to go with her to Logan Airport in Boston to pick up this 'chauffeur' because he was going to speak at a conference somewhere in Rhode Island. I went with her and learned he was the real deal. In the car, he told us he was writing a book based on diary notes he made during his years with The Beatles.

Long story short is that I ended up putting together the manuscript for him on disc. The book was later published in 1995 by Jack Edward Productions, as *Alf Bicknell's Personal Beatles Diary*. (I think the book and VHS tape are still available.) The part that struck me about this book is that while I was typing this daily diary of Beatles' concerts, and came to the August 31, 1965, entry – the one I saw – Alf had written an additional page about how dangerous that performance was and how it was the only time he had been on stage (to carry off girls) while The Beatles played. Photographs of him carrying off fainted girls in his arms appeared in the book. Also, I saw some footage of that performance recently and, when the concert was stopped because a girl managed to get on stage and grab Paul's guitar, Alf is seen behind George helping him down the steps to behind stage. I still can't believe that such a ruckus went on and, although our seats were close to the stage, we had no idea.

The Beatles return to London in early September. After a few weeks off, October and November are largely spent in the studio. December sees the group commence what proves to be their last British tour.

 # ABC CINEMA
7 DECEMBER 1965, MANCHESTER, UK

I WAS THERE: PETER HOWARD

They sounded great! Despite all I have read about not being to hear them over the screams, there were speakers overhead and so I could hear them clearly! The very strange thing about the evening was the atmosphere, which was quite remarkable and very highly charged. The sound of the girls was like being next to a jet engine! And when The Beatles finally walked on stage playing the intro to 'Dizzy Miss Lizzy' – well, it was like seeing God! It was an unforgettable night.

 # ODEON THEATRE
9 DECEMBER 1965, BIRMINGHAM, UK

I WAS THERE: JOHN BATES

I went with a friend but as in the previous year, my father and I queued up for most of the night a few weeks before to get the tickets. The tickets were just normal cinema stubs typical of that era. Sadly, I no longer have the tickets but I do have the programmes and newspaper cuttings about the concert. They only performed for about 30 minutes and were accompanied by The Paramounts and The Moody Blues.

I WAS THERE: SYLVIA ELLIS

By the second time I saw them they were even more famous. My friend Liz Russell and I decided that in order to get decent seats we should stay out all night. We both fibbed to our moms and said we were staying at each other's homes and setting out early. The problem with this idea is that we had no creature comforts like hot drinks and blankets and it was very cold! But we struck up friendships with some girls from Wolverhampton who shared tea with us. I remember one of them was a girl called Margaret from Penn in Wolverhampton who afterwards sent me autographed photos she had obtained plus a photo of George's parents on a visit she made to Liverpool. We were so excited and a cheer went up when the box office opened after a long and chilly night. We got two end of row seats on Row L and we were elated to go home with our precious tickets. Roll on 11th October!

When the day came the excitement was overwhelming and off I went with my sequinned sash, with Paul carefully sewn on it. But, unfortunately, it was stolen from me by a steward when I waved it in the air when the band came on. I was gutted. The poor supporting act, which I cannot recall, had no chance as we all wanted the boys to appear. I will never forget being in the darkness and the anticipation and then the twang of the first note of 'I Feel Fine'. That was practically all I heard as the screams were deafening and this continued throughout. I remember Paul taking a position on his own and we assumed it was for 'Yesterday', but we couldn't hear that much! It went by so quickly, like a dream.

Next day, I couldn't speak through screaming. I had decided at the concert that I may as well join in with everyone else and I thought I had gone deaf. Despite this, I would not have missed it for the world. The lads had on grey or electric blue mohair suits. They looked great whatever, even if we could not hear them!

I WAS THERE: SANDRA LONGMIRE

Fast forward to 1965 and we heard that The Beatles would be appearing at the Birmingham Odeon in December. By this time, they were worldwide famous so tickets were like gold dust. A very good friend of ours called Bernie went and queued all night to get the tickets for us. Our tickets were in the balcony, but it was good to see our idols again. We didn't all have cars in those days and we went to Birmingham by train, not thinking to find out what time the last train was. On arrival at Birmingham New Street, after the show had finished, the train had of course long gone, probably at 9pm! We came home on the milk train at about 3am. There were no mobile phones in those days so I guess our parents must have been worried. Teenagers, eh?

I WAS THERE: PAUL LUTON, AGE 14

We queued up all night long to get our tickets. I remember the queue stretching all around the back of the cinema and us being quite a way from the front and hoping that they wouldn't sell out before it was our turn. After many hours standing in the queue it was our turn. I purchased two tickets, one for me and one for my best mate, and we got the 15-shilling (75p) ones which were the better seats. We were so excited and, looking forward to the show, we soon forgot the long wait the night before.

The main thing I remember about the show itself was that the noise was so loud with the crowd screaming and shouting that you couldn't hear a word that The Beatles were singing. But that didn't really matter as we were seeing the greatest ever band live right in front of our eyes. I can't remember how long they were on but it didn't seem too long compared to today's artists. When you tell people that you have seen The Beatles live, they are almost in awe of you, such was the kudos of seeing the greatest band ever actually performing. I can't believe it was nearly 60 years ago.

HAMMERSMITH ODEON
10 DECEMBER 1965, LONDON, UK

I WAS THERE: ROGER GOUGH

In mid-1963 I moved to London and joined the Met Police and after training was transferred to Hammersmith to serve in uniform there. The Beatles played the Hammersmith Odeon to full houses more than once and I was employed with many others on crowd control. Many years later, on retirement, I had moved to Ham in Surrey and spent quite a bit of time in a local betting shop. In doing so one makes many acquaintances. One guy I regularly chatted to called John had been born and bred in Hammersmith and lived on the same street there as me. He was, shall we say, a rough diamond but despite him knowing of my time in the Met he was always willing to chat. One day, talk turned to The Beatles and he volunteered the story that as a young scallywag he had shinned up the drainpipe at the Odeon when The Beatles were playing there one night, got into their dressing room and nicked John Lennon's wallet. On reaching the ground again, he stole money from the wallet and then threw the wallet and John Lennon's driving licence down a drain! He bemoaned the fact that he didn't keep the licence. How true his story was I don't know, but he seemed a genuine type of guy who had perhaps matured over the years.

I WAS THERE: CHRISSIE OWERS

My dad loved John Lennon and managed, through a friend of Brian Epstein, to get five tickets – for him and Mum, my 14-year-old brother, me (aged twelve) and my seven-year-old sister. I remember Mum kicking off about how much they had cost. We all set off to the Odeon in Hammersmith in Dad's Austin Somerset. We lived in Finchley so the drive was not long. I remember I was wearing a red tartan dress with a white collar. I can't remember being so excited about anything in my life. There were lots of bands playing before they came on. When The Beatles came out, the screaming was so loud you could hardly hear them. I screamed too. Paul was my future husband (I had decided). Sometimes there was a break in the screaming but never for very long. My brother spent his time picking up items thrown at the stage. It was quite a haul – perfume, sweets, etc. Driving home, my ears were ringing and I had a sore throat but I was the happiest girl on the planet. I remember telling the girls at school but nobody believed me. I still play their music and still love a bit of Paul.

The double A-sided 45, 'Day Tripper'/'We Can Work It Out' is released in the UK on 15 December 1965.

Between January and June 1966, The Beatles keep a low profile, concentrating on recording and other activities until performing a handful of dates in Germany in June and then one off shows in Japan and the Philippines.

'Paperback Writer' is released as a single in Britain on 22 June 1966.

ERNST MERK HALLE
26 JUNE 1966, HAMBURG, GERMANY

I WAS THERE: ANNETTE HANL

In 1963, I was 12 years old and very innocently went to my friend's birthday party. The girls were playing games, but one of the presents my friend received was the single, 'I Want To Hold Your Hand'. Curious, I put it on the record player, not knowing what was about to happen. The music started to play and it was as if lightning had struck me! I was no longer interested in playing games with the other young girls. I sat glued to the record player, lifting the arm of the player over and over to the beginning of the song so I could listen to it. The melody went right into my heart, the feeling was so strong and I felt something unique had happened. It was overwhelming; this music somehow lifted me to another sphere.

It was music just for us young ones. Our parents, who were rigid and authoritarian, had no access to it. It was ours. But it also gave us, and me, a feeling of being taken into another world that was out of reach for our parents. I could feel the music physically. I was totally in love with the music but also with the lads... and especially with Paul. We all were...

In Germany, we had a teen magazine called *Bravo*. Each week, they published parts of the image of a star in a feature called 'Star Cuts'. Over several weeks we would assemble these parts until we had a star on our wall. We had been fans of Winnetou, a fictional Apache chief from novels written by Karl May and played in movies by Pierre Brice. The Winnetou star cut was removed and replaced by the Beatles photograph. Winnetou was history now...

At school, we talked about the music and who was a fan of which Beatle, hoping we weren't in love with the same Beatle as our best friend. I was lucky; one friend loved Ringo and the other one George. We waited impatiently for the next single or album release. I only had a little pocket money and could not afford the LP, but my boyfriend owned *With The Beatles*, and we sat in his room and listened to their music.

We learned everything we could about them; how only three years earlier they had started their career in Hamburg at the Indra, the Kaiserkeller, the Top Ten and the Star Club. Being only nine years old then, I missed all that, but it felt great to know they had been walking in the streets of my home town. I even started to eat with my left hand in adoration of Paul. I could not become a complete left-hander but ever since then I have eaten left-handed!

The TV programmes changed and music for young people got more air-time. We were glued to the screen waiting for news from The Beatles and other groups. We followed all the news about them – where were they playing, what they were up to, including news about *A Hard Day's Night* and *Help!*

And then came the news we all had been waiting for; they were coming back to Germany. The Bravo Blitztournee! I had to see them. I needed to get a ticket. I sneaked out the door of my home very early on the morning the tickets went on sale to stand in line with lots of other fans. And guess what? I got my ticket! I could hardly believe I was holding it in my hands. I would see them for real! I was so happy.

And then... tragedy. Just days before the concert, I came home from school with a bad grade in maths or history, my worst school subjects. My father was so angry that he forbade me to go to the concert. I was devastated, crushed. I burst into tears, I could not believe he said that... In my despair, I went down on my knees in front of him in prayer pose and begged him: 'Dad, please, don't do that to me, please let me go, pleeeease!' Tears were running down my face. I felt numb... I don't recall how long that went on but I got through to him and he let me go! I probably I would have run away from home if he hadn't.

It was a crazy atmosphere in the music hall. I was pretty close to the stage, on the third row, and stood on the left side. I was never the girl screaming; I just stood there in disbelief that they were there, in front of me, playing, and I silently cried tears of joy. I was so happy.

Their music was so so important to me... it carried me through adolescence, it was not easy at home, but their music soothed and comforted me, I could bathe in it and it relieved the pain and distress. My father was a classical music fan and he did not understand this music of ours. 'Turn off that fake music,' he would say. 'This music will be gone soon, it is nothing compared to Bach and Beethoven.' Well, little did he know that, 60 years later, in 2022, there would be a programme on TV heralding Paul's 80th birthday in which the commentator said what Paul and the boys achieved and the influence they have had on the music scene ranks with that of Mozart and Beethoven.

I once created a Beatles tour through St Pauli for my photography group, leading the participants to the different places, including the Bambi Kino and the Jägerpassage where John's photograph was taken in the doorway... it was fun. The Beatles have been and always will be an important part of my life. I am so grateful to have been part of those days. Even though I was a little too young to see them in Star Club times, I walk around St Pauli knowing that this is where they used to walk and this is where it started. All you need is love!

On 11 August 1966, The Beatles fly from London to Chicago to begin what is to be their last tour of North America. Or anywhere.

 # INTERNATIONAL AMPHITHEATRE
12 AUGUST 1966, CHICAGO, ILLINOIS

I WAS THERE: ALBERT HERNANDEZ DE LEON

If we were lucky to have seen The Beatles twice in 1965, we were even luckier in 1966, when me and my two girlfriends, Lin and Rhon, got second row right in front of Lennon at the Amphitheatre with only a cordon of policemen and a six feet high stage separating us from them. Both my girlfriends were huge fans of John while I was rather fonder of George. The scene was even more chaotic in a closed environment. I thought my friends were going to faint, as many gals did. There were many guys in the audience this time around but not as many nor as frenzied as I. First came The Ronettes, then The Cyrkle and finally The Beatles. The roar of the crowd was deafening. Even mothers and their pre-teen daughters were there, as well as a few grandfathers. The sound was better this time but from the second row it was hard not to catch a few notes.

 # OLYMPIA STADIUM
13 AUGUST 1966, DETROIT, MICHIGAN

I WAS THERE: SEAN EDDY, AGE 5

I don't remember it but my mom says that I asked her to make all the girls stop screaming so that I could hear the music.

I WAS THERE: VALERIE H WARD, AGE 15

The first time I saw them was in 1964. I had just turned 13 years old and was way up in the balcony. The second time, I was just one row off the floor and way in the back. But I remedied this. I caught a glimpse of Paul behind a curtain at the stadium. He was wearing a red shirt. I was a *Datebook* magazine teen interviewer and I wanted to get behind the curtain and do a brief interview. I had my 'press' badge but the police security would not let me through. Hey, I gave it my best shot!

  The Beatles wore pin-striped suits for the performance. Even though I sat straight in front of them I was quite far back. There was such commotion. I managed to leave my seat and found my way up to the fourth or fifth row from the stage. No one was in their seats anyway. I found an empty seat and quickly took it. A couple of times, I left my camera on the floor next to my seat. At one point, I did not even care if I lost the camera, I was too caught up in the moment and all I wanted was to touch them. I never thought that this would be the last time I ever saw them as The Beatles.

CLEVELAND MUNICIPAL STADIUM
14 AUGUST 1966, CLEVELAND, OHIO

I WAS THERE: BONNI GRANATO, AGE 15

$5.50 seemed such a bargain for that ticket. I only got $1.00 a week allowance back then, so I had to get a loan from my mom and went for five and a half weeks without so much as a ten-cent cherry coke in all that time. It was the best sacrifice I ever made! I remember The Cyrkle, and Bobby Hebb singing 'Sunny', but not any of the other groups, as we were there to see a phenomenon that we had never witnessed before. About ten minutes after The Beatles came on, the chain link fence that was there for security was broken down and the crowd rushed the stage. You could barely breathe due to the pushing and shoving. It was mass hysteria. My leg was caught between other fans' legs and kids were climbing and standing on our legs for a better view. Some of the guys were grabbing girls' breasts because they could get away with it.

  The Beatles were taken off stage and would not be brought back out unless everyone returned to their seats. Once the massive frenzied crowd returned to their seats, the fence was erected again. Looking back down on the field, there was a sea of trampled clothing, crushed umbrellas, broken cameras, shoes, etc. The Beatles returned and began playing. Who knows what song it was because you could never hear them. The fence was broken down again and I made it to the front of the stage. The Beatles were laughing and Paul motioned the girls forward. I jumped up to touch his boot and got hit with a policeman's billy club. I saw stars! They took The Beatles off stage and the concert was over. The next day at school, I was covered with bruises from the frenzied crowd and had a big goose egg on my forehead that I was very proud of. It was the night of my life!

I WAS THERE: LINDA MADON, AGE 20

Only two Beatles concerts were ever stopped by the police. Both of them happened in Cleveland, and I was at the one in 1966. Cleveland Municipal Lakefront Stadium was a huge baseball venue. The stage was situated on second base, with the rest of the field empty except for a phalanx of police. I was a 20-year-old art student at the time. The opening acts were The Ronettes, Cyrcle, Bobby Hebb, and The Remains. They were all terrific, playing their hit tunes of the day. The Beatles finally appeared. They were wearing dark green, double-breasted suits with green satin lapels (I had binoculars). The crowd went ballistic! During the third song, the crowd rushed the field, all but emptying the lower stands. As the cops lost control, the boys unplugged and ran for their lives to a trailer at the back of the stage. Mayhem ensued.

Everyone waited as the cops cleared the field. We were all afraid that the concert was over, but after 55 minutes everybody was back in their seats. Thankfully, the boys came back out and picked up where they left off. I was sitting in the front row of the upper deck. I could see that the crowd was policing itself. Every time somebody tried to jump the fence, the crowd would pull them back in, knowing it would all be over if anyone stepped on the field again.

I was lucky to be seated near a speaker, so I could hear them quite clearly. They played so tight they could have been lip-syncing, if not for the minor variations from their recorded material. I recall their harmony on 'Baby's in Black' was sheer perfection. It was an incredible evening that I'll never forget. Oh yeah, I paid $5.50 for my ticket. I still have it.

DC STADIUM
15 AUGUST 1966, WASHINGTON DC

I WAS THERE: NEIL FAUGNO

I saw The Beatles during the period where John Lennon had made the statement that 'we are more popular than Jesus' and there was some concern for their safety, especially in the south. There were opening acts, of course, to get the crowd all anxious and excited and then a limo pulled onto the field behind the stage and all eyes were then on the car in anticipation of their arrival. Well, nothing was happening and then I heard some cheering and looked down and The Beatles were standing outside one of the dugouts, waving at a crowd that mostly thought that they were in the limo. They were then escorted to the stage and started to play.

There was screaming and flashbulbs galore but the sound was poor and as a musical event it fell short. But there was one very interesting happening. A young man got on the field and raced to the stage with police and security in hot pursuit. The band was playing 'Ticket to Ride' with John singing the lead. The man made it to the stage, climbed up and John hit him with the butt of his guitar, sending him into the arms of security. John never missed a beat.

I WAS THERE: BETH KAPLAN

I saw them in Washington DC in August 1966, just before they stopped touring for good. And for good reason – it was a terrible experience, a vast football stadium and so much noise. It was hideous and deafening, and impossible to hear anything. I feel very fortunate that my Paris experience was in a very small venue and so tightly controlled by the French authorities that we could see and hear everything. It was a great blessing and is one of the great memories of my life.

I WAS THERE: JACKI REESE, AGE 11

By 1966 they were playing stadiums. My sister saw them at DC Coliseum in 1964, which is smaller but still pretty good size. I wore my first miniskirt to The Beatles' concert at DC Stadium. It was bright orange and came to the middle of my knee, so it really wasn't as 'mini' as I thought it was. Though we were a good 500 feet or more from the stage, my friend Susie and I were convinced that Paul looked at us! I had seen the Rolling Stones the year before. The ticket cost six dollars.

I WAS THERE: DAVID BRYANT

1966 found The Beatles under a cloud of controversy because of John's comments about them being 'more popular than Jesus'. Some in my family encouraged me to destroy my records and never see them again, but on 15th August I went to Washington DC on that same bus trip to see them one more time. Their last tour!

This time I carried a portable battery-operated reel-to-reel tape recorder to try and capture the concert experience on tape. Well, I did capture some music and mostly screaming but it was fun to listen to it and let my friends hear it. My girlfriend went with me on this trip and I thought I was going to have to carry her back to the bus after the concert. Once again, the experience was incredible and I will never forget it. Sadly, my mom, who was so instrumental in me being a Beatle fan and even paying for my trips to see them, tossed my ticket stubs and tape recordings in the trash while cleaning out the attic one day. Oh well. I still have the memories!

'Yellow Submarine'/'Eleanor Rigby' is released as a single in Britain on 17 August 1966.

MAPLE LEAF GARDENS
17 AUGUST 1966, TORONTO, CANADA

I WAS THERE: SUSAN VALLEE, AGE 15

My mom was born in Liverpool so some of my cousins went to school with them. My cousin Barbara lived next to George Harrison's family. She would bring him to school when he was the new kid on the block. He was eight or nine and Barbara was 13. I was hooked on The Beatles since I was 12 in 1963. I saw them in 1964 on *The Ed Sullivan Show* and that was it! In 1964, The Beatles came to Montreal but I couldn't go – my dad was against it. I was too young at 13 and at the time I was living in Quebec. The next year, they came to Toronto and two of my best friends won a trip plane to go and see them. I was so sad that I could not go, as all this time I had been in The Beatles fan club.

The next year, 1966, I learnt that they would tour again so I bought a ticket in January to see them in August in Toronto with the fan club, and with my beat friend that saw them the year before, and with Rodrigue, who is now my husband. The tickets were $5.50, and the bus to go from the city of Quebec to Toronto took eight hours or more and was $50. We left two days before. The bus was full and it was Beatles songs for all the trip.

We went to the airport hoping to see them but they had gone before we got there. We went to the Sheraton Hotel and waited to see them there, but no luck, and then we went and sat outside the Maple Leaf Gardens listening to the afternoon gig. I was just so happy knowing that I would see them in the evening.

We finally got to the evening show and it was just magical, 25 minutes of pot-pourri. And the screaming! It blew my mind. I was just in heaven and got back home two or three days later. I was so blessed and lucky because that was the last year of them touring.

Later on, I saw George live in Montreal with Ringo and Ravi Shankar, Paul in 2008, Ringo in October 2014, and Julian Lennon in 1987. I treasure all my beautiful memories. I've been to Liverpool twice to visit my family and to visit Beatles places. I've been to Abbey Road in London. My hubby is a drummer and our life is full of Beatles stuff. I still live by them. They still rock my world.

I WAS THERE: PETER MEISNER

I bought two tickets for my friend Tom and I to attend one of the first rock concerts we had ever enjoyed, and a first in Toronto! In the following years, we would be regulars at every good concert coming through town, including the Rolling Stones, Rod Stewart, Elton John, Billy Joel and Jimi Hendrix (just to drop a few names!). But the Beatles concert was something special and unique, for us and the world. There was lots of fan noise with little in the way of a light or stage show.

Clockwise from top left: JoAnn Grubbs was at Shea Stadium; Nancy Richy remembers 'the single most exciting and exhilarating experience of my life'; Elaine Bender caught her second and third Beatle shows at the Sam Houston Coliseum; Pamela Lord was screaming and shouting along with everyone else; Chrissie Owers and her family travelled to Hammersmith in her dad's Austin Somerset; Pam Mazzuchelli didn't realise the Cow Palace show was nearly ended by stage invaders; The Beatles inspired David Bryant to form a band called The Morlocks, and wear a top hat.

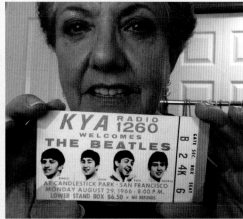

BEATLES REUNION: IT MAY BE JULY 5

THE PROSPECT of a Beatles comeback concert took a dramatic turn this week with the news that American promoter Bill Sargent has already set a tentative date for the event. He hopes to stage it on America's Bicentennial Day, July 5, though it would not necessarily take place in the United States. Sargent has told the Beatles that he would set it up in whatever location offered them the best tax advantage.

This is an extremely relevant point, because it now appears that the Beatles could earn as

much as £100 million from this one gig. Sargent has already increased his original guaranteed offer to £25 million, and the group would also take a percentage of the profits. These are likely to be immense, since the concert would be screened on closed-circuit TV throughout the world, and it would also be filmed and recorded.

It has always been understood that George Harrison was the main obstacle to a comeback because — unlike John Lennon, Paul McCartney and Ringo Starr — he was reportedly not keen on

the idea. But this problem now seems to be overcome. Although Harrison remains silent on the project, his father has stated that George has now agreed to do the show. He added that there is a distinct possibility of the Beatles remaining together for subsequent shows, although there is no question of a long-term reunion.

Lawyers representing the four Beatles have reportedly been instructed to sort out the details of the proposed comeback concert. There are apparently no serious difficulties, but various contractual issues have to be resolved.

Clockwise from top left: Bonni Granato saw The Beatles in Cleveland (two photos); Linda Madon took her binoculars to the show; Dianne Hicks has been waiting to meet Paul for nearly 60 years (two photos); a Beatles reunion was regularly mooted in the press, this time in 1976; Vickie Schall was at Shea Stadium.

SUFFOLK DOWNS RACETRACK
18 AUGUST 1966, BOSTON, MASSACHUSETTS

I WAS THERE: SHAMO JANIE BISHOP

I went to two more Beatle concerts, in 1966, one in Boston and then back at Shea. I worked at a cookie factory to get enough money that summer for the concerts and for the train fare to NYC. I loved all four of The Beatles. Each of them was so unique and, as they grew, I grew as well. I even ended up at the *Concert for Bangladesh* and, later, in India. Together they were such magic and the voices for a generation.

I WAS THERE: PAM GIORDANO, AGE 15

I was a hopeless Beatlemaniac, as were a few of my friends. We lived in Maine and spent every day talking about them and dreaming of meeting them. When we heard they would be performing in Boston, 170 miles away, we knew we had to find a way to go. We saved our money. I even sold my bike to be able to afford to go. We sent for tickets and drove the postman crazy until they arrived. I think we paid $5.75.

Then came the task of getting there. We bribed two of the mothers to chaperone and drive us. We all chipped in for gas and paid for their hotel. My parents were not going to let me go but, after many tears, they finally agreed! There were eight of us so there were two cars.

When the day finally came, we decorated both cars with Beatle posters and signs that said 'Boston or Bust'. We were quite the sight on I-95. We got there only to find out our room was not available because of an airline strike so they put us up at The Robin Hood Inn. We all stayed in one room and the chaperones in an adjoining room. It turned out to be more fun.

Well, we made it to the stadium. They were nose bleed seats but we were there and the excitement was electric. The Beatles finally took to the stage in dark green suits with pearl buttons to the deafening sound of screaming. Little did we know this would be their last tour together. I believe they ended the show with 'Yellow Submarine' but don't quote me – it's been more than 50 years! We were all in a daze and we all had laryngitis after the show.

Needless to say, none of us slept that night. We bought out every newspaper in the hotel as soon as they were delivered, to the dismay of the other guests. We woke our chaperones at the crack of dawn to take us to the airport to see the Fab Four off – they weren't too happy with us! We climbed fences to get closer but security kept us at a distance. We got our final look – a lot closer then than we got at the stadium. They waved as they boarded the plane. It was a quiet ride home, our eyes red from crying and voices hoarse from screaming, but our dream had come true.

I'm still friends with Jane, who was one of the girls who came on that trip. I look back 50 years later and realise how important this experience was in my life. I had a rough childhood and I believe if it had not been for these four guys I would not have got out as well. They were my distraction. They shaped me as a person and my love for music.

I WAS THERE: MAUREEN SMITH

I have been a fan of the Beatles since I saw their first appearance on *The Ed Sullivan Show* in February of 1964. Like most teenage girls, I was totally in love from that moment on. I could not wait to buy their first album and get every teen magazine their faces adorned. When I heard they were coming to my city, the excitement was overbearing. Thanks to my mother who stood in line to buy tickets for me and my friend while I was in school, I was going to Boston Garden to join all the screaming girls and scream along with them. That was September of 1964. I was only 14 years old but that day changed my life forever.

Now you would think that would be enough to please a young girl at the time... but when I heard they were coming back to the USA in 1966, nothing would stop me from going. This time they would appear at Suffolk Downs, an outdoor venue located in East Boston. But the story gets even better. Since I had the best seat possible, little did I know that to get to the stage John, Paul, George and Ringo would be passing right by me. Their hair blowing in the breeze as they rushed by me, their faces so young and handsome. My heart was in my throat. I will never forget that night. It was spectacular and the chance of a lifetime. Now I have created a Beatles page on social media to have people share their comments and experience of the greatest band in history. It's named 'Yes I Saw The Beatles Live In Concert' and I can say I truly did.

I WAS THERE: LAUREEN STAROBIN, AGE 16

It was my very first concert. When people started sobbing, fainting and running toward the stage, I looked overhead thinking maybe a plane was dosing us with something. I didn't get it yet. But I loved every moment of the music and have been hooked ever since. What an introduction to concert going!

MID-SOUTH COLISEUM
19 AUGUST 1966, MEMPHIS, TENNESSEE

I WAS THERE: JANIE MILLER, AGE 16

I got my best friend Gwen to go with me. I found out they were coming via *Teen* magazine before it was advertised locally and sent my money in to the local ticket office in Memphis, not even sure at that point if my parents would let me go. The tickets were $5.50 each. I was so excited I could hardly stand it. We lived in a small town called Cleveland, Mississippi, 110 miles south and two hours away from Memphis. After the tickets came, my mom called my friend's mom to work out the details and they decided that we could spend the night at my friend's grandmother's house, which was down the street from the venue in Memphis.

There were two shows that day and we were at the night show. The Ku Klux Klan was in the parking lot, as this was right after the statement that Lennon made about the Beatles being 'bigger than Jesus'. They were protesting because of that and there were some people who were burning their albums also in protest of his statement. It was a tense time, but I never felt any of that and was oblivious because of my excitement.

Our seats were about the 27th row on the floor of the Coliseum so not too bad, much better than up in the stands. There was so much noise when they came out, you could not really hear the songs. It did not matter though, just being in the same room with them was enough and such a huge thrill. The opening acts were The Cyrkle and Bobby Hebb. They were both good but it was so hard to contain our excitement for The Beatles to come out.

When they did come out the roar was almost deafening. It felt like a dream. My friend was not quite as into them as I and was a little reserved. Everybody was screaming around us and we weren't. I guess we were both shy about that but finally I said, 'I am going to count to three and let's scream' so that is what we did! We did not scream the whole time like most of the girls did, just in bursts every now and then. How funny.

The show so passed quickly and then it was over. Although we did not want to, we left immediately the show was over to meet Gwen's mother, who was picking us up from the venue. As we drove down Southern Avenue by the Coliseum to Gwen's grandmother's house, a white limo passed us. We thought it was them leaving the Coliseum. It really might have been – you did not see limos, much less white-coloured ones, in 1966, and they were on the road from the Coliseum out to Memphis airport, which was close by.

When we got to her grandmother's, we went straight to bed with visions of Beatles in our heads and it took a while for me to go to sleep. We did not know at the time, as there was way too much noise and we were too far back to see it, but a cherry bomb was thrown on stage during the show by someone at the front, scaring The Beatles. This was part of the reason they did not tour any more after that.

Because of The Beatles, I became a huge British Invasion music fan. I loved so many of those groups and still love to listen to the old songs. Music has been a huge part of my life since The Beatles landed and it continues to be so. Our parents thought we were crazy to like those Beatles but they did not understand the joy they brought. I remember getting a birthday card from my daddy and I still have that card. He enclosed a $10 bill and wrote in the card, 'Please do not buy Beatle records with this money.' The girls in my mother's day could scream over Frank Sinatra. Why couldn't we scream over The Beatles?

I WAS THERE: LINDA SCHAFFER

I've been to so many concerts that I hardly remember, except for maybe one thing – The Beatles in Memphis was horrible because people were screaming so loudly.

I WAS THERE: FLETCHER TERRY, AGE 10

My mother told me that she had heard that The Beatles had been booked to play two concerts at the Mid-South Coliseum. Since my birthday was on 21st August, Mom asked me what I wanted for my present. 'Would tickets to The Beatles concert do, Fletcher?' My immediate answer was 'yeah, Mom, that would be fantastic.' She was one of the first people to order tickets by phone. Back in 1966, there was no internet, no presales, no Ticketmaster or any other sort of ticket brokers and she managed to score tickets close to the stage for the then expensive price of $5.50 each.

As the day got closer, Mom made our travel plans. I was in hog heaven counting down the days until I was able to see my favourite band. Finally, that day arrived and we left our home in Cleveland, Mississippi to make the two plus hour drive to Memphis on Highway 61.

It seemed to take an eternity but we finally arrived and secured a parking space right outside the venue. We noticed a couple of Klan kooks with their picket signs on the way to the Coliseum and a couple of random protestors with their 'Beatles Go Home' signs, but we didn't pay them any attention. We made our way to our seats and waited through what seemed like another eternity until The Beatles hit the stage. The Ronettes were the opening act, followed by Boston band The Remains, whose set lasted about 30 minutes. The Remains were followed by the Pennsylvania group The Cyrcle, who had a huge hit that summer called 'Red Rubber Ball'. After their thirty-minute set, the last warm up act was Nashville musician Bobby Hebb whose big hit that summer was the song 'Sonny'.

Finally, after two hours of warm up acts, the moment was at hand! The Beatles took the stage around 10.30pm. The audience started screaming at the top of their lungs. I could barely hear the opening number, 'Rock 'n' Roll Music'. There were no sophisticated sound and PA systems. The Beatles would just run their Vox amps through the arena's PA. You would not believe how loud the crowd noise was. I have never ever seen or heard anything like it since. And it seemed like everyone and their brother was taking pics; I was almost blinded by all the camera flashes.

The second number they played was 'She's a Woman', which featured my favourite Beatle, Paul. He was the spokesman for the group and made small talk with the crowd after each song. The next song they played was 'If I Needed Someone'. About a minute into the song, I heard a loud explosion. I was intently watching Paul so I didn't actually see that a cherry bomb had landed close to George Harrison. When the bomb went off, Paul took a quick look to his left to make sure that his bandmates were okay. To their credit, The Beatles never missed a beat. The kid who threw the cherry bomb was arrested. Apparently, he was trying to impress his date and needless to say she wasn't impressed.

The rest of the concert went by very quickly. The only tune I could really hear well was 'Yesterday'. The gals finally shut their mouths for that one. The Beatles ended the concert with the Little Richard standard, 'Long Tall Sally'. Their entire set lasted less than 30 minutes. Mom, my sister Sharon and me slowly made our way out to the car for the long drive home to Cleveland. This show was my first concert experience. It was also one of the highlights of my life.

I WAS THERE: BETH BATEMAN SMITH

I listened to KLIF radio almost constantly those summers, listening to Beatles updates from Murray the K or other DJs who claimed to be travelling with the band. Whenever an update was announced, I was right there with my transistor radio. The fan clubs I had joined were instrumental in finding out where the band was to stay on their stops. As soon as I heard about their tour dates, we ordered four tickets for the Memphis concerts, and on August 18th Cynthia Burton and her mother drove with my mother and I to stay in Memphis at the Chisca Plaza Hotel, where the boys were to be staying.

Cynthia and I were now old pros at this fan thing. Right after breakfast, we left our moms and went riding the elevators all day in the hotel. At one point in the late morning, the elevator doors did open on the Beatles' floor and we saw several of what we thought were 'security-types'. And at a distance down the hall we *thought* we saw one of the boys going into one of their rooms. I spotted Mal Evans behind the couple of guys who were watching at the elevator doors and who politely but strongly encouraged us to stay inside the elevator when it stopped. We were in Fan Heaven!

We attended both concerts at the Mid-South Coliseum and were totally oblivious to any of the controversy that seems to have gone on around us. We did not see any KKK (or any ugliness) that day, and we were at the Mid-South location from about two hours before the afternoon show until after the evening concert was over. There were hundreds of us teenage fans milling around the area the whole afternoon and evening until the shows were both over. As 15-year-old Beatles fans, we only heard and saw anything good and positive that surrounded the band.

During the set-up of the stage equipment that day, I had enough courage to walk down and talk with Mal Evans, who was working on Ringo's drums. He was so nice and took the time to visit with this little 15-year-old fan. He could have easily been rude or tell me that he didn't have time to talk, but he did take the time and even went backstage after a few minutes, coming back with an autographed picture of all the boys. He told me he hoped I would enjoy the show and wished me well. My memories of Mal are of the nicest, gentlest person.

As we walked out of the Coliseum with the crowd, we heard through the fan grapevine that the boys' armoured truck was leaving soon, so raced around the back as fast as we could. We were able to get inside the parking garage where the armoured vehicle had backed in to a ramp and stairway in the loading area. Out came the boys, being hurried into the back of the vehicle, and at one point, George looked out at us fans in the garage – and waved! We were in awe…

 CROSLEY FIELD
21 AUGUST 1966, CINCINATTI, OHIO

I WAS THERE: CHERI BILL

I suppose organisers felt a larger venue than the small Cincinnati Gardens used for their 1964 show was needed, so Crosley Field – home of the Cincinnati Reds – was selected. I assumed we would all be going again. I was wrong. Mom wasn't going but my sister was and naturally, despite our five-year difference, I thought it was a given she'd be taking me. Nope. She wanted to go with friends. Ohhh! I burst into tears until my dad told my eldest sister to take me.

Her boyfriend drove us to Crosley Field and we presented our tickets and went in. Rain poured down but we did care? We were going to see The Beatles, or so we thought. But the rain never let up and the show was cancelled. The Beatles never emerged, the concert was called and rescheduled for the following day. An announcement was made that you had to have your ticket stub to re-enter. Many girls were crying because they had thrown theirs away. I was so glad I held onto mine! Off we went to find my sister's boyfriend, happy to know we'd be coming back tomorrow.

I WAS THERE: PAULA BROCK, AGE 13

I was now a teenager! My parents had bought me and my sister tickets to see The Beatles perform at Crosley Field, the old Cincinnati Reds baseball team's stadium. A few weeks prior to the concert, my sister and I somehow managed to get ourselves 'grounded'. My mom was mad at us and said we couldn't go to the concert. I hid our tickets and was determined to go anyway. We got out of the house somehow and made it to the stadium with some friends. And it rained and rained all day. Knowing we were going to be in big trouble for leaving the house, it all seemed worth it to us. Then something unbelievable happened. They called off the concert due to rain. It was too dangerous for anyone to go on stage. They told us we could come back the next day with our ticket stubs but I knew I would not be back, that I would be closely watched and forbidden to go since I had snuck out the day before in defiance. Oh, I cried and cried that day. I will never forget the concert I never got to see.

BUSCH STADIUM
21 AUGUST 1966, ST LOUIS, MISSOURI

I WAS THERE: DAVE BUTTIG

My dad took my sister and me and the two girls from next door to see The Beatles at Busch Stadium on their last tour in 1966. It was one of the coolest things my dad ever did for me. It was all very spur of the moment. I don't remember if my sister or I asked, or if he offered. It was raining that evening and it seemed like it took the opening acts ages to get on and get off before The Beatles started. And then, before you knew it, they were finished. Tickets were like $6 dollars as opposed to $125.00 per ticket to see McCartney in St Louis in 2001 on John Lennon's birthday. Anyway, it was a great time and when asked what was the first concert you went to, I can proudly say – The Beatles!

SHEA STADIUM
23 AUGUST 1966, FLUSHING MEADOW, NEW YORK

I WAS THERE: VICKIE SCHALL, AGE 15

Every single time I told my mother that I wanted to go see The Beatles in concert, she would tell me that I couldn't get a ticket until she was ready to get hers. Back then I lived in Newark, New Jersey. My parents were exceptionally strict and there was no way my parents were about to allow me to travel alone or even with a friend at night. Neither one of my parents drove or even owned a car.

By 1966, I got fed up with my mother's continuously putting me off about going to see The Beatles in concert so I took matters into my own hands. Back then $5.50 for a concert ticket was expensive so I saved my school lunch money and purchased a money order, filled out the form that I found in a magazine and sent for my ticket to see The Beatles at Shea Stadium. I didn't breathe a word of this to anyone, especially not to my father, who was born in Europe and was worse than a dictator when it came to certain things. My mother could be more of a soft touch once in a while.

When I finally got my ticket in the mail, I had to tell my mother and showed her my ticket. My mother immediately asked me for an order form which I very happily handed over and she sent for her ticket the same day. There was no way my parents were going to allow me to take two buses and a subway by myself at night – it would have involved taking the #31 bus to downtown Newark, then a one and a half mile walk to the street where the #107 bus would go directly to the Port Authority in New York City and finally downstairs to look for the subway to Queens, New York from the subway to Shea – and the reverse trip back home!

When the big day finally arrived, even though the weather was very warm, I wore a new dress. It was very mod – a bright green Poor Boy top and a skirt of off white, green and blue Tattersall with a bright blue belt. I wore white fishnet stockings and my babydoll shoes that were just like the ones Pattie Boyd wore in photos. I even had my hair done in a flip – I wanted to look stunning for Paul! Oh, the dreams of a teenage Beatle fan.

We finally arrived at Shea and there were vendors hawking all sorts of items. I had saved for months to be able to buy some Beatles souvenirs. I bought the 1966 tour programme, a small Beatles diary and a very cheap pair of plastic binoculars. Our seats weren't the greatest – we were in the green section – but who cared? I was breathing the same air as The Beatles! Much to my mother's dismay, her seat was 26 rows away from mine and I was given quite a lecture on not leaving my seat for any reason at all and especially not to even think of exiting at the end of the concert until she reached the row that I was in. I didn't care. I was finally going to see The Beatles and my beloved Paul in person – live at last!

I was surprised to see lots of empty seats. Murray The K was the MC and I thought he was annoying. I couldn't wait for him to shut up and get off the stage. He introduced his wife, Bobbie the K, and was dancing with her and some other dancers. It was hard to see really well as my seat was pretty high up. The opening acts were The Ronettes, The Cyrkle, The Remains and Bobby Hebb. No one seemed to care about any of them. We were there to see The Beatles and when they finally ran out onto the field to the stage, the screaming and girls standing on their seats was endless. My cheap binoculars were, surprisingly, pretty good. I joined the other girls in my row with screaming 'I love you, Paul!' with all my heart. An older woman next to me told us, 'Aw shut up, they can't hear you. He can't hear you.' Another girl around my age on the other side of me retorted 'you shut up! I don't care! Paul can so hear me!'

A nice woman in front of me turned around and lent me her high-powered binoculars for a few songs and I had a super view with them. In total they sang eleven songs: 'Paperback Writer', 'I Feel Fine', 'Long Tall Sally', 'I Wanna Be Your Man', 'Yesterday', 'Baby's in Black', 'She's A Woman', 'Nowhere Man', 'Rock and Roll

Music', 'Day Tripper' and 'If I Needed Someone'. It was during 'Day Tripper' that fans started breaking through the barriers and making a run for the stage. A couple of girls got really close before they were grabbed and carried away by the police.

Paul egged John on in booing the police and John was like 'awww, look at that.' Paul laughingly told the police, 'Leave 'er alone. I know her!' You could actually hear some of the songs but the rest were muffled by the screaming. I didn't want that night to end.

After the concert, I didn't realise I had tears streaming down my face. I was so happy to have finally have seen The Beatles and so sad that the concert had ended. My mother met me at the end of my row, and as we left the stadium she told me that a girl was there with her grandmother and that her grandmother had been giving the girl a hard time, telling her to 'stop screaming! You're embarrassing me! Everyone's looking at you!' No one really cared because all the other girls were screaming too.

My mom said she tried to muffle out the noise by sticking tissues in her ears and, if she had known it was going to be a continuous roar of screams, she would've brought ear plugs. In her younger days, Mom had gone to see Frank Sinatra in concert and she said seeing The Beatles live in concert and the way all the girls were going bananas made Sinatra's fans were tame in comparison. Then my mom said she doubted if she would ever go to another Beatles concert again ever. Who knew this would be the last concert tour they ever did? I have the ticket stubs safely tucked away in one of my Beatles scrapbooks. But I don't recall exactly which one, as I've got over 100 Beatles scrapbooks!

I WAS THERE: MITCH SILVERSTEIN, AGE 8

Shea Stadium was constructed at the same time as the New York World's Fair, which ran from 1964 through 1965. I remember the fanfare when The Beatles played at Shea in 1965; they flew in by helicopter to one of the pavilions with a heliport on the roof. My parents had tried to get tickets but it sold out. But in 1966 I saw The Beatles with my family. My parents surprised my sister and me by getting the tickets mail order. We were big Beatles fans and, needless to say, we were very excited. When the day arrived, we could not contain ourselves. We got to the stadium and I remember seeing a lot of teenage girls. We made our way to our seats on the mezzanine level, stopping to buy a programme, and then hunkered in for the evening.

The stage was set up over second base on the baseball field. The field perimeter was lined with security and police. I don't remember the warm up show too well but I do remember the local NYC radio station WMCA gave the staff a nickname – 'the Good Guys'. They came out in a group and entertained for a bit wearing their yellow shirts with a sketched logo that looked something like a smiley face. Then it was time for The Beatles. They came in through the left field bull pen in an armoured car. They got out of the back and headed to the stage and the place went wild. Every girl seemed to be screaming as loud as they could. You could barely hear the music!

I remember a couple of attempts by fans to dart onto the field and them quickly being caught and escorted out of the stadium by security. That was fairly exciting for an eight-year-old. They played for about a half hour, which was not long enough but it was still rather satisfying being part of history. As they left in the same armoured car, many fans raced out of the stands and watched from the open sides of the stadium as the car made its way out from the stadium grounds and onto the highway. A subdued quiet fell on the crowd as everyone made their way out. I also noticed the demolition of the pavilions in the adjacent World's Fair fairgrounds was quite far along. I felt two great losses at that moment but also savoured the enjoyment of these life-changing events.

 # DODGER STADIUM
28 AUGUST 1966, LOS ANGELES, CALIFORNIA

I WAS THERE: ANNE STASKEWICZ, AGE 15

By the third and final tour of 1966, the days of small venues and good seats for The Beatles were over. The stadium tours had begun. The Beatles were barely visible on the field at Dodger Stadium. At the grand age of 15 and a half, I was jaded enough to stop recording my memories. I still kept mementos like ticket stubs and the black nylons I wore, even though it was summer in Los Angeles. By the time I could drive myself to concerts, The Beatles were done touring the US. My treks to the Hollywood Bowl continued throughout the '60s and '70s. I still attend summer concerts under the stars, including a recent 50-year anniversary production of *Hair*, but I will always remember that first Beatles concert in 1964.

 # CANDLESTICK PARK
29 AUGUST 1966, SAN FRANCISCO, CALIFORNIA

I WAS THERE: JANINE BARNES, AGE 16

I went with a few friends. I always wrote the places I heard that they were coming to in the next year, so I got some pretty good seats! I paid $6.50 for my ticket. I took a bus to San Francisco then another bus to the Park. The show was great! Everyone was waiting for them. An armoured car came out to the field, so everyone thought 'here they are.' But they came out from the dug out – wow, nobody was expecting that. Girls were running down the field to get to them but got caught. I had a chance to jump over the fence onto the field but I did promise my dad I'd be good, so I didn't. The Beatles still mean a lot to me. I will always be a Beatles fan!

I WAS THERE: DIANNE HICKS (NEE WINGERT), AGE 16

I was in love with Paul from the first time I saw him on *The Ed Sullivan Show*. I can say that he was my first love at the age of 13 and imagined all kinds of ways I could meet him and imagined kissing him with my pillow. This was real teenage-girl stuff, I hate to admit. Unfortunately, I never got to meet him. I still hope I am at the right time and place for it to happen someday. I would go to my middle school with my turquoise transistor radio and listen to the local radio station play Beatle songs while I had recess and would sneak it into my lift-up desk and hide it from the teacher. I even wrote a letter to Paul when I was 14, but it got intercepted by the teacher and it got sent to the principal's office. I ended up being called into the office to explain the letter that disrupted the class. I was humiliated and never got the letter back.

It wasn't until about ten years ago that I decided to finally write and send a letter to Paul. I got his LA address on a website and sent the letter. I told no one – not even my husband. Two days later, I got a phone call from James McCartney (Paul's son, who was living in the Pasadena home). That was a shocker, that is for sure. I don't know if Paul ever got my letter but James said he would give it to him. I never heard.

I saw The Beatles three times and feel so lucky. Each time was different, each time so special. I had just turned 14 years old when The Beatles first came to San Francisco. My best friend at the time, Pam Riley, was an only child and I got the invite to go with her to see The Beatles at the Cow Palace.

We got there about 2.30pm and the show started at 8pm. As we entered, we saw the stage and the famous drum with The Beatles logo. The place filled up fast once the doors opened and I felt sorry for the acts that opened before them as the crowd chanted 'we want The Beatles' and nothing would satisfy the crowd until The Beatles were on stage. Once they entered the arena, the loudest, most piercing screams assaulted your ears. I had to cover mine because of the shrillness of the screams. As the show went on, I would get pelted by thrown jelly babies - and they hurt! All around me, the girls were screaming. I wasn't one of them, because I wanted to hear The Beatles, but that was just about impossible. After they left the stage, I walked up and collected a couple of the jelly beans from the stage and a flash cube from a camera and saved them as a souvenir. I have them to this day, except the beans kind of disintegrated... Once I got home, my ears were still ringing and I got a bloody nose from all the excitement. But it was all worth it – because I actually saw The Beatles!

In 1965, they returned to the Cow Palace and this time I was able to have a ride since my sister Mary Ann drove and was available to take us. She brought her best friend,

Joanne Mahoney. Tickets cost $7.50 a person and our assigned seats were way in the back. The Beatles looked so small, unlike my experience of the year before. I don't remember the selling of t-shirts or any kind of souvenirs. If there was, I would have wanted some for sure. There was the deafening screaming once again and a too short concert. I could hardly see them or hear them but I was there.

In 1966, Candlestick Park hosted The Beatles. My sister's boyfriend's sister Diane was a big Beatle fan like me and drove us to the South San Francisco location for what was a night time concert. We had tickets around the home plate, lower level, and there was a fence obstructing our view. In those days, I didn't have a camera with me to get any photos, unfortunately. I remember them running on the field in khaki-coloured outfits way out in the centre outfield. There was a breeze and the temperature was cool for an August night. There were the screaming girls again but I never would have dreamed it was to be The Beatles' last concert.

When I hear their music, it brings be to another place and time when life was innocent and the music made me happy. To this day, when I play their music, it brings happiness to my soul. They were a big, big, part of my teen years and way beyond. It is so hard to explain to people the craziness of the Beatle era. The whole British Invasion was the best thing that came along in the 60s. I am so happy to have been a young teenage girl with a first crush on a band that would take the world by storm. They grew up with me and I am forever grateful for the music and happiness they brought to my life.

I WAS THERE: CHARLIE GREENE

The summer of 1966 is where it all began. I had just graduated from Catholic grammar school and was ready to rock at 14 years old. Like everyone else, I was introduced to rock 'n' roll when The Beatles hit *Ed Sullivan*. On a later show, another band caught my eye. Their music was R&B and they weren't dressed in suits like The Beatles and all the other British bands. They were the Rolling Stones which I thought was a tres cool name. Finding out later that Brian got the name from a Muddy Waters song, 'I'm a Man', I could tell they were rebels.

In 1966, my best friend and I hung out at the Matrix, a neighbourhood club in San Francisco which Marty Balin had started with his band, the Jefferson Airplane. All the San Francisco bands played there, including the Grateful Dead, Big Brother (Janis) and the Holding Company, Steppenwolf (who were called Sparrow at the time), the Steve Miller Blues band et al. I also used to see them all play for free at Golden Gate Park, and I saw the Jimi Hendrix Experience play there in 1967.

On June 26,1966, my best friend and I hitchhiked to the Cow Palace and saw the Lovin Spoonful, the Byrds, Airplane and Chad & Jeremy open for the Beach Boys. It was a great show, ending with the crowd booing the Beach Boys when they came on the stage. On July 26th, my older sister and I saw the Rolling Stones at the Cow Palace. It was an awesome gig but the sound was like the Got Live If You Want It LP with all the girls screaming. And on August 29th, the two of us saw The Beatles' last paid concert at Candlestick Park. Bobby Hebb and the Ronettes opened for them. The Beatles only played for over 30 minutes and it was so windy, you could barely hear the bands. But we were there! Not a bad summer for a 14-year-old kid.

I WAS THERE: DENISE RENDON-BARRY, AGE 9

I was only nine years old when I saw The Beatles perform their last ever concert at Candlestick Park. I had no idea that I was going to see history in the making. I had three older sisters who were over the moon for The Beatles, so lucky me got to go see the concert too! I went with two sisters and one of their boyfriends. We piled into the station wagon, with my dad driving us to San Francisco, 45 miles away. We got to Candlestick and waited for The Beatles. I remember they were driven onto the baseball field in a Brink's armoured truck. They got onto the stage, started singing and all I could hear for a while was screaming and crying. I could barely hear the songs. Girls, including one of my sisters, were fainting. Just being there, amongst all the excitement, was quite thrilling for a nine-year-old and something I will never forget!

The promoter, Tempo Productions, made a loss on the show at Candlestick Park as only 25,000 of the 42,500 tickets were sold. It was to be the last ever paid performance by The Beatles.

SOHO
SEPTEMBER/OCTOBER 1967, LONDON, UK

I WAS THERE: GRAHAM COATES

I was 12 when I got a bike for Christmas in 1962. I couldn't ride it until late February due to the snow. But when I did finally go cycling with a friend around Hainault and Epping, wherever we stopped 'Please Please Me' was being played. After Christmas 1963, the family parties constantly played 'She Loves You' and 'I Want To Hold Your Hand' and that's what got me liking The Beatles. I eagerly waited for each release after that.

I first saw John, Paul and Ringo when they were editing *Magical Mystery Tour* in Old Compton Street, Soho in September and October 1967. I was working for FD&H Music Publishers at the time and used to walk over to where they were working with my friend Colin and stare up at them bobbing about on the first floor. They would be occasionally stare back. Paul would be his usual self and John on one occasion put his thumb on the end of his nose and waved his fingers at us. But on another occasion John came out and walked directly towards us. We both froze and, as he brushed past us, we looked round and he was gone. There was a door that he could have gone into but we didn't hear it open or close. Wherever he went was a mystery to us.

VARIOUS LOCATIONS
1967 - 1969

I WAS THERE: CHRISTINE TOMS

I met John Lennon and Yoko on the Brecon Beacons many years ago. They were in a Mini and stopped the car and chatted to us for some time. Julian Lennon was with them, although he was very young at the time. We took some photos but, unfortunately, I did not keep them.

I WAS THERE: NORMAN SCOTT

I got to know a singer called Bobby Shafto who was a Sixties singer who had started off as Lionel Bart's tea boy. He was a good-looking lad and he had a voice. Through him I met this guy called Terry Doran. The Beatles do that track about a man in the motor trade, 'She's Leaving Home'. Terry Doran is that man in the motor trade. He was very good friends with Brian Epstein. Apart from managing The Beatles, Brian Epstein had a car showroom and Terry Doran's first job with Brian Epstein was running Bridor Motors. It was called Bridor because of Bri after Brian and Dor after Doran. They only dealt in very posh secondhand cars – Rolls-Royces, Bentleys, Jags and things like that. I was only about 19, 20 at the time and I still lived at home. Terry Doran would borrow a posh car out of his showroom and we'd got out for the night for a drink or a meal or to go and see a show. If he came round to my parents' house, he'd come in and wait for me, so whenever he came round, we'd have a posh car parked outside. I always had to laugh because obviously my neighbours never knew it was the same guy borrowing different cars from the showroom. Terry Doran went on to become the managing director of Apple. I have his business card.

I went to a party at Brian Epstein's London flat once. Terry Doran invited me. That was rather strange. Brian was a strange man. I didn't get to know him at all really. There must have been about 15 people there. It was only a little gathering. I seem to recall drinking vodka and lime, or gin and lime, and I'd never drunk shorts in my life. The glasses seemed huge, like buckets. Brian sat on his own all night, just telling people to enjoy themselves, which I thought was rather strange. Terry Doran used to get the promos of Beatles pre-releases, which was great when I was a DJ, because I could play a Beatles record before it was out. I've got a few advanced copies of singles. I kept all those.

I WAS THERE: ALBERT HERNANDEZ DE LEON

It just could not any crazier than it did after that. I remember girls in school crying when Ringo got married, furious when John started hanging out with Yoko, and simply hysterical when rumours of a break up started circulating. By the summer of '67, flower power hit and The Beatles were in India with the Maharishi. Then 'Revolution 9' was released. To me that was a total turn off, although looking back on it I did not really listen to the lyrics attentively. But Yoko 'coming between John and Paul' was something I would not soon forgive, or forget.

APPLE CORPS BUILDING
30 JANUARY 1969, SAVILE ROW, LONDON, UK

The Beatles perform live together for the last ever time, on the roof of the Apple building.

ACADEMY OF MUSIC
28 MAY 1970, NEW YORK, NEW YORK

I WAS THERE: TOM MILLER

When I was 11 years old and the *Let it Be* movie came out, the famous New York DJ, Cousin Brucie, ran a contest on WABC radio; an essay contest on the topic of why The Beatles were culturally important. First prize was two tickets to the opening of the movie. I wrote an essay, mailed it in and forgot about it until I got a notification that I had won! So I got to go to the world's first showing of *Let it Be*. They held the official, formal premiere that night, but this was a matinee screening beforehand for the kids. Cousin Brucie himself showed up to MC. The only other sixth-grader in our suburban town who was allowed go in to New York City without an adult was this kid from Sweden whose parents were very liberal, so he ended up going with me to this and a bunch of different shows.

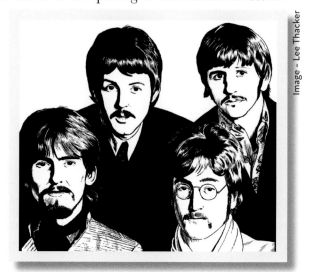

Image – Lee Thacker

GROSVENOR
(Prince of Wales Road, Norwich)

FRIDAY, MAY 17th, 1963

THE BEATLES
("From Me to You" & "Please Please Me")

also

RICKY LEE and the HUCKLEBUCKS

8—11 p.m.　　Fully Licensed Bars　　TICKET 7/6

QUEENS HALL · LEEDS
BERNARD HINCHCLIFFE presents

Jazz-'n'-Pop Ball · FRIDAY, JUNE 28th 8 p.m.-1 a.m.

BRITAIN'S BIGGEST ATTRACTIONS TOGETHER FOR THE FIRST TIME

MR.	THE
ACKER BILK	**BEATLES**
AND HIS PARAMOUNT JAZZ BAND	
RETURN BY PUBLIC REQUEST **VOLTAIRS** with SAMMY KING	with **RYLES BROS.** with GAY SAXON

Compered by North's Top D.J. **GARTH CAWOOD**

LICENSED BARS

TICKETS 10/6 from Lewis's and Vallances, Leeds; Vallance at Otley and Harrogate; W. H. Smith's, Bradford; and Music Centre, Huddersfield

ADMISSION AT DOOR 12/6

LATE TRANSPORT to Bradford, Halifax, Huddersfield, Dewsbury, Wakefield, etc.

SYDNEY STADIUM
STADIUMS & AZTEC Presents

The **BEATLES**
THURSDAY 18th JUNE
6 p.m.　RINGSIDE
Sec. 2　F 1964 11

June
DE
2
11

ENTER GATE 2

As I See It

Sullivan Wasted Time with Beatles

By PAUL JONES

If Ed Sullivan can find no better use for the time allotted him on Sunday night than to devote it to such exhibitions as he presented last Sunday night I suggest that CBS-TV find something else to put in this hour of prime time.

Why Sullivan found it necessary to aid in the phony promotion of four rock 'n' roll exponents, all of whom resemble Moe of the Three Stooges, is beyond comprehension. And why he felt it necessary to "load" the theater with screaming teen-age girls when he normally restricts his audience to grownups, is also a mystery.

It was obvious to those who saw the Beatles, four young fellows from Great Britain, that they have not attained their present notoriety on the basis of their musical talents, for the sounds emanating from their mouths were anything but melodic.

Shorn of their mop-like hairdos they would look and sound like many other inferior rock

'n' roll groups which are still attempting to keep alive the fad which died when Elvis Presley entered the armed forces.

There is nothing attractive about the looks or the sounds of the Beatles.

There is no reason why Sullivan should take part in the absurd campaign to make this group appear to be important.

But then Sullivan's program has been on the skids for several weeks. I have noticed a general deterioration in the type entertainment presented in at least three of the last four shows.

In catering to the screaming teen-agers who find this group exciting, Sullivan has shown his contempt for the vast millions who used to find his program diverting.

Tuesday, Feb. 11, 1964

THE BEATLES

WEDNESDAY SEPTEMBER 2ND
7:00 PM

CONVENTION HALL
PHILADELPHIA

Triangle Theatrical Productions
Franklin Fried PRESENTS

THE BEATLES

Milwaukee Auditorium — Sept. 4 — Milwaukee
ARENA

ODEON HAMMERSMITH
BRIAN EPSTEIN presents

ANOTHER BEATLES CHRISTMAS SHOW

1st Performance at 6-15 p.m.
MONDAY, DEC. 28th, 1964

CIRCLE £1/-/-

Block	Seat
7	**F 64**

No ticket exchanged nor money refunded
THIS PORTION TO BE RETAINED

A.B.C. CINEMA
NORTHAMPTON

1st Performance 6-30
WEDNESDAY
NOVEMBER. 6

CENTRE STALLS
8/6

Z11

No Tickets exchanged nor
money refunded
TO BE GIVEN UP

Durchführung: Konzertdirektion Kurt Collien GmbH., Hbg. 4

Sonntag, 26. Juni 1966, 15 Uhr　　Ernst-Merck-Halle

BRAVO-BEATLES-BLITZTOURNEE
Eine Karl-Buchmann-Produktion

SEITE LINKS B

DM 12.-
zuzügl. Vorverkauf

Reihe	Platz	
3	24	✱

Habusch-Druck

	THE BEATLES	
D R 7 FRONT ORCHESTRA	**SEPT'BR** **2** **1964** Wed'day Eve., at 8:00 P.M. CONVENTION HALL 34th ST. BELOW SPRUCE PHILADELPHIA, PA.	GOOD ONLY WEDNESDAY SEPT 2nd FRONT ORCHESTRA CONVENTION HALL GLOBE TICKET CO., PHILA. D R 7

Est. Price $4.87
Fed. Tax .39
City Tax .24
TOTAL $5.50

$5.50

SUFFOLK DOWNS
EAST BOSTON, MASS.

SEC 18 GRANDSTAND ROW 14 SEAT 6	**AUG** **18** **1966**	**Thurs. Eve. at 8:30** FRANK CONNELLY PRODUCTIONS — PRESENTS — **THE BEATLES** ADMISSION $5.75

The Beatles
RINGO　JOHN　GEORGE　PAUL